James Baldwin and the Heavenly City

James Baldwin and the Heavenly City

PROPHECY, APOCALYPSE, AND DOUBT

Christopher Z. Hobson

Michigan State University Press | East Lansing

♾ The paper used in this publication meets the minimum requirements of
ANSI/NISO Z39.48-1992 (R 1997) (Permanence of Paper).

Michigan State University Press
East Lansing, Michigan 48823-5245

Printed and bound in the United States of America.

27 26 25 24 23 22 21 20 19 18 1 2 3 4 5 6 7 8 9 10

LIBRARY OF CONGRESS CATALOGING-IN-PUBLICATION DATA
Names: Hobson, Christopher Z., author.
Title: James Baldwin and the heavenly city : prophecy, apocalypse, and doubt / Christopher Z. Hobson.
Description: East Lansing : Michigan State University Press, [2018] | Includes bibliographical references and index.
Identifiers: LCCN 2017046495 | ISBN 9781611862898 (cloth. : alk. paper)
| ISBN 9781609175702 (pdf) | ISBN 9781628953367 (epub) | ISBN 9781628963366 (kindle)
Subjects: LCSH: Baldwin, James, 1924–1987—Criticism and interpretation. | Baldwin, James, 1924–1987—Religion.
| American fiction—African American authors—History and criticism.
| Religion and literature—United States—History—20th century.
Classification: LCC PS3552.A45 Z699 2018 | DDC 818/.5409—dc23
LC record available at https://lccn.loc.gov/2017046495

Book design by Charlie Sharp, Sharp Des!gns, East Lansing, MI
Cover design by Shaun Allshouse, www.shaunallshouse.com
Cover Art is *Into Bondage* (1936) by Aaron Douglas © Heirs of Aaron Douglas/
Licensed by VAGA, New York, NY. Used with permission.

To the memory of Melvin Dixon
who taught me Baldwin

For they that say such things declare plainly that they seek a country.

And truly, if they had been mindful of that country from whence they came out, they might have had opportunity to have returned.

But now they desire a better country, that is, an heavenly: wherefore God is not ashamed to be called their God: for he hath prepared for them a city.

—Hebrews 11:14–16

Contents

Preface

James Baldwin is increasingly invoked today in discussions of America's unfinished civil rights reform. Behind Baldwin's uncanny ability to identify the nation's crisis and to provide a vision of hope lies his use of religious language to describe social and sexual transformation—the possible achievement of the "heavenly city" of my title. *James Baldwin and the Heavenly City* is the first book study of this topic. Its thesis is that Baldwin, in adulthood not a religious believer in any conventional sense, uses biblical ideas of prophetic speech and the apocalyptic "unveiling" of new worlds in partly but not fully secularized ways to express the possible human achievement of a new life embodying a real but undefinable holiness. Baldwin's use of this partly naturalized religious language is the master key to his work as a novelist, but has never been adequately explored.

I focus on Baldwin's six novels, from *Go Tell It on the Mountain* (1953) to *Just Above My Head* (1979)—in my estimation, the core of his achievement as an artist. While I refer frequently to Baldwin's essays, stories, and drama, the novels give most scope to his sense of human complexity and contradiction, and so are properly the form through which he explores the possibility and difficulty of change in personal and social life. I contextualize Baldwin in four ways: historically, and in relation to biblical ideas and scholarship, to African American prophetic religious traditions, and to recent models of the secular and postsecular.

In précis, my Introduction defines Baldwin's approach of "taking authority" over Bible and Gospel texts and African American prophetic religious traditions by contesting their narrowness and finding in them a liberating core that he releases and expands. The chapter that follows, "Prophetic Commissioning," deals with a single novel, *Go Tell It on the Mountain*, which, I argue, has as its main topic its protagonist's assumption of an as yet undefined, implicitly prophetic mission that involves the sense of human sacredness Baldwin sees as central to such a mission. *Go Tell It* is Baldwin's only novel to show this process in full outline.

Then follow three chapters, "Prophetic Art," "The Apocalyptic Body," and "The Apocalyptic City," that discuss those issues with reference to all Baldwin's novels—besides *Go Tell It*, *Giovanni's Room* (1956), *Another Country* (1962), *Tell Me How Long the Train's Been Gone* (1968), *If Beale Street Could Talk* (1974), and *Just Above My Head*. These chapters provide new readings—often first readings—of key episodes and themes in these works. In brief, they trace an evolution from a first presentation of prophetic art in Baldwin's 1955–1957 story "Sonny's Blues" to a portrayal of avowedly apocalyptic art in *Just Above My Head*; the utopian possibilities in Baldwin's sacramental idea of the body and sexuality, along with the social and psychic roadblocks in the way of these possibilities; and the increasing complexity of Baldwin's social vision in the later novels, which come to include ideas both of resistance and apocalyptic upheaval and of the long paths of African American history.

"Prophecy and Doubt," the last major chapter, again focuses on one work, *Just Above My Head*. While this novel's prophetic and apocalyptic ideas have been addressed in preceding chapters, *Just Above My Head* is also the book in which Baldwin systematically questions his prior ideas, creating the polarity referred to in the chapter title. The focus on this single text responds to its structural and intellectual complexity and to its status as a culminating work of major intellectual power. The conclusion assesses the prophetic potential of Baldwin's ideas of the body, society, and art from today's vantage point.

Besides these main themes, my study includes two subordinate themes. One is the importance of Baldwin's late fiction. Until quite recently these works have lived under a critical and canonical question mark. The first three novels still vastly outweigh the last three in teaching curricula and scholarship; even in the last fifteen years, it has been possible to write major books on Baldwin and religion or

Baldwin and homosexuality and barely mention them.[1] These works are, finally, getting their due in republication, as attested by the Library of America's 2015 *Later Novels* (unfortunately with small textual flaws) and in critical writing. I hope my discussions of such topics as the apocalyptic-eschatological portents in each, their views of homosexual self-suppression and self-concealment (as well as pride), their shifting social landscapes, and their formal and intellectual complexity may corroborate this new estimate of their stature.

Secondly, I stress the importance of Gospel music in Baldwin's imagination. Despite some recent revaluations (e.g., Field 109–12), commentaries still routinely treat Baldwin as above all a blues artist and relegate Gospel to a place well behind blues in his thinking. The result is a failure both to adequately understand Baldwin's musical affinities and to fully grasp his balancing of skeptical-tragic and prophetic-utopian sensibilities, which blues and Gospel, respectively, stand for in his fiction. This juxtaposition of blues and Gospel becomes a major focus in my Conclusion. Gospel emerges in my pages as a major component of Baldwin's imagination and a key to his presentation of the heavenly city and the possible roads toward it. I hope my tracing of Gospel's thematic role, particularly in the later novels, and the inferable importance of Gospel artists like Rosetta Tharpe and Sam Cooke in Baldwin's imagination will contribute to recognition of Gospel's equal centrality with blues in Baldwin's works.

I first read *Giovanni's Room* when I was younger than its protagonist David, and working to answer the same questions; I read *Another Country*, in the resonant and unlikely locale of Eden, Wyoming (where I had a summer job), when its issues were fresh. Over a lengthy consideration of Baldwin and his works, I have incurred debts both informal and formal. The largest is also the vaguest: to the period that shaped my imagination and profoundly affected Baldwin's, the 1960s, the most recent in U.S. history when change in an unjust system seemed palpably imminent. I owe a more formal debt to my dedicatee, the late Melvin Dixon, who taught Baldwin's novels in his last active semester at the CUNY Graduate Center (1992). Melvin—we had had a previous course together and became friends—believed as I did that the novels were the achievement Baldwin would be remembered by. His dedication and care during this course showed Melvin a great teacher, as well as novelist, poet, essayist, and translator. *Vale*. I owe debts innumerable to students, some named in these pages and many others over the years I have taught Baldwin at SUNY Old Westbury and elsewhere. I am in debt to those who have read some or all of this book in its gestation—to G. A. Rosso, whose knowledge of biblical issues and scholarship has been an invaluable aid; Brian Culhane; Alcides J. Alemán; and most especially Nicholas Powers, friend and inspirer as well as colleague, and the source of some of my interpretive ideas. An earlier version of parts of Chap. 5 appeared as "Prophecy and Doubt in *Just Above My Head*," *James Baldwin Review* 1 (2015): 67–90; I gratefully acknowledge peer-reviewers' comments that improved the argument. I thank the Schomburg Center for Research in Black Culture, Manuscripts, Archives, and Rare Books Division, which acquired Baldwin's papers in April 2017, for access to the papers reflected at several points below. Finally, I am grateful for the suggestions of two readers for Michigan State University Press and for the support of my editors there, J. Alex Schwartz and Julie Loehr. I hope this work will discharge all these debts in part.

Abbreviations of Titles of James Baldwin's Works

Baldwin's essays not listed separately in Works Cited are cited from *Collected Essays*.

AC	*Another Country*
BS	*If Beale Street Could Talk*
"EPN"	"Everybody's Protest Novel," in *Collected Essays*
"FAI"	"Freaks and the American Ideal of Manhood," in *Collected Essays*
FNT	*The Fire Next Time*
"FTT"	"The Fire This Time: Letter to the Bishop"
GR	*Giovanni's Room*
GT	*Go Tell It on the Mountain*
JAMH	*Just Above My Head*
"MP"	"The Male Prison," in *Collected Essays*
"MTG"	"Many Thousands Gone," in *Collected Essays*
NN	*No Name in the Street*
"NNS"	"Notes of a Native Son," in *Collected Essays*
"PI"	"Preservation of Innocence," in *Collected Essays*

"SB"	"Sonny's Blues"
TAC	*The Amen Corner*
TMHL	*Tell Me How Long the Train's Been Gone*
"UB"	"The Uses of the Blues"
"WR"	"White Racism or World Community," in *Collected Essays*

INTRODUCTION

Baldwin, the Bible, and the Heavenly City

> They were the despised and the rejected, the wretched and the spat upon, the earth's offscouring; and he was in their company.
>
> —*Go Tell It on the Mountain*

> We are made as the filth of the world, and are the offscouring of all things unto this day.
>
> —1 Corinthians 4:13

The governing idea in James Baldwin's six novels is the pursuit of the heavenly city, New Jerusalem, "that city which the people from heaven had made their home" (*AC* 436). Baldwin's fiction sees this city in largely but not fully secularized ways. The terms and vocabulary of his vision are derived from his Pentecostal church background but revised so that the mortal body and the earthly city, condemned in his church tradition, are potentially holy, while his characters' relationship to organized churches is at first antagonistic and finally warily respectful. The city, then, is a renovated earth, and the revelations of its possible future existence come not from angels but from a double descent into the lower world: that of the body and its sexuality and that of the nation and its night places that reveal truths hidden by day (*AC* 261, 348). What is revealed there is a secularized equivalent of biblical apocalypse (in one sense, "unveiling") in that "the meaning of revelation is that what is revealed is true, and must be borne"; and the revelation provides the basis for new life because at bottom the truth revealed is that "everything God made is *holy*" (*AC* 206, 121). At the same time, the goals and agents of transformation are not entirely freed from their religious origins. The interplay between secular ideas of reform or revolution and underlying but always present biblical ideas of salvation gives the best of Baldwin's fiction its characteristic tensile strength. That Eden, fall, redemption, and apocalypse—the sequence within which biblical history occurs—can happen *to* imperfect humans and *through* human actions is the premise of Baldwin's fiction.

Baldwin, then, seeks secularized—not fully secular—equivalents for biblical patterns and ideas to express the great possibilities for human change that are the base-stones of his vision, and he consistently uses biblical and Gospel music echoes to evoke them. The central biblical ideas for him are those of apocalypse and prophecy. Though these terms are rare in his fiction, he repeatedly suggests the ideas themselves in the way just described. The first—variously denoting the revelation or "unveiling" (Greek *apokalypsis*) of God's purposes; the sense of an approaching eschaton or end-time when those purposes are realized and a renovated world is born; and frequently both—suggests for Baldwin two linked ideas. One is an apocalypse, or revelation, of the holiness of the body and sexuality, especially homosexuality, a shift in awareness and action that anticipates but also differs from recent ideas of sexual-homosexual liberation and queer sexuality, yet, for Baldwin, cannot by itself achieve liberation within an inimical society. The second is a potential transformation in society, or advent of a new life, in which earth's outcast and dishonored carve out a path to dignity, power, and the end of oppression. Prophecy, in turn—biblically, the act of speaking warning, judgment, or promise to the nation, and increasingly the promise of a renewed earth—Baldwin transfers to the sphere of art. For him, prophetic art, more than political action or religious speech, awakens us to the sacred possibilities we can attain, though with immense difficulty, in our bodies and our society.

From here to Baldwin's heavenly city is a long journey. In biblical terms it is the journey from the garden (Gen. 2:8) to the city (Rev. 21:2) and encompasses all human history, and in metaphor this is the journey in *Another Country*. In terms of Baldwin's works the journey is broached in *Go Tell It on the Mountain* (1953) and still remains as an ambiguous promise in *Just Above My Head* (1979). In personal testimony, Baldwin affirms his belief in a mid-career interview in the documentary film *James Baldwin: The Price of the Ticket*:

> The day will come when you will trust you more than you do now, and you will trust me more than you do now. We can trust each other. I do believe, I really do believe in the New Jerusalem, I really do believe that we can all become better than we are. I know we can. But the price is enormous—and people are not yet willing to pay it.

But this affirmation would mean nothing without the evidence of Baldwin's fiction that his art does point to the city. This art suggests that the signposts toward the city are unclear and the costs indeed immense: many start the journey only to die, or live, in the ash of despair. The novels, then, speak not only of the heavenly city but also of what Revelation calls Babylon, the city of empire and oppression, self-hatred and self-laceration, betrayal, submission, connivance, and defeat that we live in and against (Rev. 17:5). This reality leads to the third term in my subtitle, referring to Baldwin's awareness of human incapacity and limitation, his doubt of the promise he nonetheless sees and holds to. The balance of these qualities—prophecy, apocalypse, and doubt—invests Baldwin's fiction with toughness and resilience, and, in *Just Above My Head*, becomes his subject. The novels do not, in the end, take us to the city. They only point somewhere "up the road," expressing doubt about what lies there and blinding sorrow for the fallen (*JAMH* 583–84). There is no sure guide to this road, nor can there be, since Baldwin's tenuous conviction is only of possibility.

The complexity of these issues may help explain my primary focus on Baldwin's novels. To be clear, I am not proposing a theorization of Baldwin's overall approach to the novel, or placing him within one—either would require its own study, especially in light of the varied discursive traditions Baldwin draws on. Rather, I am studying one central and underdiscussed aspect of the novels, the way in which key religious ideas shape their themes and structures. This aspect of Baldwin's art appears chiefly, and most fully, in his novels. (By way of contrast, these practices do not figure importantly in a drama like *Blues for Mr. Charlie* [1964], which, though using some biblical allusions and debating the church's role, makes its decisive points through character confrontations.) The reasons why Baldwin uses these expressive modes most in his novels lie in the form's comprehensiveness, flexibility, and ability to accommodate multiple discourses. Baldwin's six novels, first of all, while not formally linked, constitute a career-spanning exploration of repeating themes—those I call prophetic art, the apocalyptic body, and the apocalyptic city—with growing complexity of form and idea. Further, within individual works, the novel as a long form allows full development of characters' complexity, contradictions, and capacity or incapacity for change—what John Grimes in *Go Tell It on the Mountain* intuits as the truth that "the heart [is] a fearful place" (210). On a more specific level, the novel form provides scope for the long scenes that are a Baldwin love, in which character and themes unfold over extended time, frequently with pinpoint specificity of occasion and place (Rufus's last night in *Another Country*, 3–88; Christmas Day and the next in Harlem in 1950, in *Just Above My Head*, 103–52). Alternatively, the form's flexibility allows bypassing less-important events (*TMHL* 341–46) and accommodates the recursive chronologies Baldwin often uses. Finally, crucially for my topic, the novel's openness to distinct discourses lets Baldwin bring these complexities of character, scene, setting, and time, evoked through primarily mimetic means, together with a partly nonnaturalistic, in fact prophetic and revelatory, body of ideas, and enables these disparate elements to reinforce and deepen one another.

Baldwin, Religion, and the Postsecular

As this précis suggests, a seemingly paradoxical mix of mimetic and religiously-inflected artistic modes is critical to Baldwin's novels. His use of this mix, we will see, is an outgrowth of his intellectual fluency in the overlapping secular and nonsecular traditions in U.S. thought.

This mode of expression is not, on biographical evidence, a product of personal belief. Baldwin does not affirm a belief in God in his published writings, and during his last illness told David Leeming that "he did not 'believe' in God," though adding that, particularly when alone, he felt there was "something out there" (Leeming 384). Baldwin more than once speaks of God, in a quasi-Feuerbachian way, as a human creation—"man's most intense creation," whose nature human beings "expand and transform" in their own "act[s] of creation" ("PI" 596; "WR" 755). Moreover he directly condemned the Christianity of white churches, addressing the World Council of Churches, in the second of these essays, as "one of the creatures, one of God's creatures, whom the Christian church has most betrayed" ("WR" 749). On the other hand, he stops short of a full rejection of faith, particularly when speaking in a public persona: in this same address, Baldwin also tells church leaders that African Americans had "won our Christianity, our faith, at the point of a gun, not because of the example afforded by white Christians, but in spite of it" ("WR" 750), apparently affirming in some qualified way, not further defined, that African American Christianity contains an element of valid belief. And Baldwin could be cagey regarding personal beliefs, describing himself in a 1985 open letter to Bishop Desmond Tutu, for example, as "not a religious or, more precisely, a churchgoing man" ("FTT" 215); but he never defines the implied sense in which he is "religious." Religious reference in Baldwin's fiction remains, then, on the balance of evidence, a matter of literary expression, not creed.[1]

Baldwin's writings have been viewed, variously, as affirming, correcting, or basically opposing conventional Christianity.[2] The work of Clarence E. Hardy III offers an extended example of the last approach that, while not accepted by several recent writers,[3] remains influential and is worth addressing in counterpoint to my own. Hardy's "basic claim" is, first, that Baldwin critiques an African American Christianity involving unreturned love "for a Christian god who is depicted as both silent before black suffering and as white—that is, actively opposed to the flourishing of black life." Secondly, "there is, therefore, an implicit criticism throughout [Baldwin's] work that understands the principal backdrop to black people's conversion to Christianity in the United States to be shame and not hope" (x). Hardy further believes that Baldwin denounces "this white Christian god . . . more strongly over time" (xiii). Finally, he acknowledges Baldwin's "failure to disconnect entirely" from church culture, but sees this failure as revealing "how tragic the black exilic experience in the United States truly is" (xi–xii). Hardy, that is, views African Americans' acceptance of Christianity as tied to a critical acceptance of the United States that he also sees as self-limiting and "tragic" (112).

Some elements of this schema ring true. Baldwin creates characters who live and die in outrage at a God seen as unresponsive to his children: Rufus Scott, in *Another Country*, plunges to his death telling God, "*all right, you motherfucking Godalmighty bastard, I'm coming to you*" (88); Leo Proudhammer, in *Tell Me How Long the Train's Been Gone*, wants to strike out against "the monstrous blood-guiltiness of God," though concluding, significantly enough, "that this horror, precisely, accomplished His reality and undid my unbelief" (98). And both Rufus and Leo, in common with many African Americans of the 1940s and 1950s, conceive God as white (*AC* 22, *TMHL* 425). Baldwin also uses the "white God" idea in essays, in both personal and historicized ways—God, the young Baldwin felt at the time of his conversion, "is white"; freed slaves after Emancipation prayed to a God who "had made [them], but not in His image" (*FNT* 31; "EPN" 17). The same idea also appears in a more sociological sense, as the views of the cultures under examination, in keeping with the Feuerbachian approach just mentioned.[4]

Over the course of Baldwin's fiction, matters become more complex, and the weakness of Hardy's study is that, except for *Go Tell It on the Mountain*, it does not deal in a sustained way with Baldwin's novels, particularly later ones. While the idea of a white God does appear in the novels, as just noted, it is not a major preoccupation, and is not referred to at all by major groups of characters who may or may not share it.[5] Further, the indictment against an indifferent God, reaching a kind of climax in *Tell Me How Long the Train's Been Gone*, recedes in *If Beale Street Could Talk* and *Just Above My Head*, which instead stress a long African American struggle against human opposition. The families these novels center on, moreover, are occasional churchgoers; the main religious opposition they present is not between God's unkept promises and human suffering, but between these characters' broadly tolerant, profane, yet still religiously observant lives and others' narrowminded and hypocritical "sanctified" religion. In addition, as early as *Another Country* (1962), Baldwin offers a qualified corrective regarding the African American church, creating ministers and church laypeople who embody what we would think of as genuinely Christian humility and love, such as Reverend Foster in this novel (120–23), or serve quietly and effectively in the everyday perils of the civil rights struggle (*JAMH* 435–52). These points suggest, at least, a sense on Baldwin's part of the importance of Christian belief in African American life and a truce of sorts in his attitude to this belief. In important ways, then, Hardy's thesis misses a rapprochement with religious affiliation in Baldwin's later work, one that other critics note (e.g., Scott 126).

Most basically, an approach that largely omits Baldwin's fiction also misses his use of core prophetic and apocalyptic paradigms as a fictive language for human possibility. Prophetic and apocalyptic texts, of course, are not univocally liberatory. Recent studies have identified imposition of cult orthodoxy and a sometimes malevolent misogyny, for example, as threads in the prophetic literature.[6] This said, most studies of these variegated texts also see in them an emphasis on justice and righteousness (understood as fair treatment and substantive beneficence, especially to the community's weak and poor). Prophets, one overview states, frequently "spoke on behalf of those without power [and] those oppressed by the powerful," and in doing so "were indicting societal structures as well as the behavior of individuals" (Petersen, "Introduction" 8, 21). Similarly, most scholars of biblical apocalypticism find in it a call for ultimate justice for the sufferers.[7] In any case, these ideas became central in African American preaching and reading traditions. And, with other convictions reaching back to Richard Allen and beyond, such as of God's opposition to oppression,[8] they should be seen not as naïve misreadings but as considered emphases, acts of theological interpretation.[9] Baldwin in turn practices a similar, nontheist "theological interpretation" toward both general Christian beliefs and African American prophetic traditions, appropriating but also reshaping them.[10]

These aspects of Baldwin's writing raise the question of his relevance for the idea of the "postsecular"—roughly, what scholars since the mid-1990s have addressed as the persistence or resurgence of religious thinking in a modern era once assumed to be marked by cumulatively increasing secularism. Baldwin's fiction fits but also inflects this construct, in ways that can only be sketched here but that following chapters illustrate. Baldwin, in his thematic use of religious ideas in fiction, shares postsecular writers' rejection of what Gauri Viswanathan describes as the once-consensual understanding of literature as "a secular vehicle for ideas whose possible religious origins were . . . effaced as religious sensibility became absorbed into aesthetic form and imagery" (466). Baldwin, it is true, lacks some hallmarks of the recent postsecular, such as a role for the nonmaterial or supranatural or characters who seek the nonsecular as a way out of constricting secularism. In their place, however, we find a more basic trait of his fiction already sketched above, its vesting of the sacred in the secular while maintaining its sacral character. This vesting is never complete; Baldwin's practice of depicting a biblically-inflected reformation through mainly but not fully mimetic narration maintains a distance between sacred and secular ideas, and this distancing is itself a point of contact with more recent postsecular fictions typified, John A. McClure argues, by a balancing of secular and religious spheres (3–5). Yet, despite these affinities with the postsecular, there are differences as well. Baldwin's stress on redemption and apocalyptic reformation, in particular, runs counter to a basic quality in much postsecular literature: its resistance to salvational promises, preference for small-scale "contrast communities" (McClure 20) over goals of overall social reconstruction, and sense of what McClure (borrowing from Gianni Vattimo) calls "weak religiosity" (19).[11]

These differences, as well as the periodization of his work, much of which came before postsecularism emerged as a major trend, imply that Baldwin should be seen as anticipating and related to the literary postsecular rather than part of it. In this respect, his example jibes with recent scholarship questioning a neat division between "secular" and "postsecular" and suggesting instead a persistence of nonsecular sensibilities throughout modernity (see, e.g., Morrissey 100, Viswanathan 474–75). African American literature provides other notable examples. Countée Cullen's "The Black Christ" (1929), for instance, with its staging of basic questions of faith, skepticism, and evil through reenactment of Christ's sacrifice, postdates by fourteen years Wallace Stevens's "Sunday Morning" (1915), a defining text of modernist naturalization of the divine. Clearly Stevens's text and Cullen's participate in differing, secularizing and nonsecular, dynamics. This of course does not mean African American literature in general is nonsecular, but Cullen is evidence, with earlier and later writers, of an ongoing nonsecular thread in this literature over much of the presumed eras of naturalism and secularism. Even more specifically, Baldwin's work, with its roots in African American church cultures and their ideas of the prophetic and apocalyptic, matches Viswanathan's emphasis on Christian "heterodoxies" as among many elements of spiritualized thinking remaining outside the secularization of culture (475).[12]

With such persistences in mind, and without specific reference to the postsecular, Joanna Brooks, in a pathmaking 2010 essay, posits, alongside the familiar American Studies narrative tracing secularization from "Edwards to Emerson," an alternative "working narrative" of religiously based descent in U.S. thought "From Edwards to Baldwin" (441; essay title, 439). Brooks's analysis needs qualification—Baldwin remains fully conversant with empiricism in general culture and naturalism in literature—but it points to the twin lineages of religiously and secularly inflected expression in U.S. culture. Baldwin should be seen in this larger, temporally more extensive context.

Baldwin's work raises, as well, issues not addressed in many discussions of the postsecular, most centrally, for my purposes, the relation between ideas of basic social reformation and the secularization/modernization linkage. Jürgen Habermas's influential "Notes on Post-Secular Society" (2008), for example, outlining what he calls the "normative" postsecular, focuses on how secular and nonsecular groups can act together in an assumedly inclusive democratic state not requiring basic change (21–29). In contrast, Baldwin's emphasis on the prophetic and apocalyptic draws on deep beliefs in possible social transformation and substantive justice held by excluded and dishonored individuals and groups the world over, in past times and now. These beliefs, indeed, would seem to have contributed both to the secularization of culture in the nineteenth century—when they were commonly attached to secular ideologies like Marxism, nationalism, and labor reformism—and to reactions against secularism today, when these ideas have collapsed as apparent forces for basic change. The relation between prophetic belief and stalled hopes of social reformation, like other points raised here, will require further discussion in my conclusion. For Baldwin, however, the effect of a linkage between transformative belief and a biblical and Gospel music inheritance is clear: his fluency in an alternative, nonsecular and nonempiricist mode of thought, I argue later, helped him stay partly outside existing culture while functioning within it—to be "in the world but not of it," as his religious tradition would say. This complex of intellectual attitudes let Baldwin live and work in the successive milieus of post–World War II liberalism, civil rights radicalism, and the post-civil rights restabilization of U.S. society while remaining independent of dominant assumptions and able to project an alternative way of living.

Baldwin and the Bible

Baldwin's appropriation and revision of biblical language situate him within a long African American practice of taking authority over the dominant culture's beliefs and turning them to African Americans' own purposes.[13] Absalom Jones and Richard Allen, for example, were taking authority in this way when, in 1794, they spoke of "how hateful slavery is in the sight of that God, who hath destroyed kings and princes, for their oppression of the poor slaves" (24), as was James H. Cone, in 1970, in appropriating Matthew 11:28 for his own foundational statement that "it is impossible to speak of the God of Israelite history, who is the God revealed in Jesus Christ, without recognizing that God is the God *of* and *for* those who labor and are overladen" (1). These thinkers were selecting and emphasizing Bible teachings so as to reshape Christianity. Baldwin similarly reinterprets and reapplies biblical ideas so as to take authority over, largely humanize, and extend and radicalize them.

The most important biblical book for Baldwin, by far, is Revelation, to which he alludes or refers directly in most of his novels. Also salient are Isaiah, especially its redemptive later chapters, and Ezekiel, Daniel, John, and the Second Epistle of Peter, biblical source for his most famed title, *The Fire Next Time* (2 Pet. 3:6–7). Finally, a major and perhaps surprising source for Baldwin's imagery of apocalypse, discipleship, community, and the body is Paul, and Baldwin's treatment of Paul can be used to illustrate his general approach to biblical material.

The major Pauline works for Baldwin are First and Second Corinthians and Hebrews, which he takes as Paul's.[14] Baldwin refers or alludes to these texts throughout his fiction and essays, notably in *Go Tell It on the Mountain* and, crucially, *Giovanni's Room*, *Another Country*, and *Just Above My Head*. Many nonfiction references treat Paul as the legalistic, antisexual figure who is often seen as antithetical to the spirit of Jesus.[15] In *The Fire Next Time*, for example, he is "the mercilessly fanatical and self-righteous St. Paul" (44), although in Baldwin's 1954 essay on Gide, "The Male Prison," Paul stands for self-sacrifice in faith—asking if homosexuality is natural is like asking if "it was natural for St. Paul to suffer for the Gospel" ("MP" 232), an important clue to Baldwin's use of Paul in fiction. By comparison, the fiction engages with Paul in a more sustained and probing way.

Baldwin's uses of Paul seem to draw crucially on three passages in the First Epistle to the Corinthians. These concern different immediate topics—two the calling of apostolic service and one the status of different members of the faith community—but all involve recognition of the small or "weak" as against the great or "strong," a unifying theme in this letter, and feature repeated images whose common thread is God's exalting of what is low and despised in the world's eyes:

> But God hath chosen the foolish things of the world to confound the wise, and God hath chosen the weak things of the world to confound the things which are mighty;
>
> And base things of the world, and things which are despised, hath God chosen, yea, and things which are not, to bring to nought things which are. (1:27–28)

> For I think that God hath set forth us the apostles last, as it were appointed to death: for we are made a spectacle unto the world, and to angels, and to men.
>
> We are fools for Christ's sake, but ye are wise in Christ; we are weak, but ye are strong; ye are honourable, but we are despised.
>
> Even unto the present hour we both hunger, and thirst, and are naked, and are buffeted, and have no certain dwelling place;
>
> And labour, working with our own hands: being reviled, we bless; being persecuted, we suffer it:
>
> Being defamed, we intreat: we are made as the filth of the world, and are the offscouring of all things unto this day. (4:9–13)

> But now are they many members, yet but one body. . . . Nay much more those members of the body, which seem to be feeble, are necessary;
>
> And those members of the body, which we think to be less honourable, upon these we bestow more abundant honour; and our uncomely parts have more abundant comeliness.
>
> For our comely parts have no need: but God hath tempered the body together, giving more abundant honour to that part which lacked. (12:20–24)

The rhythms and antitheses in all three statements emphasize the same teaching that God favors the low and dishonored over the great, and the passages' repetitive oppositions between similar word pairings (*despised, dishonored, base* against *chosen, honored, honor*) show how close is the inner thinking in each.

These passages, Dale B. Martin's study of First Corinthians' intellectual contexts shows, form part of Paul's challenge to entrenched status hierarchies in the community of believers at Corinth, a guiding purpose of First Corinthians as a whole. To balance the sway of "the Strong" at Corinth—essentially the social elite among Jesus's followers there—Paul needed to "advance an alternative system," which he found in Jewish apocalyptcism's narrative of "an alternative, hidden, and vastly more powerful empire: the kingdom of God," and in the corollary assumption that "[u]ltimately, the last would be first, and the first would be last" (Martin 60, echoing Matt. 19:30 and similar passages). Paul's "confound the things which are mighty" is, as well, a key teaching in African American prophetic tradition, adding to its resonance for Baldwin.[16] These passages would suggest for him the exaltation both of the world's outcast and, I will propose, also of the sexually degraded. Though he directly paraphrases just one of the passages (the second) in his novels, his repeated uses of "despised," "honor" and "dishonor," and "filth" suggest familiarity with all three.[17]

These texts form a crucial part of Baldwin's overall encounter with Pauline ideas. For Baldwin, Paul is first of all an apocalyptic writer. In biblical contexts, as already noted, apocalypse involves both the revelation or "unveiling" of God's purposes and power and, especially in Revelation, the announcement of the transformative advent of God's city (Rev. 21:2). These were originally distinct ideas, the latter building on conceptions of a change between ages, and ultimately of a culminating end-time (eschaton), that appear in late prophetic writings and in some, but not all, apocalyptic works. Revelation, Daniel, and Pauline and other epistles all involve this sense of end-time change as well as of revealed knowledge. In Revelation, this transformation is presented, too, as a pervasive destruction of the present world, and this idea—more or less what "apocalypse" now means in common usage—adds its implication of cataclysmic force to the fused senses of apocalypse.[18] But the destructive imagery in Revelation also, and primarily, signifies the end of an evil world and the coming of a new one. This new world, God's city, is not to come *in* heaven but "down from God out of heaven" (Rev. 21:2). Elisabeth Schüssler Fiorenza argues that "the center of the theological vision and rhetorical movement of Revelation is the earth. . . . Revelation's vision of salvation centers on the earth" (109), and Christopher C. Rowland observes of one of its major events, the general resurrection (Rev. 20:13), "Resurrection transforms death into new life in a renewed world. It is not an escape into a world beyond" (Rowland, "Revelation" 716).

With these ideas as underlying assumptions, Baldwin, as seen later, uses Paul to signify understanding of hidden truth in *Giovanni's Room*, and Hebrews' "For here have we no continuing city, but we seek one to come" and "he [God] hath prepared for them a city" (Heb. 13:14, 11:16) to imply the goal of the heavenly city in *Go Tell It on the Mountain* and, by allusion, in *Another Country*. But while treating Paul, Hebrews, and Revelation with complete respect, Baldwin adapts and revises their meanings. The "city" he envisions will come into being—if it does—not in response to divine judgment but out of human actions; the resurrections spoken of by Paul and John of Patmos (1 Cor. 15:51–57; Rev. 20:13) will be, by implication, a rebirth of those living today.

Baldwin further appropriates and revises Paul's teachings on discipleship and community. Besides valuing the voluntary suffering of discipleship—an idea Baldwin responds to in his Gide essay and expands in *Go Tell It* to imply willing immersion in the community of the despised—Paul bases his idea of community on the analogy of the body of believers to Christ's body, "one body in Christ, and every one members one of another" (Rom. 12:15). This central Pauline tenet builds on the "social body" metaphor that was "a commonplace in the Greco-Roman world" (Sampley 947). For Paul, the diverse men and women making up the believing community, who should be bound together in faith and equal or comparable in status, quite directly represent Christ's "body" in this world. The same idea enters later Christian thought in the form of the church as Christ's body, frequently with the narrowness and exclusivity latent in such an identification. Baldwin gives the idea a more general sense: rather than the church or the faithful, humanity constitutes a community whose members should practice fraternity; in *Another Country*, love and hate between members of this community synecdochically stand for love and hate in the social body.

Possibly Baldwin's most surprising and far-reaching response to Paul is his appropriation of the apostle's teaching on the body. Here as elsewhere Baldwin applies the method of "taking authority," recasting an oppressive word as one of freedom; doing so in relation to sexuality and homosexuality means he is revising much African American church teaching as well as Paul's. Baldwin surely knew Paul's pronouncements in First Corinthians against "abusers of themselves with mankind" (6:9) and in Romans against both female and male homosexual acts (1:26–27), statements that figure in Pentecostal teachings on sexuality.[19] Victor Paul Furnish summarizes that in Paul's eyes, both men and women who take part in homosexual acts "are thereby disqualified from participation in the kingdom of God" (83; see also 84). Baldwin also knew and rejected Paul's view that the flesh (*sarx*) is the gateway for pollution in the flesh-spirit continuum that is the body, with its corollary that in resurrection, "this corruptible must put on incorruption" (1 Cor. 15:53)—implying that the resurrected body will be "without earth, flesh, blood, or even psyche," for ancient culture a fine substance rather than immaterial (Martin 135).[20] Baldwin refers polemically to this and similar teachings in addressing the World Council of Churches, saying that black bodies are "the flesh that St. Paul wants to have mortified" ("WR" 754, probably referring to Romans 8:13 or Colossians 3:5). Despite his rejection of these doctrines, it is, nonetheless, the Paul of First Corinthians 13:11, "When I became a man, I put away childish things," that Baldwin will turn to in dramatizing his protagonist David's painful self-acceptance in *Giovanni's Room* (168), and he will take Paul's view of the "mystery" revealed in the eschaton as applying to the "mystery" and potential "revelation" inherent in his protagonist's "flesh," generally, and sex organs specifically (*GR* 168–69).

In these revisions, Baldwin extends Paul's apocalypticism, without biblical authority and thus on his own authority, from what he has already read as an apocalypse of the world and society (*Go Tell It*) to a revelation of the body's holiness. In part, as later uses of "filth," "honor," and "despised" suggest, Baldwin finds his authority in his own extension of the passages on God's choosing "things which are despised" and on the apostles' status as "the filth of the world" (1 Cor. 1:27, 4:13) to include the sexually reprobate. In this way, Baldwin locates in Paul's apocalyptic reversal of the world's judgments his own reversal of Paul's judgment against "abusers of themselves with mankind" (1 Cor. 6:9).

Additionally, Baldwin has, if not authorization, nonetheless a basis for his appropriation in the third passage, which resonates closely with the others. The body's "members," Paul says to the "Strong" at Corinth, though all different, are all "necessary," and indeed, "those members of the body, which we think to be less honourable, upon these we bestow more abundant honour; and our uncomely parts have more abundant comeliness" (1 Cor. 12:23). Paul's point is the need for accommodation between upper- and lower-class followers of Jesus at Corinth; his treatment of the faith community as a "body" allows the metaphor. But equally, the passage's reference to the genitals, the body parts often thought shameful and ugly, is plain; indeed, Martin notes that "the penis was euphemistically called the 'necessary' member" by Artemidorus and other ancient writers (95, 269 n. 22). So besides a symbolic application of this passage to the poor and outcast—one he would welcome on its own terms—Baldwin may have been alert to the literal meaning that the sex organs should receive "more abundant honour," and perhaps possess it intrinsically.[21] While Baldwin never quotes or alludes to this passage directly, his presentations of his protagonist David's body and "sex" as "the incarnation of a mystery"—a phrase combining traditional terms for Christ's taking human form and for the Trinity—and of another protagonist, Arthur, licking a lover's "sacred balls" replicate Paul's teaching on the "uncomely parts" (*GR* 168, *JAMH* 211). If, indeed, Baldwin paid attention to the literal meanings of Paul's "more abundant honour" and "more abundant comeliness," then, in this doctrine that the genitals should be exalted, he would have found a basis for his own belief, as well as a point of tension in Paul—between according the genitals honor in rhetoric and in analogy to the despised of society (1 Cor. 12), and insisting that the flesh is the source of contamination and must be put off entirely at the resurrection (1 Cor. 15). In that case, the three passages I have discussed offered a way to use Paul against Paul, in what is sometimes called "intra-canonical correction" (A. Smith 36). As the first two passages help Baldwin respond to Paul's dicta on homosexual acts, this part of First Corinthians offers a basis for Baldwin's view of the body and genitals as sacred as well as an answer to Paul's negation of the body.

Baldwin and African American Prophetic Traditions

Besides using and reshaping biblical language, Baldwin takes authority over and inflects African American prophetic traditions. He does so in two ways. Most directly, he sets his vision against the church traditions he grew up closest to, those of Pentecostal churches infused with Holiness or "sanctified" beliefs. These terms refer to distinct but partly overlapping church bodies and traditions, with major followings among both African American and other Christians. "Holiness" denotes a group of churches and fellowships, white and African American, that diverged from Methodism in the late nineteenth century. They placed preeminent emphasis on the experience of "sanctification" and stressed the need for believers to enter "a covenant of personal holiness for the glory of God" ("Holiness Churches"). "Pentecostalism" refers to a development originally out of Holiness Christianity, primarily in the first two decades of the twentieth century, involving both black and white leaders and congregations and, sometimes, interracial congregations, and ultimately spreading widely to other denominations. Pentecostal teaching stresses speaking in tongues as a key sign of receiving the Holy Spirit, and often shares Holiness theology's emphasis on bodily sanctity.[22] Baldwin rejects what he sees as these churches' narrowness, antisexuality, and complacency toward social oppression (see *FNT* 39). Against these perceived ills Baldwin practices both "intra-canonical" correction and the "extra-canonical correction" of appeal to secular experience (A. Smith 37). Characters such as Gabriel in *Go Tell It on the Mountain* embody the ills Baldwin indicts, while nonchurch or marginal church characters who despise church sanctimony and hypocrisy, such as Esther, Royal, and Richard in *Go Tell It*, the young Caleb Proudhammer in *Tell Me How Long the Train's Been Gone*, and the Rivers and Montana families in *If Beale Street Could Talk* and *Just Above My Head*, provide critique or corrective. (The last two families are sometime churchgoers, as noted earlier, who prefer Baptist to "sanctified" worship.)

Baldwin's second way of taking authority over African American prophetic traditions is more complex and far-reaching: he draws eclectically on at least three major threads in African American prophetic religious thought, largely secularizes them, and combines them in ways of his own.[23] These traditions are particularly important to Baldwin's ideas of the apocalyptic city and the roads toward it. But in contrast to his oppositional or "corrective" stance to church traditions on morality and the body, Baldwin responds to those in thinking about social progress by placing himself within them and filling them with his own content.

By far the most important such tradition for Baldwin is that of millennium and apocalypse, biblically based on Daniel, Revelation, and sections of Matthew, Mark, and the Pauline and general epistles, and including both broad ideas of a coming millennial age of peace and those of near-term eschaton and apocalypse. This varied

African American tradition reaches from the early-eighteenth century beginnings of Christianization (Frey and Wood 66) to twentieth-century Pentecostalism and beyond. In this tradition lie such sermons as John Jasper's "The Sun Do Move" (1877) and "The Stone Cut Out of the Mountain without Hands" (1884), which trace God's covenant with the downtrodden, discuss conduct in the post-Reconstruction world of entrenched injustice, and extend hope for the fall of the present world and the coming of God's kingdom. From these roots, too, comes the itineracy of Elder (later Bishop) Charles H. Mason of the Church of God in Christ, jailed more than once during World War I after "I took a scriptural stand against the ungodly deeds of the various races, about how many souls were being hurled into eternity without chance of seeking God for their soul's salvation. . . . I told them [his hearers] not to trust in the power of the United States, England, France or Germany, but trust in God."[24] Baldwin approaches this, his natal tradition, with respect but also opens it out into a two-sided vision of the transformative power of bodily and social love. At the same time, since Daniel and Revelation do not see human agents as initiating apocalyptic events—the initiative comes from the world above—Baldwin naturalizes the sources for the change, finding them in conscious acceptance of what is deepest in the psyche and in acts of love and rebellion in the social world.

To accomplish this naturalization, Baldwin turns to two other foundational traditions in African American church prophecy, themselves closely tangent. These tap ideas based in Exodus and Deuteronomy, on the one hand, and in the prophetic books, especially Isaiah and Ezekiel, on the other. From Exodus, African American general and religious tradition takes the fundamental assumption of a God for whom slavery and oppression are "hateful" (Jones and Allen 24) as well as a figural identification between the race and biblical Israel (Raboteau, "Blood" 53). Prophetic thinking further takes from Exodus and Deuteronomy the idea of a long history before reaching freedom—the forty wilderness years after Sinai and, even more, what Gerhard von Rad calls the "colossal arch" spanning the hundreds of years from the promises to the patriarchs until entry into Canaan (*Old Testament Theology* 1:134). Finally, these books, in which the law is given, contribute to a central African American belief in God's law—in itself, and as assumedly reflected in founding U.S. documents—as guide for the race and test and challenge for the larger nation. Baldwin, who mainly views law as unjust and oppressive,[25] has little interest in the last point, but takes from Exodus-Deuteronomy thinking the idea of a communal road to liberation spanning generations or centuries and marked, for him, by the growth of a rich, accretive common culture. To this part of Baldwin's thinking, too, belongs his use of one of African Americans' most remarkable appropriations from the oppressors—of the United States itself as chosen home and arena for struggle.

Baldwin further takes up African American uses of the prophetic books, including prophecies of communal restoration and resurrection in Isaiah and Ezekiel and, importantly but less centrally for him, the idea of a reform or "turn" that will save the surrounding nation from catastrophe, exemplified in Ezekiel's call to Israel, "Repent, and turn yourselves from all your transgressions; so iniquity shall not be your ruin" (18:30). While these ideas originally focused on the assumedly sinning nation of Israel, African American prophecy tradition applies the "turning" idea primarily to the United States' sins of slavery and exclusion and that of redemption to African Americans and their allies, as well as the larger nation once reformed. The latter idea, then, no longer refers only to a lifting of deserved punishment but to deliverance from undeserved affliction.

Importantly for Baldwin, these related traditions meet in believing that God works redemption in history by inspiring African Americans themselves to labor for it: "I believe that our cause can be helped by prayer," says Francis J. Grimké, a towering late nineteenth and early twentieth century exemplar of these traditions, but this belief "doesn't mean that we are to do nothing but pray, that we are to fold our arms and expect God to fight our battles for us." Prayer means, rather, "that in the midst of the conflict, while we are doing all we can, . . . we are at the same time to lay fast hold of the Almighty, to keep ourselves and our wants ever before Him, and to look to him for help in every time of need" (Grimké 1:289). This approach involves its own political tradition, which I elsewhere call prophetic integrationism, in which African Americans envisioned full participation in a future nation of justice and equality, one not yet existing, which they and their children would help bring by their own efforts.[26] These are, of course, partial and selective ways of reading biblical texts, as religious interpretations of scripture always are, but they have been foundational in African American prophetic thought.

Among these varied ideas, Baldwin makes that of "turning" central in some of his best known works, *Another Country* in fiction and *The Fire Next Time* in nonfiction. Yet, ultimately, it is less basic to his thinking than those of communal effort over time and ultimate liberation of the sufferers—ideas in which the Exodus-Deuteronomy and Isaiah-Ezekiel threads in prophecy entwine with those of Daniel and Revelation. For Baldwin these conceptions coalesce, with those of communal redemption and struggle through time standing as buttresses on either side of his sense of the reality, in some partly naturalized sense, of revelation of the hidden and of a future holy habitation. This amalgam is his own. In African American prophetic history, beliefs in long historical process and in communal redemption, themselves closely related, have borrowed at need from millennial-apocalyptic ideas of supernal justice, but have not fused with them. Likewise, millennial and apocalyptic thought has stood somewhat apart from these other traditions, the mainstream in prophetic social justice thinking. It is Baldwin who constructs a type of eschatological-apocalyptic thinking that incorporates and relies on processes of long evolution and communal restoration.

This Baldwin construct, in its turn, considers but places on one side a fourth strand in African American prophetic thought that, like biblical Jeremian prophecy, finds the oppressing nation so steeped in evil—affliction of the weak and worship of false gods of power and exclusion—that it cannot "turn" and must be destroyed or left for a new life elsewhere. This mode of thinking—in secular life the Black Nationalism common in the Harlem of his youth and in the national politics of his maturity—appears in Baldwin's fiction in the ideas of some characters. In nonfiction, Baldwin comes nearest this stance in *No Name in the Street* (1972), whose conclusion envisions a seemingly irreversible decline of U.S. world power and a decades-long world revolutionary struggle signifying a new world "ready to be born" (196), perspectives mixing Jeremian downfall of the sinning nation with apocalyptic birth. Yet this outlook proves transient, both because the expectations it embodies collapsed in the later 1970s and because, *Just Above My Head* will show, for Baldwin the core opposition was between hope of winning African American freedom in a society transformed as a whole, and losing redemptive hope altogether. Jeremian thinking as such remains marginal for Baldwin, while the three entwined threads in prophetic tradition already mentioned are central.

All these, however, presuppose the essential function of prophetic witness—the ability to make future possibility seem visible and real in present life. Consistently with this point, Baldwin's fiction is deeply concerned with prophetic office, the need for prophetic vision, and the truth, possible falseness, and costs of this kind of thinking and speaking. Logically, then, the prophet's commissioning is the subject of his first novel.

CHAPTER 1

Prophetic Commissioning

It came to him that he must testify: his tongue only could bear witness to the wonders he had seen.

—*Go Tell It on the Mountain*

Also I heard the voice of the Lord, saying, Whom shall I send, and who will go for us? Then said I, Here am I; send me.

—Isaiah 6:8

The subject of Baldwin's first novel, *Go Tell It on the Mountain* (1953), is the commissioning of the prophet. As readers know, the protagonist, John Grimes, a young man of intellect and individuality in Harlem in March 1935, initially longs for escape from the miserable circumstances of his community and his family life, especially from the strictures of his stepfather's churchliness and the general expectation that he himself will be a minister one day. In the novel's climax, he undergoes a carefully foreshadowed, yet dramatically unexpected, religious conversion experience. Concurrently, though this point is not explicit in the text, he has been moving toward a homosexual awakening that, in the aftermath of his religious experience, he accepts, though it is not clear how fully he understands it yet.[1] These circumstances set up the most obvious parameters for John's future development: will the conversion prove illusory or temporary, leaving John free to explore his own nature, or, alternatively, will commitment to an antisexual religion ultimately crush both John's emerging sexuality and his individuality? These are real possibilities and Baldwin explores them in portions of this and other books. Here, however, Baldwin sketches a third path. In the moments following his awakening, it comes to John, with conviction, that he must "testify" to "the wonders he had seen" (210), and his determination to do so grows in the remaining pages.

The evidence of Baldwin's text is that John's life will follow neither of the courses just indicated, but he will speak both the external and interior truths he has witnessed and continues to witness, testifying as well to some version of the conclusion his vision has persuaded him of—that the faithful will one day find "a city out of time, not made with hands" (207, paraphrasing 2 Cor. 5:1). John will be free in one way—from social convention—but bound in another, fated to speak what he alone can speak. In biblical terms, John has been called, or "commissioned," as a prophet—not through God's command but through inner sureness. However, the evidence is that John's future will not fall within bounds his church would bless but will take him in paths it would see as profane, and that he will fill the emptied vessels of church prophecy with new content. The novel only hints—but does hint—at this content: victory and transcendence for the bloodied multitudes in John's visionary experience (206–7), victory and transcendence for the dishonored body; the two great premises of Baldwin's fiction.

Baldwin's central story of prophetic vocation builds on a scaffolding of Old and New Testament ideas that are assumed but not made explicit.[2] In Old Testament tradition the prophet is selected (commissioned) by God or an agent of God, as recorded for Moses, Joshua, Isaiah, Ezekiel, Jeremiah, and Amos, and implied by the "word of the Lord" formula used for several others.[3] His or her function is not to foretell the future—an incidental though real element in biblical prophecy—but to speak God's word of warning, judgment, or promise to the nation, often a word it does not want to hear: "Go, and tell this people, Hear ye indeed, but understand not; and see ye indeed, but perceive not" (Isa. 6:9). In this mission the prophet may suffer rejection and mistreatment—may live "in watchings often, in hunger and thirst, in fastings often, in cold and nakedness," as Paul recalls of his ministry (2 Cor. 11:27), words Baldwin will appropriate for his protagonist.

As this tradition of calling and possible suffering indirectly indicates, the prophet's mission, at least in the important social justice strand in prophetic tradition, involves witness against those with social power and on behalf of the poor and defenseless, who are testing stones of the nation's justice. David L. Petersen comments about Isaiah specifically that he "indicts those who act unjustly to [the vulnerable]—princes, judges, lawyers, those who take bribes, those involved in illicit real estate transactions—in sum, those of high status and with access to power in the society" (*The Prophetic Literature* 90). These aspects of prophecy, which in historical real time vied against more complacent prophetic teachings, became central to the genre in a later process of canon formation that sought to understand Israel's disastrous history as, in part, a result of social injustice (with religious violation). In the New Testament, such statements as Jesus's "Come unto me, all ye that labour and are heavy laden" and "Inasmuch as ye have done it unto one of the least of these my brethren, ye have done it unto me" (Matt. 11:28, 25:40) powerfully continue this focus on the poor and outcast, and these aspects of prophetic and Gospel tradition became central in African American thought.[4] Yet, in contrast to this type of prophecy, canonical tradition also speaks of false prophecy—not simply untrue prediction but wrong orientations for the nation in its need. Though too neat historically, it is part of this tradition that while the true prophet speaks "things that cause himself and his audience to become apprehensive," the lying prophet "speaks the things he and the people desire" (Mowinckel 92–93). With regard to Revelation, a governing text for this novel, Christopher Rowland reminds us that in its view, "a prophet who claimed to speak for God but who also compromised with the existing order . . . is to be repudiated" ("Revelation" 735).

Ultimately, as Rowland implies, prophets' roles are not limited to denunciation and warning, but extend to visions of a new existence. With the historical development of eschatological and apocalyptic prophecy in post-exilic Israel and then in Greek and Roman times, and finally with the Gospel proclamations, apostolic writings, and Revelation in the New Testament, ideas of prophecy came to encompass the transition between old and new worlds and to include what Acts calls "the restitution of all things, which God hath spoken by the mouth of all his holy prophets" (3:21). Apocalyptic-eschatological prophecy becomes the word of hope for a new kind of existence, "new heavens and a new earth, wherein dwelleth righteousness" (2 Pet. 3:13; see comparable passages in Isa. 65:17 and 66:22 and Rev. 21:1). Baldwin's novel will speak of these and prophets' other roles, evoking biblical tradition yet redefining it.

The Need for Prophecy

Go Tell It on the Mountain uses multiple fictional techniques—narrative structure, epigraphs, characters' names, and imagery—to suggest the need for prophecy in its fictional world, its protagonist's prophetic affinities, and, to some extent, the content of the prophecy he will speak. This content, which will become evident in John's visionary experience, involves a sense both of accepted membership in a community of the despised existing across time and of a future transformed time in which that community will gain dignity and honor. The fictional techniques just mentioned treat these prophetic elements as latent dimensions of the narrative plot, suggested by implication.

Baldwin implies the need for prophecy through his novel's structure, in which the first and last sections focus on the seemingly private experiences of John's religious and sexual awakening, while middle sections delineate other characters' sexual and social lives against the historical backdrop of U.S. black experience. This structure puts John's life and conversion into a larger context, makes his fate of significance to the community, and, at the same time, suggests a long-term impasse in African American society. Tying these sections together is the novel's examination of African American Holiness and Pentecostal (or "sanctified") churches, their role as a shelter and rallying point for the overburdened, and what Baldwin sees as their narrowmindedness, antisexuality, and isolation from society. The cultural crisis turns around these churches' incapacity to lead toward the redeemed future they present as hope and aspiration, and this unmet need, in turn, implies the need for an alternative prophetic vision.

The Holiness and Pentecostal affiliations of the novel's church are clear from its name, Temple of the Fire Baptized, and the designation of the saved as "saints." In Holiness thought, the precursor to Pentecostalism in U.S. church history, the "fire baptized" were those who had experienced an ecstatic reception of the Holy Spirit, and many churches with this name eventually became Pentecostal (Synan chaps. 3, 6). The use of "saints" for the saved came into Methodism from English Puritanism (the ultimate derivation is from Daniel and Paul) but was particularly common in "sanctified" churches.[5] Holiness followers shunned "worldly" practices such as wearing decorative clothing or earrings, dancing, and watching movies (*GT* 32), and engaging in any sex outside marriage. "Holiness denominations," writes Peter Kerry Powers, partly drawing on personal experience, "believe that the body is the site within which the spirit is dramatically transformed [to experience] the indwelling of the Holy Spirit. . . . Paradoxically, despite its attention to matters of the spirit, Holiness Christianity encourages a meticulous attention to and monitoring of the body" (788).

This concern with bodily sanctity—which eventually generates Baldwin's contrary conception of the body's inherent holiness—stems originally from John Wesley's promulgation of "entire sanctification" or "Christian perfection," his "most distinctive contribution to the Christianity of his day" (Rack 552), as a cornerstone of eighteenth-century Methodism. Though Wesley's varied glosses of "perfection" could be modest—for example, it could mean an ability to adhere to God's law in action—he came to accept that sanctification might come in an instantaneous conversion-like experience, a "second blessing" or "second work of grace," and might confer "salvation from sin" in both thought and act, though sin was only "suspended," not "destroyed" (Wesley 187–88, sec. 26). (In contrast, Wesley's great rival George Whitefield rejected the possibility of ending the "in-being" of sin in life, and Baldwin was also deeply convinced of human imperfection.) Despite Wesley's qualifications, and his not emphasizing sexual over other kinds of sanctity, many of his nineteenth-century followers turned belief in "entire sanctification," especially regarding bodily purity, into hardened doctrine, spurring the formation of Holiness groupings within an increasingly worldly Methodism, their eventual exclusion, and their emergence as distinct churches, many of which later became Pentecostal.[6]

Disciplining sexuality was intrinsic to this stance. As John L. Peters's classic account of the Holiness development indicates, late nineteenth-century Holiness teaching evolved in part around beliefs in what an 1885 doctrinal statement called "a full regeneration of sinful habits and associations" and the "entire extinction of the carnal mind, the total eradication of the birth principle of sin" (137)—beliefs, we will see, mirrored in one of Gabriel Grimes's sermons.[7] These preconceptions are seen in Baldwin's portrayals of Holiness or "sanctified" worship in *Go Tell It on the Mountain* and later works, and in some characters' lives.

Additionally, though less saliently, the novel's setting, with no present-time scenes outside Harlem apart from John's midtown trip in Part One, shows the congregation's spiritual life as inward-looking, shunning involvement with or challenge to the larger society and awaiting a future transformation in a stance of patient nonengagement. In this social dimension as in its moral-sexual dimension, *Go Tell It* implicitly tests the Holiness culture's capacities against the unmet needs of the novel's historical world.

Epigraphs add to the implication of the novel's structure. As will be Baldwin's practice in later novels, epigraphs are thematically important and demand knowledge of their contexts; full meaning often depends on verses preceding or following those quoted. *Go Tell It* uses biblical epigraphs to head the book as a whole and Parts One to Three, and these restate and concretize the suggestion of a need for prophecy. (Chapter epigraphs, taken from Gospel and hymn music, focus on individual characters.)

The general epigraph, adapted from Isaiah 40, "They that wait upon the Lord shall renew their strength; they shall mount up with wings like eagles; they shall run, and not be weary, they shall walk, and not faint" (40:31), is part of the redemptive promises to Israel that begin in this chapter of Isaiah. This assurance, addressed to "Jacob" and "Israel" (verse 27), general terms for the nation, promises strength and renewal to those who serve, or "wait on," God. By implication, it applies as well to God's servants the prophets: they will have the strength to continue without tiring and to mount high.[8]

The remaining biblical epigraphs enact a shift from apocalyptic promise to the prophecy needed to work for it. The first is from the closing verses of Revelation:

> And the Spirit and the bride say, Come.
> And let him that heareth say, Come.
> And let him that is athirst come.
> And whosoever will, let him take the water of life freely. (Rev. 22:17; *GT* 1)[9]

Almost the last words in Revelation—the four final verses announce its completeness and pronounce benediction—this verse sums up the promise of the heavenly city detailed throughout the last two chapters: the city has descended to earth and in its midst is the fountain whose waters are for all (21:6). Thus, the context for Baldwin's examination of African American history, church evangelism, and their importance in his protagonist's life is the assurance of an end to suffering, a world in which God "shall wipe away all tears from their eyes" (Rev. 21:4). We do not yet know, however, whether to read this assurance as a serious sign of a transformed future or an ironic reference to false hopes.

The epigraph for Part Two is also from Revelation: "And they cried with a loud voice, saying, How long, O Lord, holy and true, dost thou not judge and avenge our blood on them that dwell on the earth" (6:10; *GT* 57), words spoken by "the souls of them that were slain for the word of God," who are granted robes of promised redemption and told to "rest yet for a little season" (6:9, 11). In counterpoint to the first, this epigraph denotes the present world of social and personal suffering that Part Two details in the stories of Deborah's rape by whites; Florence's failed marriage and approaching death; Gabriel's affair with and denial of Esther and his son Royal; Royal's own life, defiance, and death; Richard and Elizabeth's failed love; Elizabeth's suffering; and the continuing contexts of night riders (62–64), itinerant labor (134–36), white mob actions (140–43), and police oppression (169–70). Biblically, Revelation 6 leads on to the full disclosure of Babylon-Rome's arrogance and terror, before its destruction (chaps. 12–18); Baldwin does not deal with this material but it is felt in the gap between the two epigraphs. *Not yet*, this epigraph might answer its implied question and the promise of the first.

The third epigraph moves forward from this seeming impasse. Biblically, however, it moves back—from Revelation to the prophets and from the city to the event that must precede its advent, the prophet's selection. If the promise is not to be presently fulfilled, either it must be repudiated or ironized, or prophecy is required to guide us toward its fulfillment. Baldwin quotes Isaiah:

> Then said I, Woe is me! for I am undone; because I am a man of unclean lips, and I dwell in the midst of a people of unclean lips; for mine eyes have seen the King, the Lord of hosts. (6:5; *GT* 193)[10]

In immediate narrative context the words refer partly to John's sense of sexual sin—already suggested in his thoughts of boys, his fascination with his churchmate Elisha's physicality and imagined nights, and their wrestling (11, 6, 8, 48–49, 56). The words refer, as well, to the conversion now beginning, when John like Isaiah will sense God's presence. Biblically, however, the verse belongs to the genre of prophetic commissioning narratives (Ex. 3:2, 4:17; Jer. 1:4–19, etc.) and its meaning depends on its continuation, which Baldwin leaves to readers' knowledge. The quoted verse, from Isaiah's vision of himself at God's throne, registers his sense of unworthiness to see God, and leads on to his selection as prophet:

> Then flew one of the seraphim unto me, having a live coal in his hand, which he had taken with the tongs from off the altar:
>
> And he laid it upon my mouth, and said, Lo, this hath touched thy lips; and thine iniquity is taken away, and thy sin purged.
>
> Also I heard the voice of the Lord, saying, Whom shall I send, and who will go for us? Then said I, Here am I; send me. (6:6–8)

Touching the prophet's mouth with the coal signifies not only forgiveness of his sin but delivery of the commission, since the lips are "the vehicle of the word" (Childs, *Isaiah* 56).[11] Baldwin's part-epigraphs thus imply movement from the Revelation promise (*GT* 1) through the present reality of suffering and oppression (57) to the selection of a prophet figure to carry hope of the city to the community (193).

To suggest his protagonist's prophetic affinities, Baldwin uses both biblically resonant names and the chapter epigraphs associated with him. In Luke, Gabriel speaks to Elisabeth and Mary, foretelling the births of John (the Baptist) and Jesus respectively (1:11–20, 26–38). The former story, of the child to be called "the prophet of the Highest" (Luke 1:76), provides the names and the pattern for the Grimes family, with its ambivalent mother; father who, unlike biblical Gabriel, fails to announce the prophet; and son who ultimately emerges having heard the call to prophesy. Baldwin's John later recalls this one, "the prophet, John," who "came out of the wilderness," as an example of faith and witness (208). A coequal referent for the book's John is John of Patmos, the John of Revelation, who announced the struggle of Lamb and Beast, the end of empire, and the descent to earth of the heavenly city, seen from a "great and high mountain" (21:10) as in Baldwin's title. These references for John's name are underlined by the book's part-titles: that for Part Two, "The Prayers of the Saints," echoes John of Patmos's prophecy, and that for Part Three, "The Threshing Floor," John the Baptist's (Rev. 5:8, 8:3–4; Luke 3:17).[12] The novel's focus, then, is on the prophet's role rather than the savior's birth, as the traditional song of its title might suggest; indeed, the role of foretelling is implicit in the song as well, whose singer, in one version, calls herself/himself "a watchman / Upon a city wall."[13]

Complementing these Bible references, John's chapter epigraphs, "I looked down the line, / And I wondered" (3) and "Then I buckled up my shoes, / And I started" (195), show a shift from doubt to readiness, pertinent to his acceptance of prophetic vocation. They are from the same Gospel song, most significantly recorded by Rosetta Tharpe (1939), and show Baldwin's deep grounding in this music genre:

> Then I looked down the line and I wondered
> And I wondered
> And I wondered
> I looked down the line and I wondered
> Just to see how far that I was from God. . . .

Then I buckled up my shoes and I started
    And I started
    God knows and I started
I just buckled up my shoes and I started
    Just to see how far that I was from God. (Tharpe, "I Looked" 1–5, 11–15)[14]

Though still far from her goal, the song's seeker has "started," as John, by the novel's end, has also done.[15]

To suggest the content of the novel's prophecy, Baldwin uses several ways of approaching biblical imagery that he will repeat in later work, making them worth analyzing in some detail. Baldwin's typical procedure of appropriating biblical language and ideas while reversing or revaluing their meanings works in two ways in this and later novels. One inverts the values attached to this language—a text or image traditionally read salvationally becomes for Baldwin a sign of error or negative development, or one usually taken negatively signifies positive possibilities. In a fairly simple use of this inversion, when Elizabeth meets Gabriel, after the suicide of John's biological father Richard and John's birth, she feels she has begun an "upward climb—upward, with her baby, on the steep, steep side of the mountain," and that "her safety lay before her, like a hiding place hewn in the side of the mountain" (185, 189). Mountains traditionally signify holiness and closeness to God, and we understand that this imagery encapsulates Elizabeth's own conscious judgment, yet in doing so it reveals its falseness. Readers understand that, with Richard, Elizabeth was simply living on the same plane (of premarital sex and love) as millions more, one perhaps equivocal but human and defensible, and that the "mountain" and "safety" that she now values are arid and loveless, results of a restrictive morality and a false conception of holiness.[16] As used for Elizabeth, then, the mountain bears a meaning informed by but opposite to its biblical senses.

An alternative, more complex use of biblical and church imagery accepts such references in their customary positive or negative tonalities but modifies their content or supplies new content. Application of the "Canaan" idea to John (226), as noted later, provides an example. Canaan, the land promised Abraham and the Israelites' destination in their march from Egypt, resonates in African American usage through figural identification, as the place or condition of the promised future. Baldwin, always skeptical toward such traditions, does not necessarily affirm the identification overall but still applies the Canaan image to John at the novel's end, though he is bound toward a state his church would consider unholy.

Canaan, then, retains its traditional meanings of liberation and promise, applied to far different conduct.

Images of the sea and mountains, and downward and upward movement, which recur throughout this and later works, are used in both ways—sometimes with inverted meaning, sometimes attaching their traditional valuation to revised content. The two images have biblical roots. The "deep" or "waters" of Genesis 1:2 signify primordial chaos.[17] God's subjection of them is a fundamental manifestation of his power, remembered in Isaiah 51:10 and elsewhere, and replicated in the sea miracle (Exodus 14) and Jesus's calming of the sea (Matthew 14 and analogues in Mark and John). The mountain in contrast is the very seat of God's power, "the hills, from whence cometh my help" (Ps. 121:1), and in prophecy, a site of vision or of God's self-manifestation.[18] The mountain embodies, finally, God's glory in the time of redemption, when, God promises, "They shall not hurt nor destroy in all my holy mountain" (Isa. 65:25).

Baldwin often inverts these values in dealing with secondary characters, notably Gabriel. Water or chaos, negative in biblical uses, is for Gabriel a saving element he should but cannot embrace; the mountain, or holiness, represents his false piety and arrogance. Thus, Gabriel immerses himself in baptismal "water" whose only effect is to outline his "nakedness" and "black body" under "thin white clothes" (69). On his conversion, he hopes to leave his former life "at the bottom of the sea of forgetfulness" (88); memories of this life erupt "with the violence of water that has burst the dams" (91), but he subdues them. Later, experiencing a subsidiary temptation that leads him to marry Deborah, he is again immersed in liquid—his semen, in a wet dream—and, in a second dream, labors up "the steep side of [a] mountain," in response to what he takes as God's voice, until, "wearing long, white robes" (a dream transformation of the semen and his baptismal clothes), he emerges on an upland (107–9). In these linked descriptions, water connotes not the disorder and chaos of Genesis but that of the body, including its color and sexuality, and so should be confronted and experienced, not shunned; climbing the mountain, which Gabriel takes as an ascent to holiness, works as a dream symbol of rising from the body and its tumultuous desires. Here, then, water and mountain images have the opposites of their biblical values.

As used for John, the same images are refigured, but in ways not immediately obvious. Early in the novel, the mountain is evoked in tandem with the heavenly city as John surveys midtown New York from a hill in Central Park (26–29).[19] He experiences a complex temptation: he will enter the city as a welcomed "conqueror" and "live in this shining city which his ancestors had seen with longing from far away. For it was his; the inhabitants of the city had told him it was his; he had but to run down, crying, and they would take him to their hearts and show him wonders his eyes had never seen" (27). Yet, recalling church members' warnings of the city's sinfulness and his own sense of being a "stranger" there (27), he believes that to run down the hill, as he eventually does, is to "hurl away, for a moment of ease, the glories of eternity" (28, alluding to Heb. 11:25). The most obvious reading of these images is as a secular reimagining of their biblical senses. John's vantage point recalls Mt. Nebo in Deuteronomy (34:1) and the mountain of John of Patmos's vision. The city is New York, and the locations John encounters—Fifth Avenue (riches), the Public Library (learning), and a Times Square theater (entertainment and art)—are ones his church warns against and his white teachers have indeed implicitly promised (12–13).[20] So the mountain-and-city image seems to promise a city more humane and meaningful than that of Revelation. To turn to the biblical holy city along the "narrow way," which John associates with Harlem's streets and hallways, with "humiliation" and "growing old and black with hunger and toil" (28), is neither desirable nor even consistent with the biblical subtexts, since Harlem is behind John on his hilltop, not before him. Descent to the secular city, then, seemingly signifies liberation, as indeed the "ironic voice" John hears on the "threshing floor" (196 and later) will insist.

But ultimately the mountaintop image cannot be taken in this way, as a simple secularization of its biblical meaning. To do so would require ignoring the city's real warnings of its race prejudice (27, 30–31). Morally, it would mean seeing the church's "saints" and Harlem's "sinners" or non-churchgoers (7, 4) in John's dismissive terms—as contemptible because dirty and poor. Further, John's view of the city as one his ancestors had seen "with longing" (27), false to African Americans' overall history, true for the mood of the early twentieth-century migrations, is belied by the lives of Florence, Elizabeth, Richard, and Gabriel, who all find disappointment or undeserved death in the city. To interpret New York as the longed-for city, in sum, is to embrace a vision that separates the individual from the community, accepts or minimizes the pain of discrimination, and internalizes a partly true but historically inadequate sense of African Americans' place in the United States. These perspectives may be possible for John at this early stage, but the narrative urges their falseness. John's vision can be other than a bitter irony only if in some meaningful way it indeed refers to the city of Revelation 21:10—a city transfigured spiritually, democratically, or in another way. The contradictions of reading John's hilltop fantasy as a simple secular revision of biblical meaning, then, call for a reading in which his imagery retains its visionary biblical sense but with transformed content. This content will later require of John a descent not to secular New York but into the terrors of the self and a vision of the saints and the city that is neither his church's nor New York's, and that embodies the prophetic promise of the novel's biblical epigraphs. If such a reading makes sense, then Baldwin will have suggested the master idea of his fiction, the need to strive for the heavenly city, within the opening pages of his first novel.

False Prophecy

Gabriel is *Go Tell It on the Mountain*'s paradigm of the false prophet. He is presented both as a cruel and hypocritical individual and as a type, representing the evangelical church ministry and, in his own mind at least, that ministry's idea of a prophet. While the smug, worldly ministers at Gabriel's early revival and, in present time, the vigilantly antisexual Father James round out the picture (96–105, 9–10), Gabriel himself, particularly in his early ministry, is Baldwin's main example of this social type. Through Gabriel, the novel shows the arrogant and implicitly anti-working-class character of the church culture, and so its unreadiness for redemptive mission.

Baldwin's portrayal of Gabriel and those around him shows the falseness of Gabriel's prophetic self-conception—and so the need for John's acceptance of prophetic vocation—in several ways. First, the terms used for the faithful, "saints" (97; above), "chosen" (105–6, used by one of the elders at the revival and echoed by Gabriel), and "elect" (109, in Gabriel's dream), reveal part of the intellectual foundation for the church community's self-righteousness and censoriousness. In the view implied by Gabriel's dream, the elect are those who have experienced conversion and sanctification in the church and now occupy a superior status, signified by their presence on the mountain upland. The arrogance this idea can prompt is visible in Gabriel's conduct throughout the novel. Since Baldwin sketches Gabriel's early ministry as generally evangelical, rather than specifically Holiness-affiliated,[21] this part of Baldwin's critique applies to evangelical culture generally. (However, Gabriel's struggle to achieve sexual sanctity and his preaching emphasis on sexual sin typify Holiness attitudes and prefigure his later affiliations.)

Gabriel's ideas about his prophetic role, and his preaching, show his misconception of this role. Gabriel is specifically called a prophet just twice—once when his thoughts refer to his unborn child as "the seed of the prophet" and once in scorn by Florence (127, 217). But this is his self-conception from his conversion on. He hopes "to know himself to be the Lord's anointed, his well-beloved" (89), and feels God has given him "signs of His favor" (111). He believes he will father "a royal line" (105), that God told him his "seed" would be among the elect (109), that his dream contained a "promise" valid across the years (112). His words recall Isaiah's claim of being "anointed" by God (61:1), similar references to Israel's kings and the nation as a whole,[22] and Paul's uses of "beloved" for particular disciples and for the believing community (e.g., 1 Cor. 15:58, 2 Cor. 12:19). But as used by Gabriel, the terms convey self-importance and self- entitlement, senses that continue in his view of ministerial vocation. His expectations that his calling will confer "authority" in speech and the status of a "master" (89), and his anticipation of his first sermon as a "performance" that can win "the prize" (97), are understandable for a novice minister, and yet Gabriel's thoughts show no sense of prophetic mission to the community—Isaiah, for example, says he has been "anointed" to "preach good tidings unto the meek [and] proclaim liberty to the captives" (61:1). Absent, finally and crucially, from Gabriel's use of "promise" is the sense that the promise is God's to the community, rather than personally to the prophet. Gabriel's use echoes but contrasts with one of the great texts on faith and prophecy, Hebrews 11, where the term denotes a word to be redeemed in future time, not by the prophet in present time:

> These [Abraham, Isaac, Sarah, etc.] all died in faith, not having received the promises, but having seen them afar off. . . .
>
> And these all, having obtained a good report through faith, received not the promise:
>
> God having provided some better thing for us, that they without us should not be made perfect. (Heb. 11:13, 39–40)

Gabriel lacks this sense of communal destiny and of the prophet's role of announcing "promises" that she/he, and indeed the community of a given time, may never see. Both will be aspects of Baldwin's sense of prophecy, hinted at though not fully expressed in John's commissioning.

The falsity of Gabriel's assumed status is also clear in his conventional rather than prophetic understanding of scripture, revealed particularly in the first of two sermons Baldwin creates for him—his first public sermon, on Isaiah 6:5 (99–102).[23] The text is the same that later appears as the epigraph to Part Three. Ignoring or unattuned to its narration of Isaiah's commissioning, Gabriel develops the text as a lesson in the overwhelming power of sin, mentioning Isaiah as prophet only to show that even the great are helpless before sin. The sermon uses sexual desire as its chief example of sin. Though it refers briefly to sins of envy (Cain) and presumption (Babel; the revolt in heaven), it mentions no sins of abusing power, intolerance, caste, social exclusion, or war—topics many African American sermons did stress in the time of Gabriel's youth, the end of the nineteenth century. (Examples include Alexander Crummell's "Christ Receiving and Eating with Sinners," published 1882, against the "spirit of caste," and Lucius H. Holsey's "The Work of an Enemy," published 1898, on war as Satan's work.)[24] Further, the sermon sees sexual sin not as a wrong use of a good or valid desire but as the very expression of evil desire, in line with Gabriel's previously expressed hatred for "the evil that lived in his body" (88), and consistently with Holiness teachings on carnal desire. Sin, Gabriel says powerfully, "reigns in all our members, sin is the foul heart's natural liquid, sin looks out of the eye, amen, and leads to lust," caused "the fire to fall on Sodom," and can be overcome only through Jesus's sacrifice on the cross (100, 101).

Two aspects of Gabriel's view deserve comment. First, as Gabriel's later history shows—after his affair with Esther, he is faithful to Deborah and later Elizabeth—the Holiness "monitoring of the body" already referred to (Powers 788) is possible, though difficult. But this self-policing neither alters nor even offsets pride, deceit, hostility, and cruelty, Gabriel's besetting sins. Psychically, if Baldwin does not suggest directly that sexual repression is a cause of the personality deformation that fosters these sins, he does imply that wrestling down one's sexual impulse leads to arrogance and coldness. Morally, Deborah's avowal after Royal's death that "if you'd wanted to own that poor boy, I wouldn't of nohow cared what folks said, or where we might have had to go, or nothing. I'd have raised him like my own" (148), implies that Gabriel's focus on sexual sin is entirely irrelevant to a Christianity of acceptance and forgiveness such as hers. Second, in overlooking the sermon text's relation to Isaiah's prophetic commissioning, Gabriel's sermon also neglects a salient aspect of that story, the seraph's touching Isaiah's lips with a coal (verses 6–7), signifying purification to speak God's word. It is not told of any of the prophets that they led sinless lives. Rather, God took them as they were: "The word of the Lord came unto me"; "and the hand of the Lord was there upon him" (Jer. 1:4, Ezek. 1:3). The prophet's selection does not require absence or mastery of sin but its acceptance and transcendence through the prophetic mission. John, who can accept that he is a sinner, can become a prophet, whereas Gabriel, who denies it, never can.

Falsity in pastoral and family relations also contravenes Gabriel's assumed status. Despite images of the prophet as a social outsider, many of the recorded prophets were involved in their communities and several, at least, functioned as priests, acting as pastoral caregivers as well as public tribunes.[25] One historian of prophecy speaks of Ezekiel, for example, as exemplifying, over two decades, "prophecy as a form of pastoral ministry and community leadership" (Blenkinsopp 180). Prophetic life, then, should involve active care for one's congregants and community. Gabriel shows little of this concern. In abandoning Esther and failing to acknowledge Royal after her death, Gabriel not only displays personal cowardice, but also disregards the pastor's role as caregiver and, indeed, the prophet's concern for the poor and victimized.

Baldwin's portrayal of Gabriel's field itineracy (134–36) illuminates the larger social and spiritual world that must be transformed to make love and fraternity real, and the incapacity of evangels with Gabriel's ideas to meet this need. The chronology places this episode, during Esther's pregnancy, at the very beginning of the 1900s, but its social terrain can fit any time through the 1920s. The communities Gabriel ventures into are full of women "twisting their bodies into lewd hallelujahs" who tell him of others who could "make him lay his Bible down"; the music he hears is blues and early jazz, strummed "in the lone, blue evening" or blown "in fury and ecstasy" at night. This world contains, Gabriel believes, "no man, preaching, or cursing, . . . who had not been made to bend his head and drink the white man's muddy water." He views those he is among as "a bastard people, far from God, singing and crying in the wilderness," whose "names were nothing more than dust blown disdainfully across the field of time" (135–36). These are Gabriel's perceptions, not Baldwin's: the musicians' names, as Baldwin knew, were W. C. Handy, King Oliver, Ma Rainey, Thomas Dorsey, and more; indeed, in Baldwin's work the world to which the prophet bears responsibility is largely of communities like these.[26] Gabriel manages, against odds, to retain and strengthen his faith in this alien setting, to keep in mind "that power of redemption to which he must, till death, bear witness" (136). But this is a victory of personal sanctity alone; Gabriel, and the evangelical culture he represents, remain disdainful of this group, unable to respect them or find how to care for their souls.

Finally, Baldwin's depiction of characters around Gabriel who reject his assumption of righteousness—Esther, Royal, Florence, and, in her own way, Deborah

—allow the novel's church skeptics and reprobates to speak in direct or indirect judgment of the "elect." The two most important such scenes involve Royal. In the first, Royal as a child accosts Gabriel "boldly" in the street and, after he passes with no acknowledgment, stage-whispers, "I bet he got a mighty big one!" (138). Even as a child, then, Royal sees through Gabriel's self-protecting holiness, knows that a preacher is as much a man in the profane sense as anyone, and may have divined their relationship. In a later chance meeting during the white mob attacks of summer 1919, Royal, after hesitation, is the first to acknowledge the other, with a respectful "How-de-do, sir," to which at first Gabriel can only reply in kind. Surprise, extreme danger, and perhaps Royal's flashy dress (141), a provocation to whites, then wrest from Gabriel a rebuke followed by a plea: "I just mean you better be careful, son. Ain't nothing but white folks in town today." Gabriel's generic "son" rings with the ambiguity of their unacknowledged relationship. As they separate, Gabriel blesses Royal; Royal thanks him, and adds, with a smile, "But you be careful, too" (142). Gabriel, in sum, blesses without acknowledging a bond, while Royal, without blessing Gabriel, acknowledges him as human being and perhaps as father. Royal, then, negates Gabriel's assumed superiority of status and morality by treating him as only a man, but also acknowledges their bond as men in common danger. If, in such encounters, the reprobate deny the superiority thought to lift the elect above common humanity, they also imply that pastoral and prophetic office would know only this humanity, and in this way they show the inadequacy of the church culture's understanding of its mission.

Prophetic Vocation

John's ecstatic experience on "The Threshing Floor" (193), which at first he and his congregation accept as a conventional awakening to faith, seems to pose an insoluble dilemma. If he embraces the experience in his church's terms, he must throttle his burgeoning intellect, psychic autonomy, and sexual desires; but if he remains true to these, his trajectory must lie away from his church and, seemingly, his experience cannot have been valid. These alternatives replicate those implied in the Central Park scene: will John turn back to the holy city or run forward to the secular one? In the event, he does neither. Under the epigraphs mentioned earlier, implying prophetic vocation and resolution, he descends into the depth of the self, senses there the fellowship of prophetic suffering and salvational vision, and emerges with the strength to face new experiences that confirm his sexual and prophetic identities, and to bear forward with his own vision.

Some recent commentaries have seen more compatibility between John's homosexuality and his church or community culture than I propose, while, at the same time, not accounting for the specifics of his vision. Rightly stressing that "sexual desire is inextricably linked to religious transformation" in *Go Tell It on the Mountain* and the related story "The Outing," and acknowledging the "Puritan strictures" of John's church, Douglas Field nonetheless proposes that Pentecostalism incorporates "an acceptance between Africanism and homosexuality" and, by implication, a possible berth for John (103, 139). In a similar vein, though without referring to religious contexts, Matt Brim, using work by Roderick Ferguson, argues that nonheteronormativity in African American family structure implies tolerance toward John's emergent homosexuality (46–53 and notes). These readings situate the possible acceptance of homosexuality differently—in the church and the community, respectively—but neither takes account of the strong church- and class-based African American aspirations toward heteronormative family life and conventional morality that Baldwin shows in this (e.g., Elisha's shaming, 9–10) and other novels.[27] Neither, additionally, distinguishes street tolerance from street derision and violence or the tacit latitudinarianism of some church members (e.g., Elizabeth) from the stance of church leaders. (I myself have learned from students of their own or family members' leaving Pentecostal congregations because of homosexuality, and in the last decade, not the 1930s and 1940s.) Neither accounts for John's "no matter . . . where I go, what folks say about me" (225), a plea that makes no sense if John envisions a future as a tolerated homosexual within his church. And they disregard or minimize the visionary-communitarian content of John's experience.

Baldwin's account in effect telescopes into a night events that in his life occupied the span from about his fourteenth year to his late twenties: assuming a role in the church and leaving it, coming to terms with homosexuality, growing into adult vocation, and taking up the task of articulating a partly secularized redemptive vision. It is of course not naturalistically credible that all this would happen in one night and morning, and this fact and Baldwin's veiled language contribute to the ambiguity of the novel's ending. But Baldwin's presentation conveys a clear thematic meaning.

For John's ecstatic experience, Baldwin uses imagery primarily of descent, balanced by a final "rise" (209) to rejoin the congregation. Before his fall onto the church floor John senses in the congregants' prayers "endless, depthless, swelling water" and in his own mind "a deep, deep turning, as of something huge, black, shapeless, for ages dead on the ocean floor" that begins moving in a silence like that of the "void before creation" (74–75). Later he feels his mind "like the sea itself" and feels himself "at the mercy of this sea, hanging there with darkness all around him" (145). And within his ecstatic seizure, John lies "at the very bottom of darkness," simultaneously prostrate on the church's "dusty floor" and "going down" to the "bottom of the sea"; he is "swallowed up in chaos" (196–97). The darkness, water, void, and chaos—all images from the opening of Genesis—are, then, those of John's own mind, and the chaos is partly that of sexual confusion: the "huge, black, shapeless" thing sensed on the sea floor (75) is arguably a form of both his own penis and his stepfather's, "slimy like a serpent, and heavy like the rod" (199). The latter term conflates the rod of punishment, the church tradition of Christ as "the living rod" that John hopes to grasp (199), and John's own rod, which he has already grasped more than once (11, 199).[28] The word, then, suggests the symbolic mutability of the penis as source of dread and punishment and as holy and sacred. If, indeed, the primordial chaos, according to one school in biblical interpretation, was linked to the sea dragon in other Near Eastern religions,[29] then John's fear is of his own sexuality as chaos.

This is half of what he must confront; the other half is the dread and attraction of communal identification. Earlier in the all-night service he has sensed around him the company of the faithful, their "faces, and their attitudes, and their many voices rising as one voice," and has intuited their continuity over "the terrible stretch of time" since Jesus's ministry (74–75). This vision then inspired "anguish"; John wished either to experience "a power that would bind him, forever and forever, to the love of God," or "to stand up now, and leave this tabernacle" (75), the alternatives most interpreters allow him. But his sense of this company will mutate as his vision continues.

Early in his trance, John senses an "ironic voice" (196 and later) urging him to reject the experience, go "out into the world," and so avoid becoming "like all the other niggers" (196).[30] Essentially equivalent to his earlier vision of the city as secular promise, this voice becomes silent as John finds that "irony had left him" and that "he was searching for something, hidden in the darkness, that must be found" (202).[31] That "something," the intensely emotional imaginative encounters that follow will suggest, is the truth about himself—including his likeness, despite difference, to "all the other niggers"—and the possibility of imaginative connection to the earth's despised across space and time.

Once the ironic voice is still, within his trance John faces and accepts fundamental realities. These start with the brute fact of death. Lines from the song "I Looked Down the Line (And I Wondered)," which supplies epigraphs for the opening chapter and this one, come to him: "Then I looked in the grave and I wondered"; "And the grave looked so sad and lonesome" (202). The song's answering refrain remains unstated: "Just to see how far that I was from God." John further experiences the overpowering need for love and forgiveness (202–3). Beyond these elemental emotions he senses degradation and despair, of the individual soul and of African Americans as a group: "the body in the water, the body in the fire, the body in the tree" (203). This anguish is manifested in a community of sufferers that, the text implies, is both the faithful in particular and African Americans and the exploited and subjected in general, "the despised and rejected, the wretched and spat upon, the earth's offscouring," in words partly echoing Isaiah's and Paul's (204; see Isa. 53:3, 1 Cor. 4:13). John senses that he is "in their company," that "their humiliation, anguish, chains, their dungeon [will be] his, their death his," and he envisions this "desolation" in words also drawn from Paul's about his discipleship: "Thrice I was beaten by rods. . . . In weariness and painfulness, in watchings often, in hunger and thirst, in fastings often, in cold and nakedness" (204; 2 Cor. 11:25, 27). John, in sum, learning from the prophets and apostles, envisions both his own suffering witness and that of the world's scorned. And beyond these intuitions, John gains a vision of a new world of glory, represented both in traditional song—"I, John, saw a city, way in the middle of the air"—and in biblical reference as Paul's city "out of time, not made with hands" (207).[32]

Paul's references to the sufferings of the faithful, in particular, form a pathway for John from the idea of unwilling suffering to that of suffering accepted as part of identification with a community.[33] Having earlier sensed a community of faith existing across time (74–75), John now experiences a more vivid and extensive, and differently inflected, vision of this group's long struggle. He perceives its members first in white robes at a celebration of the Eucharist and then in ragged robes, some naked, and stained with dust and blood on a long road (206), struggling against one another to reach the healing river. The road is that of communal history—"Stony the road we trod," in the Johnsons' "Lift Every Voice and Sing"—and the general history of suffering and oppression, and has upheld, yet also maimed and deformed, those who walk it. As John awakens after his trance, he perceives the church congregants in the light of this historic experience; significantly, he is now conscious, assimilating and interpreting what were raw perceptions during the trance:

> The trembling he had known in darkness had been the echo of their joyful feet—these feet, bloodstained forever, and washed in many rivers—they moved on the bloody road forever, with no continuing city, but seeking one to come: a city out of time, not made with hands, but eternal in the heavens. No power could hold this army back, no water disperse them, no fire consume them. One day they would compel the earth to heave upward, and surrender the waiting dead. (207, adapting Heb. 13:14, 2 Cor. 5:1, and Rev. 20:13)

The "army" of the faithful and the earth's wronged will, then, according to John's understanding, one day usher in a figural resurrection of those gone before, in the new city promised in Revelation. As these thoughts continue, John associates the "army" with the prophets who triumphed over fire and stopped the mouths of lions; with those in whose company Moses chose to suffer rather than live in ease; with the "scattered bones" in Ezekiel's vision, emblem of national resurrection; with those whom John the Baptist told that God's "promise was for them" (208; see Heb. 11:25, 33–34; Ezek. 37:1–15; Luke 3:4–6). It is particularly important that John envisions a struggling multitude, while his father's dream was of "the elect," and that he imagines eschatological change coming through human agency—the "army," not God, will cause earth to yield its dead. Both ideas will become integral to Baldwin's apocalypticism.

To understand the power of John's vision we must imaginatively enter the world of apocalyptic thought and *feel* the assumed redemption of both living and dead—what Blake, in another context, describes as "all that has existed in the space of six thousand years: / Permanent, & not lost not lost nor vanishd" (*Jerusalem* 13:58–59). As he sensed earlier in the service (*GT* 74–75), John now *experiences*, as direct presence, his part in a visionary community reaching across the present world and both back and forward in time. John's vision is central to Baldwin's meaning and constitutes both an early comment on the persistence of the idea of the heavenly city in African American religion and an initial statement of the importance of this idea in Baldwin's fiction.

To sustain this view of John's vision as seriously redemptive will require, however, examining its aftermath to establish that John integrates his insights within his own understanding of the world rather than abandoning them or simply reverting to his church's ideas. Four significant events after John awakens support this assessment: he senses that "the terrors of the night" are "not finished" but in fact "in this company [are] now to begin" (209); he confronts his stepfather, asserts his justification in God's eyes, and tells him he will resist "everything and everybody . . . that wants to cut down my soul" (210–11, Baldwin's ellipses); simultaneously, he resolves that he "must testify" and "bear witness to the wonders he had seen" (210); and he receives blessings from his mother, from Praying Mother Washington, from Florence, and from Elisha (210, 209, 211, 225). These events are most plausibly read as indicating John's emergence into conviction of his difference from his church's prescriptions, including some degree of self-awareness as a homosexual, and into sureness of his mission of bringing his own vision of redemption to the world.

John's request for the last blessing will be pertinent first, as it triangulates with his earlier thoughts. Having come "through" in response to Elisha's voice (205, 207), John asks Elisha to confirm that the voice was his (221), then asks if the price of faith may be "*my life*" (222); asks Elisha to "pray for me . . . for *me*" (223); struggles to tell Elisha "something more—struggled to say—all that could never be said" (224); and pleads that "no matter what happens to me, where I go, what folks say about me, no matter what *any*body says, you remember—please remember—I was saved. I was *there*" (225). These are his last words to Elisha. John, in sum, conceives that he may pay a heavy price for his belief; feels himself in need of others' prayer; wishes to tell Elisha something that not only cannot be said now, but can never be said to him; anticipates that people (inferably church members) will vilify him and that he will go elsewhere; and yet expresses his own self-knowledge and self-acceptance. These reactions may partly reflect John's already developed sense of intellectual difference, his conception of himself as a future "poet, or a college president, or a movie star," and his sense that his "hatred [for Gabriel] and his intelligence" constitute his very "identity" (12, 13)—early preoccupations, however, that he has now passed on from. His responses probably further reflect his perception, born on the threshing floor, that "the heart was a fearful place" (210), an idea at odds with his church's shallow understanding of attainable perfection and sin as a violation of specific codes. Finally, while these factors may be enough to explain some level of estrangement within his church's culture, they do not fully explain John's intuition of continuing "terrors of the night" (209) These, with his senses of something that can "never be said" and that he must go elsewhere, make it likely that John has come to some awareness, if not full consciousness, of his homosexuality and anticipates that because of it, he cannot long remain within the church. Yet, while already aware of the "terrors," John has told his stepfather that he will pray God "to make me strong" against those who would "cut down my soul"—Gabriel and others—and has asserted, with Job, "My witness is in

Heaven and my record is on high" (210–11; Job 16:19). He is saying, then, that what is "on high"—the words refer to God, but also encompass inner sureness born of visionary experience—already knows and accepts him *as he is*, and that it is for that power rather than Gabriel to judge him.

It further comes to John "that he must testify: his tongue only could bear witness to the wonders he had seen" (210). The words mark John's sense of a future vocation, as distinct from simply a conviction of being saved and accepted. They recall biblical statements about and by the two prophets whose common name he bears:

> There was a man sent from God, whose name was John.
>
> The same came as a witness, to bear witness to the Light, that all men through him might believe.
>
> He was not that Light, but was sent to bear witness to the Light. (John 1:6–8)

> And I John saw these things, and heard them. And when I had heard and seen, I fell down to worship before the feet of the angel which showed me these things.
>
> Then saith he unto me, See thou do it not: for I am thy fellow servant, and of thy brethren the prophets. . . . (Rev. 22:8–9)

The scriptural echoes establish John's future roles: as "witness to the Light" and as one of "thy brethren the prophets." The "wonders" must be specifically the content of his visionary experience—his vision of communal history and suffering and the sufferers' destination in the holy city. Further, the earlier "wonders" that he imagined receiving in the hilltop scene (27) have been displaced by those seen on the dusty floor of a Harlem church, among, not apart from, the poor and hated. Finally, since John's sense that his "terrors" will continue has prompted his determination to "testify," Baldwin implies that his prophetic role will incorporate knowledge of the darkness and mystery of the heart, his ocean floor—though it is not yet clear whether he will speak openly of homosexuality as a prophet.

The series of blessings that follow John's emergence from the visionary experience act as confirmations of his prophetic role—unwitting ones so far as the speakers do not fully understand this role. His mother urges, "You keep the faith. I'm going to be praying for you till the Lord puts me in my grave"; Praying Mother Washington tells him, "Run on, honey, and don't get weary!"; Florence echoes, "You fight the good fight. . . . Don't you get weary, and don't you get scared. Because I *know* the Lord's done laid His hands on you"; and Elisha, kissing John's forehead, says as well, "Run on, little brother. . . . Don't you get weary. God won't forget you" (210, 209, 211, 225). John receives the kiss in what is inferably a double way, erotic but also as signifying the "holy kiss" to the disciples of First and Second Corinthians and as bearing "a seal ineffaceable forever," the seal of the 144,000 righteous in Revelation 7:3–4 (*GT* 225). In the novel's last words, John responds implicitly to all the blessings: "I'm ready, . . . I'm coming. I'm on my way" (226).

These statements all are multivalent, meaning one thing to the person blessing, potentially another to John, and certainly a third to the reader who understands Baldwin's Gospel and biblical allusions. All the characters save John himself assume, presumably, that he is poised to advance toward the illustrious church career long foretold (3), and so Praying Mother Washington's and Elisha's blessings also look to this event. Elizabeth's and Florence's blessings are illuminated in their respective parts of the novel's tripartite coda (211–24).[34] Elizabeth's blessing is suffused with regret for her lost happiness and fear that John *will* grow into his church role; like her otherwise inexplicable earlier sorrow at John's vow to "love the Lord" (26), her promise, "I'm going to be praying for you" (210), and her statement to Sister Price that she prays for God to "bear him up on every side" (212) reflect this fear. For Florence, certainly, "Fight the good fight" and "don't you get scared" mean John should stand up to Gabriel. Elisha, whom John so idealizes, grins and imagines (we suppose) that John will be like Father James. Yet three of the speakers have chosen the same biblical text for their blessings—the one in the novel's general epigraph: those who "wait upon" God will "mount up with wings like eagles;" shall "run, and not be weary, they shall walk, and not faint" (Isa. 40:31, adapted). As used by the characters, the verse, promising God's strength to his faithful, implicitly blesses John as a servant of God. Further, as noted earlier, the verse promises, as well, strength and endurance to the prophets, the servants of God who will speak the promise. John's closing words, implicitly responding to all the blessings, have the same twin resonance. Drawn from the song "I'm on My Way to Canaan's Land," which begins, "I'm on my way to Canaan's land / [twice more] / I'm on my way (praise God) I'm on my way," John's "I'm on my way" speaks both of personal assurance and of the race's advance toward the figural Canaan of its destiny.

This double vision—a serious promise of a redeemed future and the emergence of a biblically-inflected, partly secularized prophetic voice to speak the promise—emerges in Baldwin in this novel, as a brief comparison with the earlier story "The Outing" (1951), which shares some of its elements, will show. In a climactic moment, the story's protagonist Johnnie "felt, suddenly, not the presence of the Lord, but the presence of David," the story's homoerotic interest (51). Thus Johnnie apparently recognizes his sexuality more clearly than John has so far. The counterposition of God's and David's "presences," however, is not repeated for Elisha in the novel; in its last scene, John seems to attest to both. Further, the scenes in *Go Tell It on the Mountain* showing John's sense of God's acceptance and the need to testify do not occur in "The Outing," in which Johnnie is not saved and which ends with him sitting with David's arms around him but feeling "panic" and "danger" (57). Johnnie, then, has awakened to possible life as a homosexual wholly within the existing world, without hope of its transformation or a mission to help bring that transformation. In sum, what *Go Tell It* adds to "The Outing" is, first, its homosexual protagonist's self-acceptance in some religiously meaningful sense and, second, his conviction of a communitarian-redemptive vision.

That vision is antithetical to the church's but also set apart from ordinary mid-twentieth century liberalism by its retention of ideas of eschatological change. Recent commentaries have accepted early Baldwin's critical distance from liberal and Cold War thinking (see, e.g., Rasberry), but have not recognized *Go Tell It on the Mountain* as an expression of this distance nor its eschatological language as the basis of its alternative outlook. It is, in sum, the core validity of John's trance experience—both of realized identity with history's bloodied pilgrims and of identification with Pauline apostolic service and suffering—that first articulates Baldwin's own mission and establishes his separateness from the liberalism of his time.

John's sense that his "terrors" are to continue has, then, been the precipitating stress that carries him beyond the temporary joy of finding oneness with God to a conception of difference from his church's ideal and a determination to withstand all "that wants to cut down my soul." This impetus does not bring about a turn toward the worldly city, as the "ironic voice" urged, but catalyzes the resolve to be a "witness" to the "wonders" he has glimpsed, both individual and general, social and sexual—everything sensed in his trance as well as the family and racial history traced in Part Two, which he knows little of but is heir to and will discover. And this sense pushes him toward oneness with the prophets who chose "rather to suffer affliction with the people of God"—as very broadly understood in his vision: the faithful, the race, and all the insulted and injured—than to enjoy the world's pleasures (Heb. 11:25; *GT* 208). John will emerge as prophet of this group's destiny and its inheritance of the heavenly city. This intuition, finally, prompts his further foreknowledge that he will not remain long in the church and his requests for prayer and acceptance from Elisha—requests Elisha cannot comprehend fully. We do not learn John's future—he makes no firm commitment either to prophecy through art, or to any other form of prophetic activity. Baldwin's predominant figure for articulating his vision, the prophetic artist, awaits definition. Yet John is justified in his sense of being, with Elisha's blessing, "on my way."

CHAPTER 2

Prophetic Art

> I seemed to hear with what burning he had made it his, with what burning we had yet to make it ours, how we could cease lamenting.
>
> —"Sonny's Blues"

> Then said he unto me, Prophesy unto the wind, prophesy, son of man, and say to the wind, Thus saith the Lord God; Come from the four winds, O breath, and breathe upon these slain, that they may live.
>
> —Ezekiel 37:9

Baldwin's fiction develops, deepens, and finally questions a conception of prophetic art, without ever abandoning it. This is an art that speaks to the community about restoration from oppression and about ultimate freedom and is embodied in an artist figure whose art has this content. Baldwin suggests varied possible emphases for this art, from largely secular to overtly sacred, and sometimes implies prophetic art by negation, showing what is lost when it is absent. In showing this kind of art, Baldwin maintains his own practice of juxtaposing mimetic narration—implicitly naturalistic and apparently secular—with the emotive force and implication of sacred possibility he draws from biblical and Gospel language; and he introduces the nature and relation of prophetic and nonprophetic art as a major concern of his novels.

The prophetic art Baldwin depicts is, usually, not narrowly programmatic. Baldwin is concerned in nearly all his works with the responsibilities of the artist and the nature of an ideal or true art, and this emphasis is to some extent independent of his focus on the prophetic. Yet in fundamental ways Baldwin portrays prophetic art as the most fully artlike, not at odds with the artist's obligation to reveal truth but an expression of it. Art that is valuable, Baldwin suggests through a character in *Another Country*, reveals what is "dark, strange, dangerous, difficult, and deep" (112), especially (but not only) the depth of sexual terror in the human soul. Art, further, must not offer a spurious or shallow hope but must recognize what Baldwin, like others of his generation, affirmed as life's tragic nature, "tragic simply because the earth turns and the sun inexorably rises and sets, and one day, for each of us, the sun will go down for the last, last time" (*FNT* 91). And yet, because art's obligation is to reveal what is true, and for Baldwin what is true is that we can live differently than now, art is at odds with contemporary reality[1] and must speak of liberation and transformation. It must do so, further, because art should be rooted not in individual vision alone but in communal experience, that of the "feet, bloodstained forever, and washed in many rivers," that John Grimes senses after his visionary descent (*GT* 207), and this community, Baldwin asserts in most of his writing, despite long tribulation can someday find relief and glory. For both reasons, art's mission of speaking truth is partly one of pointing to the future we are capable of, if we can recognize our humanity and its holiness.

This vision of potentiality, which it is the prophetic artist's responsibility to tell, builds on redemptive oracles in the Old Testament, for Baldwin primarily those of Isaiah and Ezekiel, and in the New Testament on eschatological and apocalyptic messages in the Gospels, apostolic books, and Revelation. In their evolved canonical forms, the Old Testament prophecies combine warnings of destruction with promises of restoration and, in later parts of Isaiah and the short prophecies from Hosea to Malachi, earth's transformation. In Isaiah, the redemptive prophecies in the work's late-exilic middle portion start from the fact of loss—historically the fall of Jerusalem and the Babylonian exile after 587 BCE—and offer hope for redress and restitution:

> Thus saith thy Lord the LORD, and thy God that pleadeth the cause of his people, Behold, I have taken out of thine hand the cup of trembling, even the dregs of the cup of my fury; thou shalt no more drink it again:
>
> But I will put it into the hand of them that afflict thee. . . . (51:22–23)[2]

These hopes do not negate or deny but incorporate and compensate historical suffering. Importantly for Baldwin, too, the pain from which Isaiah pledges relief is that of exiles seeking return—for Baldwin never a literal return to Africa but rather accession to a birthright in the United States. To these assurances, late-prophetic and apocalyptic texts add hopes of a redeemed Jerusalem (Isa. 60), an end to earthly empire (Dan. 2), and "new heavens and a new earth" (Isa. 65:17). In turn, New Testament writings, such as First and Second Corinthians, Hebrews, Revelation, and John, contribute ideas of suffering for truth, the importance of faith, condemnation of the present powers of the earth, and the imminent coming of God's kingdom.

These promises depend, in biblical perspective, on prophets to proclaim them. Prophets, we have already seen, are not those who esteem themselves as such, who are likely to be false prophets like Gabriel Grimes. They are those who are commanded or offer themselves to speak what is assumedly God's truth—who are shown a vision of God's throne where a plea is made for a messenger (Isaiah) or ordered to stand before the people "and thou shalt say unto them, Thus saith the Lord GOD" (Ezek. 2:4). So there comes to be an analogy between the prophet's work and the artist's, who is also laid hold of by a truth he or she cannot alter or ignore. Hall Montana, in *Just Above My Head*, expresses this parallel, and the prophetic nature of his brother Arthur's music, by saying, "A mighty work was being worked, in time, through the vessel of my brother, who, then, . . . belong[ed] to me no longer" (21)—who, that is, was lifted and driven by his mission.

Baldwin does not fully specify the source of the artist-prophet's vision, analogous to God's commanding voice in biblical prophecy. By inference it is partly the artist's inner soul, especially the depths of sexual truth that can strike with the force of revelation. In part, the source is the prophet's own time, history, and surrounding life, as in a meditation by Jimmy Miller, Arthur Montana's surviving lover and collaborator, late in *Just Above My Head*:

> The song does not belong to the singer. The singer is found by the song. Ain't no singer, anywhere, ever *made up* a song—that is not possible. He *hears* something. I

> really believe, baby, at the bottom of *my* balls, that something hears *him,* something says, come here! and jumps on him just exactly like you jump on a piano or a sax or a violin or a drum. . . . That sound you hear . . . is the sound of millions and millions and, who knows, now, listening, where life is, where is death? (576)

That great artists voice common dreams is a truism. The core of Jimmy's statement is that this action, at least for the prophet-artist, is in no way voluntary, if one is true to one's vision. The true artist, Jimmy says, "*hears* something," or, rather, "something hears *him*," becomes aware of the artist's ability and uses him or her as single-mindedly as a saxophonist uses that instrument. This "something," not further defined, is the link between the experience of millions and the artistic process that allows their sound to become the artist's. In Baldwin's use, something like Shelley's "spirit of the age," acting on and through the poet in revolutionary times (Shelley 508), reaches the prophet-artist through African American common life across generations.

So far, Baldwin has replicated in artistic terms the biblical sense of prophetic commissioning. But he revises this idea as well, having Arthur tell Hall, in their first real discussion of Arthur's homosexuality, "When you sing . . . you can't sing *outside* the song. You've got to *be* the song you sing. You've got to make a confession" (*JAMH* 52). The prophet-artist, then, becomes or is "jump[ed] on" by the song—as the prophetic idea and Jimmy specify—in part through emotional self-opening (confession), and is cleansed by no seraphic coal but by this dangerously willed self-revelation. This act in turn necessarily creates a contradictory set of impulses that in *Just Above My Head* echoes through Arthur's life: like many real Gospel and crossover artists, he is vulnerable to a sense that his body is not as holy as his song (and by homophobic guilt in general), but he will also, at a moment of deepest commitment, offer his song and implicitly his sexual nature as a "confession" at the "throne of mercy" (267). In Baldwin's extension of the prophetic-art idea, the homosexual artist, at least, exists in a kind of continuing gamble against believed dishonor and despair, without the external assurance that the biblical prophets' assumed discourse with God afforded.

Baldwin's idea of prophetic art develops through his career, shifting in content and receiving differing emphasis in different works. Initially posed in a fairly early story, "Sonny's Blues" (1955–1957), the idea of an art that points toward possible redemption recedes in *Another Country* (1962), which emphasizes the truth-seeking aspects of art as such, including its social content, but without pressing its prophetic significance. *Tell Me How Long the Train's Been Gone* (1968) then examines the inadequacy of this same type of art. In *If Beale Street Could Talk* (1974), Baldwin looks briefly at art in a time of dire oppression, subjecting it to a criterion of utility but also treating it as implicitly prophetic and perhaps apocalyptic. Finally, *Just Above My Head* (1979) returns to and elaborates the prophetic art conception, giving this art an eschatological and apocalyptic focus, even while placing this and other aspects of Baldwin's prophetic vision under a lens of doubt that will require discussion in a later chapter.

Parallel with these shifts in focus, Baldwin also broadens the musical references he uses as indicators of art's imaginative reach. While Gospel and biblical quotations help express the prophetic ideas in *Go Tell It on the Mountain*, Baldwin's middle work often emphasizes blues' ability to articulate the pain and longing in everyday life. Even here, there is a parallel emphasis on Gospel's evocation of hope and on transition between the two as indicating a movement toward hope. In later work, especially *Just Above My Head*, Gospel emerges as a primary referent for possibilities of reformation. While most commentaries continue to see Baldwin as basically a blues artist, with only incidental interest in Gospel, here and in later chapters we will come to see blues and Gospel as coequal in a complex aesthetic with analogues in Baldwin's view of possibilities for a changed world.[3]

The Genesis of Prophetic Art

"Sonny's Blues" (1955–1957) is Baldwin's first work to raise the idea of a prophetic purpose in art. It does so in a way that varies the author's presentation of similar issues in his immediately preceding important work, the play *The Amen Corner*,[4] which reflects the blues aesthetic just mentioned.

The play, though mainly directed at Holiness hypocrisy, manipulation, and restrictiveness, also takes aim at a church culture that it sees as denying life's pain, and at the Gospel music that—though it suffuses the play—it regards as complicit with this denial. The play's rejection of these evasions finds expression in the advice given to its young church pianist protagonist, David, by his father, a dying jazz musician—to live with "the things that hurt you" and learn to "use" them (*TAC* 40–41), advice the protagonist implicitly accepts as the basis for a secular art. These ideas embody what Baldwin takes as a blues sensibility. Baldwin treats the blues as primarily dealing with sorrows, losses, and pain—as he put it in 1964, with "work, love, death, floods, lynchings," a "series of disasters which can be summed up under the arbitrary heading, 'Facts of Life.'" As an attitude, Baldwin says, the blues express "the toughness that manages to make this experience articulate," and so convey a way people face disaster and "ride with it" ("UB" 57, 59). These are common views: Baldwin's statement is substantively similar to Ralph Ellison's that blues as a genre keeps "the painful details and episodes of a brutal experience alive in one's aching consciousness" and transcends pain through "a near-tragic, near-comic lyricism" (Ellison 129).[5] Both writers, then, see blues as close to the nub of lived experience. And for Baldwin, as Saadi Simawe notes in commentary on the play, this attitude has a broad philosophic dimension as well: his view that blues can help people "ultimately gain wisdom from suffering . . . may be seen as the blues connection to the Biblical concept of suffering as a way to wisdom" (16). This idea, including its biblical links, forms at least one part of Baldwin's complex musical understanding.

"Sonny's Blues," though closely related to *The Amen Corner* in time, and like it in dealing with art's ability to mediate pain, varies it in important ways: the story offers a broader treatment of suffering, finds a potentially redemptive-prophetic significance in its blues-based music, and, though incidentally, shifts the play's view of Gospel music.

Two major scenes present the thematic core of this story of Sonny, the artist, and his initially philistine older brother: the brothers' Saturday afternoon conversation a few weeks after Sonny's return from prison, partly involving a street revival meeting both witness, and Sonny's downtown jazz performance that same night. As presented in earlier narration and the brothers' conversation, the suffering that belongs to life and so is part of serious art is not only human and universal, as in the narrator's loss of his child to polio, and as it predominantly is in *The Amen Corner*, but is also social and racial. Baldwin links the pain Sonny has tried to slake with heroin to the Harlem landscape where boys much like the narrator and Sonny in youth "found themselves smothering in these houses, came down into the streets for light and air and found themselves encircled by disaster" ("SB" 112); to the long-ago death of the brothers' uncle, killed carelessly by white boys looking for a thrill (116–18); to the heartache from which their father died early and their mother in her turn. Both universal suffering and its communal forms are what thoughtful children sense gathering in the dusk outside during a long family Sunday (114–15), and what wait beyond the nightclub in the last scene, when "trouble stretched above us, longer than the sky" (140).

The capacity to suffer and to incorporate these forms of suffering in art becomes, in turn, the requirement for an art that evokes suffering's end. Baldwin presents this idea first through the revival meeting that proceeds under the brother's window as he waits for Sonny, and later through Sonny's playing at the club. Though the revival music ("The Old Ship of Zion" and others)[6] wins no converts, the brother believes those listening "underwent a change, the eyes focusing on something within; the music seemed to soothe a poison out of them; and time seemed, nearly, to fall away from the sullen, belligerent, battered faces, as though they were fleeing back to their first condition, while dreaming of their last" (129). The music, then, evokes both conditions. Further, while individually these are childhood and the end of life, or heaven, biblically they are the beginning and end of the long path of human redemption—Eden and the New Jerusalem. So the music has stirred both a memory of bliss and a hope of bliss to be recovered in some imagined future. The scene, though a detail in this story, shifts Baldwin's presentation of Gospel/hymn music away from viewing it as escapism and emotional compensation, toward recognizing its capacity to elicit serious hope, whether or not the hope is seriously affirmed.

The requirements for an art of hope, the narrative and Sonny both suggest, are stringent and in a sense ironic. Sonny, who has paused at the meeting before coming upstairs, speaks of "how much suffering she [the singer] must have had to go through—to sing like that" (132). The commonality of torment allows the singer to pull from herself the pain and longing to which her hearers respond with their own, and in this way to create an art that evokes some sense of torment's end. The point is underlined by Sonny's stopping at the meeting and, when leaving, putting money in the collection plate while "looking directly at the woman [the singer] with a little smile" (130). At the least he recognizes her as a sister artist; at most, her music has had an impact that will show in his own. That music, in the final scene, moves and grows into one that invokes hope through Sonny's medium, blues-inflected piano, as the street singer did in hers.

Sonny's playing in this scene goes through three fairly clear stages. At first, long absent from the piano and afraid to engage emotionally, Sonny hesitates and backtracks, until, encouraged by the band leader Creole, he "strike[s] out for the deep water" (138). When he does, the narrator recognizes the music's character as blues, which he sees as telling "the tale of how we suffer, and how we are delighted, and how we may triumph" (139). Sonny's playing then subtly changes. As Creole's bass line suggests that the blues' "tale" is reinvented for each generation (139), Sonny reinvents his solo; he "return[s] to the spare, flat statement of the opening phrase of the song" and through it evokes both the immediate suffering that the brother has glimpsed and experienced and, intuitively, that of the community, the "long line" leading up to those he has known:

> He had made it his: that long line, of which we knew only Mama and Daddy. And he was giving it back, as everything must be given back, so that, passing through death, it can live forever. I saw my mother's face again, and felt, for the first time, how the stones of the road she had walked on must have bruised her feet. I saw the moonlit road where my father's brother died. And it brought something else back to me, and carried me past it, I saw my little girl again and felt Isabel's tears again, and I felt my own tears begin to rise. (140)

Yet, even as it summons a history of desolation, the music has changed and is "no longer a lament," and it suggests to Sonny's brother "with what burning he had made it his, with what burning we had yet to make it ours, how we could cease lamenting" (140). "Freedom," the brother believes, is around them while the music lasts, and the song seems to mean that "he [Sonny] could help us to be free if we would listen" and that "he would never be free until we did" (140). The music, then, evokes not only the race's past and present, but its dimly sensed future as well.

Baldwin's description defines by implication a conception of prophetic art. In the brother's perception the music is prophetic both in substance, carrying conviction of the possibility of a changed existence, and in effect—through it Sonny *directly* helps his audience sense the possibility of freedom. At the same time he, the artist and prophet, cannot gain his own freedom without the community, reminding us of the fundamental idea of the prophet as forerunner and spokesperson rather than personal beneficiary of "the promises" (Heb. 11:13).[7]

The idea that art may promise a people's freedom is reinforced by the biblical allusion in the story's last sentence. Here, as Sonny begins playing again, the drink the narrator has sent him, set aside on the piano, "glowed and shook above my brother's head like the very cup of trembling" (141), words recalling Isaiah's promise to Jerusalem. The words should be read not in isolation but in canonical context, a "long line" of their own stretching in Isaiah from warning of downfall (the main focus of chaps. 1–39) through punishment and the promise of return and restoration (chaps. 40–55) to the expectation of a future in a redeemed Jerusalem whose "light is come" (60:1; chaps. 56–66). Baldwin is certainly aware of this overarching structure. The promise implied in his final sentence cannot be read, then, as signifying only family relationships or psychic attitudes; Isaiah is referring to the punishment, suffering, and redemption of a people. Only as such a promise can the final line triangulate with the two other key elements in Baldwin's description of the music, that it conjures "freedom" and that it sums up a "long line" reaching from the past to today.[8]

Besides the basic idea of art's prophetic function, Baldwin's descriptions suggest two further points that reappear in later writing. The first is the use of a transition beyond blues to represent a shift from endurance to hope. Baldwin, we know, sees blues as in some sense capturing the essence of human existence. His descriptions do not, however, indicate that blues speak of a hope of transforming existence, ending pain. The implication is that a different music does so, if any. In "Sonny's Blues," the transition in Sonny's playing as he begins his solo, when the music becomes "no longer a lament," marks a shift in genre style and feeling.[9] The music is still blues, as thrice emphasized ("SB" 139), but has reached past Baldwin's essay description of blues as a way to "ride" pain, seeming to promise its assuagement or end. In later work Baldwin will use blues and Gospel/hymn music, respectively, to signify suffering and hoped-for redemption (*Another Country*) and the shift between these genres to indicate a move to prophetic-apocalyptic utterance (*Just Above My Head*). At the same time, Baldwin's use of "trouble" ("SB" 140)—a resonant term for him, recalling Job's "Man that is born of a woman is of few days, and full of trouble" (14:1)—acts as a counterpoint, reminding us that the tragic or blues attitude is as fundamental in human life as the hope of a future when we may "crease lamenting."

Baldwin further suggests, through the image closing "Sonny's Blues," that an art pointing toward salvation may not save the artist who creates it. Sonny has told his brother that his drug use "can come again" (135). If, in the final sentence, the drink he has sipped "glowed and shook" above him, then the "cup of trembling" has not for certain passed from his hand, whether or not it will someday pass from the community's (141). Baldwin will return to this problem, with other problems of prophetic art, in *Just Above My Head.*

Baldwin's claims in the closing tableau have problematic aspects. While the brother's thoughts of his uncle, mother, and daughter dramatize art's ability to elicit empathic response, the point that art may evoke future hope rests on assertion of an emotive effect that is not shown dramatically, only stated—"Freedom lurked around us" (140). Moreover, the statements about freedom contain their own ambiguities: will the freedom be psychic—an acceptance of the tragic in life—or an actual cessation of lived suffering? Does this art "help us to be free" through understanding the pain and beauty in Sonny's life or through understanding our own and the community's lives and history? And does this art create belief in an end to affliction or, somehow, actually help us find the end? Probably, in each instance, Baldwin intends both meanings, but the links between these meanings are not found in the description of Sonny's playing but in the final image from Isaiah, once its meaning and context are understood. Thus, the plausibility of an art that can help lead us out of suffering is stated but not shown.

Yet to say this is not to negate the passage's claim. It is impossible to show that art can guide humanity toward redemption, since such an event lies in the future, but the story's conclusion is an assertion of what art *should* do. And it bears its weight of plausibility both because of our own knowledge that we need some belief in freedom and because experience tells us of art that taps deep beliefs of this kind: "I Wonder as I Wander," "A Change Is Gonna Come," and, Baldwin will remind us later, "Daniel Saw the Stone." So the tableau is a programmatic statement that art *should* have the form and function that the story has only seemed to describe.

Baldwin's suggestion of a prophetic art in this story partly resolves an earlier disjunction between art and prophecy. In *Go Tell It on the Mountain*, John feels a call to prophetic vocation but, we know, Baldwin leaves its future expression undefined. In turn, the novel's artist figure, Richard, John's biological father, does not apparently envision a prophetic art. His interest in art is aesthetic and cultural, sparked by African art and motivated in part by determination to outshine whites (*GT* 168), but is not socially transformational and is determinedly antireligious—Richard invites Jesus to "kiss my big black ass" (164). Richard belongs, then, among the novel's secular sinners and truthsayers. Similarly, David in *The Amen Corner* is a nascent blues artist. In effect, Sonny's acknowledgment of the street Gospel singer has not occurred in either earlier work.

Baldwin's slightly earlier essays on aesthetics, "Everybody's Protest Novel" and "Many Thousands Gone" (1949, 1951), which attempt to chart his own aesthetic path partly against the then-dominant example of Richard Wright, suggest that this separation of art and prophecy is no fluke. These essays tax "protest" novels (Stowe and Wright) with lacking human complexity ("EPN" 13, 16–17); in regard to African American culture, Baldwin argues that "protest" fiction implies that "in Negro life there exists no tradition, no field of manners, no possibility of ritual or intercourse," whereas in reality we have only lacked a "sensibility sufficiently profound and tough to make this tradition articulate" ("MTG" 27). So far as the essays projected Baldwin's own first artistic program, it was inferably one of seeing

African American life this way—as a web of relationships spun among individuals and within a community over time; certainly this is why *Go Tell It on the Mountain*, then in progress, centers on a family history that is also a community history. Such an art must at least be in tension with a desire to show the possibilities of changed existence that are prophetic art's concern—though of course it might show hopes for change in the culture. The art Baldwin sketches in nonfiction, in sum, is mimetic and reflects social reality and its complexity; it is in the best sense an art of manners. *Go Tell It*'s portrayals both of prophetic mission and of an artistic ambition fueled by race pride and anger (John, Richard) already take a step away from this emphasis; "Sonny's Blues," fusing artistic and prophetic functions, makes a further step. But Baldwin does not abandon the essays' program either; rather, the essays share with Baldwin's then-developing fiction a consistent concern with the forms of social life.[10] It becomes his aim both to show the complexity of African American and U.S. society and, also, to assert possibilities of liberation, while exploring in nearly all his works the responsibilities of art and the claims in it of both mimesis and prophecy.

Art and Commerce

Another Country focuses on art in general rather than prophetic art, yet also provides the latter idea's necessary foundations. Among other topics, the novel explores the polarity between art and commerce, in relation to deep-based, unpalatable, potentially chaotic truths about the psyche and society that, it suggests, the true artist must bring to light. The aspirant who can face these truths has the capability of becoming a true artist. If not, she or he can never become one, but may succeed in the world of commerce, which absorbs and destroys not merely the facilely ambitious but the apprentice of real promise who turns from art's dangers because of fear, hunger, or false ideas. True and false art, then, exist in an antagonistic tension and in an asymmetric relation to the buried truths that, in the first, are burdensome yet vivifying to artist and audience, and that the second shuns. In exploring this polarity *Another Country* pays relatively little attention to the prophetic in art; yet it implies that genuine art is transformative in bringing truth to light, and, further, that it is social in reference, exposes the corruption and oppression beneath society's surface, and exists in some kind of relation to social struggle. Finally, so far as Baldwin sees prophetic art as actual art—not proclamation—*Another Country*'s examination of what is valid in art applies to it as well.

As signifiers of serious art, Baldwin uses references to artists high in the modernist canon, such as Proust, Henry James, Beethoven, and Stanislavski, as well as to blues, Gospel, and expressive jazz—for example in an extended description of Rufus's young saxophonist bandmate "blowing with his lungs and guts out of his own short past" (*AC* 9). Vivaldo's socially serious novel-in-progress serves the same function, as Richard's crime novel does negatively (75, 160–62). Popular fiction, formulaic jazz, and television signify low or commercial art, with Broadway and films as contested terrain.[11] *Another Country* facilitates this focus on art as such through its time scheme; while the novel was completed in 1961, its action, extending over roughly eight months from November (Rufus's suicide) to July or the start of August, most likely takes place in 1955–56.[12] In the United States, this period falls between the Supreme Court school integration decision (1954) and the first major school integration struggle (Little Rock, September 1957); two salient intermediate events, the opening phase of the Montgomery bus boycott (from December 1955) and Autherine Lucy's admission to and expulsion from the University of Alabama (February 1956), fall in the three-month narrative break between Rufus's funeral just after Thanksgiving and the Silenskis' party in early March. Internationally, the novel's time period lies in a "cold war" lull between Austria's reunification and neutralization (October 1955) and the crises in Suez and Hungary (October 1956), well before major U.S. involvement in Vietnam. Whether or not Baldwin planned all this out, the novel's period is one of relative social inaction when questions about art could be asked without considering art's duties in time of crisis.

The novel most fully expresses its conception of serious art in Cass's rumination on Vivaldo's inability to connect with his past and Vivaldo's later answering intuitions when just starting to do so. Vivaldo, on their way to Rufus's funeral, has told Cass how, in his teens, he and his friends sexually terrorized a young "queer"—evidently, material he is mulling over for his novel—and Cass reflects on the bloodlessness of his narration:

> He had not gone back into it—that time, that boy; he regarded it with a fascinated, even romantic horror, and he was looking for a way to deny it.
>
> Perhaps such secrets, the secrets of everyone, were only expressed when the person laboriously dragged them into the light of the world, imposed them on the world, and made them a part of the world's experience. Without this effort, the secret place was merely a dungeon in which the person perished; without this effort,

> indeed, the entire world would be an uninhabitable darkness; and she saw, with a dreadful reluctance, why this effort was so rare. Reluctantly, because she then realized that Richard had bitterly disappointed her by writing a book in which he did not believe. In that moment she knew, and she knew that Richard would never face it, that the book he had written to make money represented the absolute limit of his talent. It had not really been written to make money—if only it had been! It had been written because he was afraid, afraid of things dark, strange, dangerous, difficult, and deep. (112)

To drag secrets "into the light of the world," impose them "on the world," and make them "part of the world's experience" is definitionally the aim of art in a modernist aesthetic; in this meditation the "things dark, strange, dangerous, difficult, and deep" are the content of meaningful art. The "secret place," never defined, appears variously as the "deep, secret place" in which Ida holds herself away from Vivaldo, the "dark place" in which Eric has buried his boyhood, the "mysterious, hidden source" of Eric's tenderness for Yves, the "cavern behind the eye" that Vivaldo will intuit in a moment of terror, and "the secret place of the eyes" in Eric's face in his French film (172, 193, 225, 302, 330). It is, then, the place containing sexual anguish and truth as well as human terror and love in varying forms. In society, it is the place, in Ida's words, "behind all them damn dainty trees and shit" where "people are screwing and sucking and fixing and dying," (348) and the "secret place" of Ida's black culture which Vivaldo cannot yet enter (313). Art's mission, then, is to bring the contents of this place to light.

Later in the novel, and months later in time, Vivaldo himself experiences a complementary intuition. Drinking at a Village bar, at a troubled point between himself and Ida, he is depressed about his and his friends' relationships, the passing of youth, his equivocal class and racial positions, and attraction to a young woman he sees through both his own and the dead Rufus's eyes (300–1). Under these pressures he feels that

> something in him was breaking; he was, briefly and horribly, in a region where there were no definitions of any kind, neither of color, nor of male and female. There was only the leap and the rending and the terror and the surrender. And the terror: which all seemed to begin and end and begin again—forever—in a cavern behind the eye. . . . What order could prevail against so grim a privacy? And yet, without order, of what value was the mystery? . . . When people no longer knew

> that a mystery could only be approached through form, people became—what the people of this time and place had become, what he had become. (301–2)

Roughly, Vivaldo is becoming aware of an idea Baldwin expresses elsewhere, that race, nationality, sexuality, and the like are invented categories that neither describe nor even reach the complexities of human behavior.[13] Vivaldo has briefly been both black and white, male and female, homosexual and heterosexual. But with no differentiation of any kind, his response implies, behavior is merely chaotic. Art's role, then, is to reject accepted categories and find or create others that more truly express the human "mystery," a "form" that renders it comprehensible. Implicitly this will be one that preserves complexity and irrationality while ordering them, so that neither convention nor chaos will destroy us.

Baldwin is making four main claims for genuine art. First, it not only should but can reach the "secret place" and express what lies there; it is distinguished from false or commercial art by a mission and possibility of expressing truth. Second, it can find a "form" to express the "mystery" and "terror" (302) it uncovers. These are modernist conceptions. They posit hierarchy in artistic worth and, while rejecting traditional forms and ordering principles, also reject the idea that all forms and ordering principles are equally artificial; some, by implication, better represent human reality. Third, Cass's meditation assumes that art can make unearthed secrets "part of the world's experience" (112)—change how we think and what we are. In this respect, art's aim is like prophecy's, though Baldwin does not pursue the point here. Finally, both Cass's and Vivaldo's thoughts assume that a deeply truth-telling art of this kind, though frightening, helps and guards us—can keep the "secret place" from being a "dungeon," the world from being "darkness," and us from being what without it we have become (112, 302). Commercialized art, implicitly, does none of these, because of conventionality, failure to confront deep truths, and the like.

The novel's clearest examples of the art-commerce duality are Vivaldo himself and Ida. They embody the duality in asymmetric ways: Vivaldo struggles until, with Ida's help, he touches chaos, terror, and truth and is thereby freed to advance in his art; Ida begins with genuine if unformed art and squanders her capital, though perhaps not irreversibly.

Through most of *Another Country* Vivaldo is blocked on his novel, whose characters remain lifeless (127). The obvious, even schematic, reason is that he fears depth and complexity, responding to Rufus's hours-long talk on his last night alive by feeling "tired of the strain of attending, . . . tired of the troubles of real people" and wanting "to get back to the people he was inventing, whose troubles he could bear" (71), who are thereby revealed as shallow and false. Behind this situation lies an unconsciously willed racial and sexual fatuity. Vivaldo lives a fantasy of racial comity in which personal open-mindedness blanks out public bigotry—earlier, when Rufus mentions an obvious danger of bias, Vivaldo answers, "I really don't want to hear all that shit" (35), as if not listening could erase both his difference from Rufus and Rufus's risk. And, though genuinely concerned for Rufus, Vivaldo is psychically and sexually afraid of his intense need. His later confession that, on the last night before Rufus disappeared, he shrank from holding him close, "afraid that he wouldn't understand that it was—only love" (342), is a terrible self-indictment; to be frightened by homosexuality away from expressing love, though common then and now, is to become almost non-human.

From this unpromising start Vivaldo does move forward, primarily through continuing confrontations in which, with terrible verbal blows, Ida forces him to recognize both his racial obliviousness and the shallowness of his love for Rufus and for her (165–70, 261–62, 277–81, 317–25, 408–31). He advances, as well, through a sexual confrontation with himself partly under these blows' impact. This confrontation takes him from his moment of polymorphous terror at the bar through the ensuing night of drugs and rooftop utopian visions, when he falls asleep with Harold's head on his chest (315), to his night, morning, and afternoon of confession and sexual union with Eric (332–44, 381–98). Vivaldo realizes then that he loved Rufus (382–83); paradoxically, he must realize this before he can recognize that, at least in part, he also "envied and feared him" (413). He has begun, then, to face his depths and contradictions. When he is further bludgeoned by Ida's revelation of her affair with another man and his own timid complicity in it, can acknowledge his cowardice, and feels Ida's anguish without "the distance called pity," Vivaldo experiences the epiphanic moment in which he sees that his coffee pot, the cooking pork chops, and cigarettes are "real," and the detail he has long sought for his novel falls "neatly and vividly, like the tumblers of a lock, into place in his mind" (426, 427). The revelations he has accepted, in sum, have opened him to the reality of other people, mediated as that of the objects around him, and his novitiate can begin.

Among Ida's multiple roles in *Another Country*, that of compromised artist deserves more sustained attention than it has had.[14] Ida's ambition to become a singer is already formed, though guardedly expressed, when first mentioned (162). At least in her retrospective view, the ambition was rooted in the need to escape Harlem—"hit the A train"—and, when she saw how degrading it was to try to do so through sexual affairs with whites, "That was when I decided that I ought to try to sing" (418, 419). Amid these negatives, we can forget that Ida does have talent. In her first appearance, sitting in with a downtown band as arranged by the television producer Steve Ellis, she performs first a blues-inflected pop number, then a traditional blues ballad, and finally Gospel (253–56)—a version of the progression from music of the everyday to music of hope that Baldwin suggests elsewhere. Ida compensates for restricted range and skill with a "sense of the self" both "profound" and "powerful," but also has been "working" to build technique; her final number, Thomas Dorsey's "Precious Lord," in which she boosts herself on her strong emotions about Rufus, has deep power (253–54).[15]

Ida backslides for both personal and artistic reasons. Most obviously, while enunciating racial home truths in her relations with white friends, she herself is trying to hotwire a career through a sexual relationship with Ellis, at inevitable cost to artistic and moral self-confidence. More fundamentally, while she takes voice lessons that Ellis has arranged (320), it is not indicated that Ida thinks consistently or carefully about the nature or direction of her art, its emotional roots in her dependent love for Rufus, or her anomalous position vis-à-vis the musicians who work with her only because she is a powerful man's protégée. Rather, she deflects her feelings about Rufus into homophobic spite at Eric (257, 265, 322–24) and those about Ellis into racial resentment of Vivaldo. Finally, she is unable to admit how deeply she loves Vivaldo until it is almost too late. She has thus lost touch with what Baldwin would see as the experiential bases for genuine art. So, the character who is clearest on the need to "pay dues" (277, 325, 350) and to replace dreams with "reality" (357) does not do the first personally or artistically and does the second only when her world crashes. Yet, by the time of her last scene (430–31), Ida has at least begun to pay the price in suffering that, "Sonny's Blues" implies, art demands. There is a basis for her to resume her apprenticeship, entering this time through the street door, but Baldwin leaves unspecified whether she will do so.

The novel's figure for commercial art, Ellis, sketched schematically but incisively, is a liberal television producer who uses Negro actors and has recruited a Negro to his publicity department, as he brags in front of the man in question (151, 356). He aggressively defends popular art (161) and showily scorns highbrow critics (262). He is chiefly important in terms of others' reactions. Ida, quick to score Vivaldo for liberal condescension (280), must be silent as Ellis condescends to his black employee (356). Vivaldo, scornful and rude to Ellis (162, 264), but cowed by his success, still realizes that the important question is "how he [Vivaldo] was to discover his possibilities and become reconciled to them" (164).[16] Eric, Baldwin's emblematic artist in formation who has served his apprenticeship of suffering and self-purification, and pursues art as serious study, is not swayed by Ellis's vision at all and is merely "mortally bored" (262).

What is sketched through these characters, then, is dedicated art in general, without reference to prophetic possibilities. Yet art must deal with social as well as personal life, and *Another Country* emphasizes serious art's social dimension. Vivaldo's novel "about Brooklyn" (162) potentially includes both the sexual terrors and brutalities of his adolescence (112) and the racial confrontations of his present, triggered by thoughts of bringing Ida to meet his family in that borough (277–81). Yves's reading includes works by Blaise Cendrars and Genet, mythologists of Africanness and of the homosexual as social rebel (195). The play Eric will appear in, briefly sketched, features industrial and labor bosses and the struggle and social equivalency between them (286); *The Possessed*, for which he is doing a screen test, is Dostoevsky's most direct study of revolutionary nihilism.[17] Eric's French film, finally, despite "helplessly frivolous" politics (329), is a signifier of art's social dimension, climaxing during an insurrection or urban guerrilla war (330–31). Tracked in a long shot, Eric's face, and especially "the secret place of the eyes," becomes an emblem not of the human condition as such, but of "the twentieth century torment," and the implication of martyrdom is accented by Eric's only line, spoken just before he is shot by a sniper, "*Nom de Dieu, que j'ai soif*"—"God, I'm thirsty," echoing Jesus's "*J'ai soif*" or "I thirst" (Jean / John 19:28; *AC* 330). To bring forth what lies in the "secret place," then, is partly to stand as witness to political oppression and sacrifice, if not necessarily to point toward ending them.

Mimesis and Prophecy

Baldwin's fourth novel, *Tell Me How Long the Train's Been Gone* (1968), centers on an implied comparison between mimetic and prophetic art.[18] The former, we know, is the art of reality as it is, while the latter tries to discern the possibilities of a changed reality. Few commentaries, however, focus on the novel's treatment of art, and those that do have overlooked its central polarity and misread its protagonist's artistic impasse.

This work's meaning turns on a single Bible passage that crystallizes the protagonist's artistic ambition in youth, echoes in his achievement of artistic maturity, and yet also reveals the limits of his artistic vision. That passage is Ezekiel 37:1–14, the vision of the valley of bones. Taking Ezekiel to the valley "in the spirit," God asks him, "Son of man, can these bones live?" and instructs him to prophesy to them to join together, and, further, to prophesy to the wind, "Come from the four winds, O breath, and breathe upon these slain, that they may live" (37:3, 9). The bones, God says, are "the whole house of Israel," and he commands:

> Therefore prophesy and say unto them, Thus saith the Lord God; Behold, O my people, I will open your graves, and cause you to come up out of your graves, and bring you into the land of Israel. . . .
>
> And shall put my Spirit in you, and ye shall live, and I shall place you in your own land. . . . (Ezek. 37:12, 14)

The prophecy belongs to the redemptive visions in the latter part of Ezekiel, dating probably from the first and middle years of Israel's sixth-century exile, and forecasts Israel's eventual restoration and new life.[19] More basically, the passage signifies the viewpoint of prophecy as against that of what we call "real life." In a meditation on the verses, Katheryn Pfisterer Darr notes that belief in corporeal resurrection was uncommon in Ezekiel's time and that the passage speaks of "seemingly impossible events":

> In recounting his vision, Ezekiel challenges his fellow exiles and generations of his readers to view their circumstances not through their own, limited vision, but through God's eyes. Can these bones live? Of course not. But look at them through God's eyes, and watch . . . as God's spirit, which heals hopelessness, infuses them, so that they rise up—a great army testifying to the power of Yahweh. Can corpses be brought forth from graves and become living beings again? Absurd! But look through God's eyes, and watch them come up, receive God's spirit, and return home. . . . "I can't believe my eyes," we say when we have witnessed an utterly unanticipated and/or seemingly impossible event take place. But we can believe God's eyes and, looking through them, glimpse unimagined reasons to keep on hoping, though the desert be dry and dark, and the promised land far, far away. (1502–4)

This is the power Leo Proudhammer, *Tell Me How Long*'s protagonist and narrator, has not found in his art. Leo is an actor whose midlife heart attack on the book's first page would seem to signal an artistic crisis. The book's title, taken from a song refrain ubiquitous in both blues and Gospel culture, underscores the point: Leo has, or may have, arrived too late at the station.[20] The crisis is not easy to understand, however, since Baldwin has not written a moment of full insight for Leo into its nature and instead provides a pattern of references from which the reader must construct its meaning. It is not clear to all readers that there is a crisis: one of the novel's best interpreters, Lynn Orilla Scott, sees *Tell Me How Long* as "a 'success' story that could not be used as a salve for the white conscience; it does not equate the 'success' of an individual with the progress of a nation" (25). That, for Scott, is the novel's point: it presents not an artistic but a national crisis. Leo exemplifies "the black artist as a survivor and successful public figure," who seeks "a socially responsible role" (48, 46) but cannot alter the nation's slide into preapocalyptic chaos. Such a reading is, I think, too limited in its conception of art because it envisages only mimetic and not prophetic art. And it does not fully account for Leo's senses that he is and has been "a very frightened man—a very frightened boy"; that his life has involved "the creation of a role"; and that his youth held "a vanished, a blasphemed beauty, a beauty which I had never recognized and which I had, myself, destroyed" (*TMHL* 9, 17, 73).

While each of these reflections has other meanings—childhood fears, Leo's relationship to his brother Caleb, sexual and racial beauty—all can be associated with a loss of artistic direction, if only because Leo's heart attack occurs during a stage performance—"the creation of a role." But what is the nature of the crisis? The novel's major focus on the "Actors' Means Workshop"—a satire on Lee Strasburg and Cheryl Crawford's Actor's Studio, which Baldwin saw as unable to choose between dedication to "commerce or to art" (Leeming 239)—may prompt an inference that Leo has betrayed serious art by agreeing to perform "oppressive discourses" in order to succeed (Oforlea 70), so that the novel focuses on how "[f]ame supplants honesty" as a goal and reveals Leo's "inability to bring any level of truth to his art" (Jones, *His Tale* 114, 117). Alternatively, the novel's shift in emphasis to the figure of Christopher, the Black Nationalist revolutionary who is Leo's young lover, may suggest that Leo's crisis is one of art versus political commitment. There are aspects of both problems in his predicament. Yet there is no indication that Leo has fundamentally compromised the dedication we will witness in *Tell Me How Long*'s breakthrough scene (432–37). This artistic triumph, however, has left Leo unable to guide or save those he most reveres, Caleb in youth and Christopher in maturity, and has placed him, thirteen years after that youthful moment, in his present impasse. The reason is not lack of artistic service, but the nature of the art he serves.

This point leads back to Baldwin's use of Ezekiel. Early in Book Two, near the beginning of his summer in New Jersey with the Workshop, Leo, then eighteen or nineteen, stands on the Workshop's deserted stage while stealing time from an errand on a rainy afternoon (136).[21] Before this afternoon, Leo has not ventured onto the stage. He has worked at sorting and filing the troupe's props and costumes, stored in an attic—military uniforms, shoes, shirts, and the like—and they have reminded him of the "reality . . . which would one day overtake me and all my styles and poses and all my uniforms"; the garments had been worn by "real people" who had "put their hands on their hearts and delivered their vows, and the curtain had come down" (136). So Leo's reflections begin where Vivaldo's end, in the human reality, here of death, whose recognition makes serious art possible. Leo cannot, then, if he remains true to this intuition, make shallow art of the kind Richard and initially Vivaldo attempt in *Another Country*.

Leo now evokes Ezekiel: "These costumes," he recalls, "were like their [owners'] dispersed, indifferent bones, and the attic always reminded me of Ezekiel's valley, and Ezekiel's question: Oh, Lord, can these bones live?" (136).[22] On the afternoon not long after when he stands on the darkened, vaulting stage, Leo takes up the thought, wondering

> if my destiny could be involved in such a place. . . . For I desired, I realized one day—if these bones could live—to stand here before those living with whom I would fill this dusty void, and hear them bearing witness as now I heard the sound of the rain. . . . I merely suspected in the chilling height, the dusty, roaring darkness, the presence of others, each of whom was myself. But these others could not know it, and neither could I, unless I was able, being filled by them, to fill this theater with our lives. (137)

Leo's dedication to acting thus begins in the desire to recreate real lives, to let the bones live. And it begins with the hope for a pact of truth with other lives—we hear an echo of Sonny, whose "life contained so many others" ("SB" 140)—so that he may recreate "*our* lives" (my emphasis).

At the climax of his retrospective narrative, Leo implicitly revisits this moment. After some years of intermittent professional experience playing butlers, a few white roles cast nonracially, and the like (341–46), he is cast as the male lead in an experimental production of Emlyn Williams's *The Corn Is Green*, using African American actors for the Welsh working-class roles. The play is an apt choice for

Baldwin (and for its director, Konstantin Rafaeleto, loosely based on Elia Kazan) both because it uses color differences—the young miners are called "black-faced" in a stage direction and "nigger-boys" by a character (23, 24; Act 1, scene 2)—and because of a reformative theme. Miss Moffat, who tutors Morgan Evans (Leo's character) for an Oxford scholarship after his composition paper about the mine captures her attention, urges him to become "a great man of our country. 'If a light come in the mine' you said.... Make that light come in the mine and some day free these children" (82; Act 3). The audiences in the small off-off-Broadway theater are themselves partly African American, including cast members' families and friends from Leo's night job. Singing the prologue song backstage—Merle Travis's coal mining lament "Dark as a Dungeon," added for this production—Leo feels "from beyond the curtain, something sweeping up to me, life sweeping up to me, carrying me and my song" (*TMHL* 432).[23] That is, as he hoped years earlier, he senses "those living with whom I would fill this dusty void" (136). And in the scene in which his character awakens to awareness of his talent, Leo

> played [the] scene for all that was in it, for all that was in me, and for all the colored kids in the audience—who held their breath, they really did, it was the unmistakable silence in which you and the audience re-create each other—and... I realized the fabulous extent of my luck: I could, I *could*, if I kept the faith, transform my sorrow into life and joy. I might live in pain and sorrow forever, but, if I kept the faith, I would never be useless. If I kept the faith, I could do for others what I felt had been done for me, and if I could do that, if I could give, I could live. (433)

Leo then has answered for himself the question "can these bones live?" (136). He has answered in the senses in which he understood it: can art, drawing inspiration from the lives around the artist, recreate life in such a way as to make the play's bones live with those lives' truth? Leo feels, as the curtain falls, that he has "not betrayed"—neither the director, the play, himself and his loved ones, nor "all that history which held me like a lover," implicitly the race's and nation's history (435). Despite later enjoyment of fame, there is no indication that Leo does betray. Indeed, in an earlier episode in which he speaks at a civil rights rally and in the book's closing pages in which he sees the earthly city, San Francisco, on the edge of destruction, he is a witness to the history invoked here (108–14, 476–82).

Yet the Ezekiel references—explicit in the scene on the empty stage and subtextual here, conveyed by the phrases "I could live" and "transform my sorrow into life"—insistently ask a second question: can art do what prophecy does? Ezekiel 37, we remember, is the prophecy of Israel's restoration and entry into the land. Powerful as they are, the terms of Leo's vision are those of mimetic art: he hopes in his beginning and is able in his breakthrough to recreate the lives around him, those he has known, his and their history. He cannot or does not envision doing in his art what Sonny is said to do: play so that his hearers sense "how we could cease lamenting" ("SB" 140); in Ezekiel's terms, lead audiences to imagine that which will "cause you to come up out of your graves, . . . / . . . [and] place you in your own land" (37:12, 14).

But, *Tell Me How Long the Train's Been Gone* implies repeatedly, prophecy is a lifeblood need in the social world; its absence felt every day. "We need a prophet," Leo's father says when Leo is a boy, "to straighten out our minds, and lead us out of this hell" (22–23). Leo, anticipating Christopher's likely future martyrdom, wonders if God will then "raise up a people who could understand" (331)—a half-remembered biblical reference, probably to Isaiah's second "Servant Song" and verses following, which call the Servant "to raise up the tribes of Jacob . . . : I will also give thee for a light to the Gentiles, . . . / . . . That thou mayest say to the prisoners, Go forth" (49:6, 9). Leo is asking if a martyr's sacrifice can awaken his people and the surrounding nation and set the prisoners free.[24] Most resonantly, the styles of the Sixties signify for Leo the need his father felt: Christopher's friends arrive at Leo's house "with their beautiful black kinky hair spinning around their heads like fire and prophecy" (454).

Several of these references are highly ironized. Though Leo's father believes "that Jew's hand" is holding down the fish-shop scale, Leo hasn't necessarily seen it doing so (22), and Leo comments that "God's batting average fail[s] to inspire confidence" that he can raise a righteous people (331). Such comments point to Leo's ambiguous role in the narrative, as skeptic but also witness to a process of potential upheaval. Significantly, the only such reference presented nonironically, to Christopher's friends' hair, comes when Leo has overcome some of his estrangement and is attuned to the period's prophetic currents, if not fully part of them.

Other plot elements support the importance of prophetic art. One is Leo's realization of a blues attitude that does not, in fact, provide adequate guidance for his life or art. In a passage already mentioned, the young Leo wants to strike out against a God whose "horror filled my nostrils," yet realizes that the very intensity of this need "accomplished His reality and undid my unbelief" (98). He senses, then, that he must process hate on his own. As his thoughts proceed, Leo begins to grasp what Baldwin would view as a blues sensibility. He realizes he is in a "universal trap. I was human, too," and so is subject to unassuaged pain, and he begins to see "the possibility of creating my language out of my pain," treating it, in words recalling Baldwin's 1964 essay on blues, as "the horse that I must learn to ride" (99). Leo resists this idea, wondering if he might flick his life out the window as he does his cigarette. But, significantly, instead he plays the blues for the party he is attending—adopting and "using" a stereotyped role; and this act leads to his acceptance at the summer workshop (99–100).

Leo's thoughts constitute an indirect comment on Rufus in *Another Country*: to die cursing God for our pain, to jump from a height as Rufus does and Leo imagines, is not to have learned to ride pain, and to learn this is, for Baldwin, not only the indispensable condition for bearing life at all, but the requisite for creating real art. But, Baldwin shows, this nascent blues outlook is not able to orient Leo's life choices or art. In a long scene (151–99) that I return to subsequently, he pulls back both from immersion in black life and from a possible love relationship that would require that immersion—chances that will not recur for decades. And, as just noted, the art he imagines, while serious, lacks ability to touch its audience's need for another way of living, a way forward from pain. And so Baldwin's treatment contains a respectful critique of the aesthetic he has espoused in earlier work: to "ride" pain, without a perspective of possibly ending it, is not to have enough reason to endure one's own pain, or a means to assuage others'.

This lack is most strongly evoked in Leo's night dialogue with Caleb late in the book about Caleb's own trial of the soul (386–405). The scene is one of Baldwin's most masterly because it presents with full fidelity a viewpoint opposed to the protagonist's, thereby showing the limits of the latter's thought. Set after hours in the Village Caribbean restaurant where Leo is working in the winter of 1945–1946, the conversation begins with questions about art from Caleb, now a minister in Harlem: "'Leo,' he [Caleb] asked me, after a moment, 'can you tell me what it is—an artist? What's it all about? What does an artist *really* do?'" (386). In the ensuing exchange Leo's answers sound flat and unsatisfactory even to himself: the limits of his art are on display in his justifications, years before the career-launching performance discussed above. Leo stammers that an artist "creates— . . . You know . . . paintings, poems, books, plays. Music," and is compelled to add, "Not all of them are *good*" (386–87). Caleb asks, "But those that are good—what do they do? Why are they good, when they're good?" (387). Leo's answer, "They make you—feel more alive" opens him to an obvious rejoinder: "That's what drunkards say about their whiskey" (387). So far, then, Leo has not distinguished art from anodyne. He next offers, "I think it—art—can make you less lonely," and finally that in art, "a man you've never seen—well, he tells you something about your life. And it doesn't seem as awful as it did before" (387, 388). Leo, in sum, awkwardly defends mimetic art: it shows us our lives in a way that helps us understand ourselves and our oneness with others. Caleb in turn criticizes this art from the standpoint of salvational theology: those artists he has known through his day employer may have "had gifts, but they didn't think the gift was for others, for the glory of God. They thought it was just for self. And that's what made them like they were—that they just thought of self. And that offended God, and so they lost the gift" (388).

Caleb now tells his own tale (390–403). In brief, it is of a battlefield homosocial friendship and later rivalry with a white upper-class soldier whose sexual envy and race resentment lead him to betray Caleb, and whose treachery leads Caleb to plan his murder under cover of combat. This resolve is frustrated by a preemptive enemy shot when he has already called out to the man, so that the rival has "gone into eternity believing I'd killed him" (402). In the din of combat Caleb is brought down, still unwounded, by an exploding shell and hears the screams of a soldier next to him stop.

> It was a pain I had never felt before, a heartbreak I had never felt before. I saw my whole life stretching ahead of me forever like this, in lust and hatred and darkness, and to end like this, face down, hugging the earth, and you feel your bowels moving for fear, Leo, and to be like that until the earth covers you. I struggled up to my knees. I knew, I knew for the first time that there was a God somewhere. I knew that only God could save me, save *us*, not from death but from that other death, that darkness and death of the spirit which had created this hell. Which had sent men here to die. I cried out, I cried out something, I remember I was thinking, *Lord, send the angel down,* and then I was struck. It didn't hurt. It knocked me flat on my back, it knocked me out of my body, and I remember I thought of Frederick's eyes and I thought, Well, now, I can tell him I didn't pull the trigger. And it seemed to me God's great mercy that I hadn't, and I praised Him for His mercy, that He'd held me back from mortal sin, and was taking me home now, washed of my sins, forgiven. I thought I was dying, but I wasn't afraid. I understood for the first time the power and beauty of the love of God. (403)

Caleb's answer to Leo's hopes for art, then, is the human need for redemption, freedom from hatred and its degradation, hope for a new way to live. By the time of this recollection, more than a year after the events, Caleb has changed in ways repugnant to the younger brother who once idolized him. In his role as minister, he has become self-righteous and aloof; his resolve to change his life has cost him his bright spontaneity, his intellectual openness, and at least a portion of his sexual being. Leo, however, has no answering hope that could save Caleb from these costs. An art that cannot offer such hope, Baldwin implies—that is, a mimetic rather than prophetic art—cannot match evangelical theology's power.

Tell Me How Long the Train's Been Gone, then, makes clear through structured allusion and character relations what is never clear to its protagonist, the need for an art of prophecy in a society of violence, chaos, and hatred, both of and among the oppressed. Baldwin's story is neither of his own artistic crisis nor of the artist as successful survivor and witness. Leo's theater career does indeed embody an aspect of Baldwin's art—not simply the craving for visible success, but more fundamentally the art of observation and recreation of social life already suggested as his early aesthetic. *Tell Me How Long*, however, through its protagonist's crisis, portrays this art as inadequate in an apocalyptic time; and the novel is, itself, an architectonically structured example of prophetic art that depicts a society in chaos and asks, through negatives, for an art to tell us of that society's potential movement from death to life.

Usable Art

Baldwin's last two novels return to the idea of a prophetic art, presented through allusion or in direct plot representation. They also treat this art as possibly or definitely apocalyptic, in that it speaks not only of future redress for injustice, but of tyranny's end, a new world of righteousness, or both. These presentations in turn build on a shift toward apocalyptic social scenarios found in *Tell Me How Long*'s closing pages and in its two successors, though questioned in the last. *If Beale Street Could Talk* (1974), in particular, responds to the semi-insurrectionary mood current among black and white leftists in the early 1970s, as well as to the awareness of prison injustice stemming from events like the deaths of Jonathan and George Jackson (1970, 1971) and the Attica rebellion (1971), though it does not deal directly with the period's oppositional movements.

Ideas of prophetic and in part apocalyptic art, an important though subordinate thread in *Beale Street*, are conveyed through its main characters, Tish, the narrator, a nineteen-year-old Harlemite, and Fonny, her twenty-two-year-old lover wrongly imprisoned for rape and the father of her child, whose birth begins on the novel's last page.[25] The novel places their story in the larger context of W. C. Handy's "Beale Street":

> If Beale Street could talk. If Beale Street could talk,
> Married men would have to take their beds and walk. . . .(15–16)

The novel then is Baldwin's effort to let Beale Street talk, to voice contemporary African American reality "on the street," as one said in the 1960s and 1970s—its surface oppression and violence, its underlying realities, its hidden prophetic and apocalyptic truths. Tish, working and living among the streets of lower Manhattan and Harlem, is the primary vehicle through which "the street" talks. Her narration signals Baldwin's own partial departure from mimetic art, in that it violates what she can have first or second-hand knowledge of and swings between a streetwise, savvy diction and characteristically Baldwinian phrasing, inconsistencies that make Tish, in effect, a vessel for larger truths than she is directly aware of.[26] Tish's counterpart, serving as vehicle for ideas on art, is Fonny, a beginning sculptor, whose art starts as mimesis and is reconceived as utilitarian and by implication prophetic and perhaps apocalyptic.

This shift takes place in the book's last pages, but its context is Fonny's overall artistic growth. He began sculpting more than two years earlier, with no formal training, at first stealing tools and materials from his vocational high school (30). He sculpts mainly in wood, though also in stone (36, 51), and it is important that wood is the traditional material of African art—*Beale Street* and *Just Above My Head* both incorporate a sense of African Americans as part of a diaspora as well as irreducibly American. Fonny's initial artistic self-conception and aesthetic are not detailed and must be inferred from his work. One of his first pieces, a small figure in black wood, shows a naked striding man, with one foot seeming "planted, unable to move," and the figure's motion expressing "torment" (30). A later intended work comes to Fonny in a dream in jail: a block of soft brown wood meant for a bust of Tish, which he has not yet begun to cut. He is "waiting for the wood to speak. Until it speaks, he cannot move. I [Tish] am imprisoned somewhere in the silence of the wood, and so is he," and as Fonny makes the first cut he awakes (149, 150). The first piece, then, is representational and expressionist, its form inferably a token of the entrapments Fonny and others live each day. The second is a dream representation of future artistic intentions; though it is conceived as a bust, its eventual form and style are unknown. The latent figure in the wood, standing for sculpture's canonical role of liberating forms already contained in the material, also represents Fonny's own emergence as a mature artist and, proleptically, his agonized self-liberation from his first artistic ethos.

Fonny's statement of a new aesthetic follows on his experiences in the jail system (and others' he has learned of). In the book's plot, Tish's mother Sharon's mission to Puerto Rico, seeking a retraction from Fonny's accuser, has failed, the woman has retreated to a remote village, and the New York District Attorney's Office—which probably controls her actions—has postponed Fonny's trial indefinitely (155–57). In the months covered by the closing pages, Fonny comes to understand "why he is where he is now"—as a way for "the righteous" to uphold their control over "the damned" (161–62). He is beaten, loses a tooth and almost an eye, is placed in solitary for resisting rape (164). Earlier, he has learned the prison experiences of his friend Daniel, including witnessing a gang rape and being raped himself (85–91, 145).[27] In consequence, "Something hardens in him, something changes forever, his tears harden in his belly" (164). He has moved, we infer, from victimhood to resistance.

His closing statement on art is made on the day when Tish's labor will begin. Fonny tells Tish, "*Now.* I'm an artisan. . . . Like a cat who makes—tables. I don't like the word artist. Maybe I never did. . . . I'm a cat who works from his balls, with his hand. I know what it's about now." He adds, "And I'm going to *build* us a table and a whole lot of folks going to be eating off it for a long, *long* time to come" (163). Fonny's distinction between artisan and artist implies a focus on usable art. This art, he suggests, will be made *as* an artisan builds tables, will function *like* a table, and will be made both to last, like all true art, and to benefit the community ("a whole lot of folks"). Fonny's "table," then, is first of all a metaphor for art that serves the community, as distinct from pure or disinterested art.[28] But his metaphor, as Scott notes (65), also suggests the "welcome table" in African American churches and homes. It recalls, too, the table prepared "in the presence of mine enemies" in Psalm 23:5, and Jesus's words at the Last Supper, "I appoint unto you a kingdom . . . / That ye may eat and drink at my table in my kingdom" (Luke 22:29–30). To build "a table," then, is to create, in art, a place of succor amid terror and destruction not only for the family in the novel but for the population they are part of, and potentially to promise those outcast a place of honor in the apocalyptic kingdom.

Tish's narration gives Fonny's words a prophetic and semiapocalyptic frame. She prefaces his speech by saying that, when she visits, his "eyes burned, now, like the eyes of a prophet" (162); as she recalls his words later, shortly before her labor begins, she feels her child ask, *"Is there not one righteous among them?"* (163). Tish suggests, in part, that Fonny as artisan will exercise a kind of prophetic office. (His "enormous, slanted" black eyes in the same description also inevitably recall Baldwin's.) The question she imagines for her child as it moves in her alludes to Abraham's pleas to God to stay judgment against Sodom and Gomorrah (Gen. 18). So the child's imagined question, which uses "righteous" nonironically, as distinct from Fonny's earlier thoughts, suggests an approaching quasiapocalyptic time of punishment as one setting for Fonny's art. Tish's thoughts also imply an answer to an issue unresolved in Fonny's statement, whether his art will serve African Americans alone or others as well: the righteous, by the tradition of Genesis 18, are those in every community who protect God's own. Tish's moment of prophecy—it is one—does not answer whether Fonny's art will speak directly of this approaching time, but it is at least possible that it will.

If Beale Street Could Talk, then, as part of what "the street" would say, presents positively what is implied in *Tell Me How Long the Train's Been Gone* through critique: a move from mimesis to prophetic, partly apocalyptic art and from an "artist's" art to art that is graspable and serviceable, like a table. This art is not necessarily programmatic or prescriptive; it is visionary, as a "table" that people will use long into the future must be. And it continues art's mission to disclose the hidden and dangerous (*AC* 112), extending this idea in a direction *Another Country* implies but does not explore. For the subsurfaces of society that will be revealed "if Beale Street could talk"—hidden but true relations of power, the potential for resistance and retribution—are what an art that unveils denied truths would bring to light.

Nonetheless, there is a pragmatic or utilitarian emphasis in Fonny's formulation that remains open to a determination of art's mission by social purpose alone, whereas usually for Baldwin—as in *Another Country*—art's social utility stems from its capacity to uncover truth. *Beale Street*'s presentation, in the upshot, is not one Baldwin holds to: his last novel offers a partial corrective to the model of serviceability by presenting apocalyptic art as born both of deep inner conviction and of social need.

Apocalyptic Art

Just Above My Head presents the evolution of an apocalyptic-eschatological art, whose emergence can be traced in the Gospel lyrics its protagonist Arthur Montana sings, first as an adolescent in the short-lived Trumpets of Zion quartet and then solo. Allowing for the variations of any singer's repertory, songs that illustrate Arthur's development move from a general Gospel embodying prophetic hopes through an eschatological hymn sung amid the civil rights movement's terrors to an apocalyptic Gospel envisioning the fall of empires that shapes a climactic late scene and also provides one of the novel's part-epigraphs. This evolution occurs over a period stretching from about 1950 into the 1960s, in one of Baldwin's most formally complex texts.[29] Baldwin's decision to build the novel's prophetic and apocalyptic hopes on a scaffolding of Gospel and hymn music completes the revaluation of Gospel noted earlier: though blues and "standards" are important in a few scenes—and commentaries have tended to focus on the novel's blues affinities—Gospel is the dominant music in *Just Above My Head*, serving to evoke both sexual transcendence and the overarching hopes of the civil rights era.[30]

The novel's most general evocation of music as prophetic art occurs during rehearsals for and at the debut of the Trumpets, the ensemble Arthur has formed, when just fifteen, with his friends Red, Peanut, and Crunch. Three linked scenes present a view of art's meaning for the artist, Gospel's meaning in African American life, and finally the partly prophetic meaning of a Gospel staple. Though the word is used only in one of the group's song lyrics, these passages present a view of art as a prophetic calling that lifts its practitioners above their ordinary selves and also—with everything else in a destructive society—threatens their ease and even their lives. Music, according to Paul Montana, the brothers' father, a jazz pianist who is coaching the quartet for a Christmas debut, consumes the artist who sings it—it is "going to burn him [Arthur] up, burn him every hour that he lives, char the flesh from the bone, man, and leave that for someone to gather up and bury" (92). Paul's prescience states a major theme, already known to the reader from the novel's recursive structure: none of the quartet's former members will live out a full, happy life (31–33). Artists are not, however, heroic figures who choose their calling out of high commitment; they are ordinary persons with talent and perhaps dedication who are lifted toward transcendence by what they sing. The quartet members, aged about fifteen to eighteen on that long-ago Christmas, probably in 1950, are "street boys" who "stole, they lied, they fought—they cheated," and yet their "faces and their voices held the promise of the Promised Land" (89–90). This transcendence, a central mystery of art in this novel, is similar to the prophet's. We recall that Isaiah is "a man of unclean lips" whose "iniquity is taken away" by the seraph's live coal (Isa. 6:5, 7), so like the "burning" Paul foresees. The singer, then, like the prophet, is both selected as a "vessel" for the song (21) and also raised high by it.

Transcendence in this sense means that, besides possessing talent, singers of this type must be able to tap their songs' roots in common life. Hall suggests the connection:

> Niggers can sing gospel as no other people can [Hall believes] because they aren't singing gospel—if you see what I mean. When a nigger quotes the Gospel, he's not quoting: he is telling you what happened to him today, and what is certainly going to happen to you tomorrow. . . . *Oh, there wasn't no room,* sang Crunch, *no room! at the inn!* He was not singing about a road in Egypt two thousand years ago, but about his mama and his daddy and himself, and those streets outside, brother, just outside of every door. . . . (109–10)

So Gospel music, like blues, deals with "disasters" ("UB" 57), as known through shared experience, but in the register of hope—taken as certainty—of better to come.

But the song Hall recalls from the Christmas debut (89, 110–11) is not the occasion-specific "No Room in the Inn" but Rosetta Tharpe's classic "Savior Don't Pass Me By" (1939), and this song presents the book's conception of Gospel music as a call to prophetic witness. It is based on two incidents in Jesus's ministry, in which he healed a blind man and a woman "diseased with an issue of blood" (Matt. 9:20; analogues in Mark and Luke). Baldwin quotes the song's version of the second incident:

> Now, when Jesus
> was passing by
> He heard
> a woman cry. . . .
> She said,
> Savior! don't you pass me by! . . .
> If I could but touch
> the hem of His garment

I would go,
and prophesy. (110)[31]

The song significantly varies the Bible stories, in which the woman is healed but does not speak of prophecy; this element is a Gospel music addition. In the song, the woman's reaching out to Jesus constitutes, in effect, a self-commissioning, like Isaiah's (6:8): touching the garment confers prophetic ability. And the song itself becomes a call to its hearers to reach out—"Savior don't you pass me by"—to receive the same gift. Music here is redemptive and prophetic in a general way, promising that seeking is not in vain and attesting the importance of prophesying as an outcome of faith. Yet the prophecy at this point remains a general one of gospel tidings and redemption, rather than the more focused promise of an end to suffering and a new world coming that we associate with apocalyptic prophecy.

The possibility of such a world enters the novel when Baldwin situates prophetic art in the civil rights movement of the 1960s. In Book Four, which moves the characters to early maturity and extends from the beginning of desegregation to the height of the civil rights campaigns (about 1955 to 1963), Arthur, accompanied by Hall as manager and Peanut as pianist, undertakes a southern tour singing at movement events (396–452). The tour is cut short when Peanut is kidnapped and presumed murdered after a church rally near Atlanta, supposedly the South's most progressive city. Among several of Arthur's songs, Francis Bottome's "The Comforter," which he sings minutes before Peanut disappears, is particularly significant:

Go spread the tidings round, . . .
Wherever man is found,
Wherever human hearts
And human woes abound
Let every mortal tongue
Proclaim the joyful sound,
The Comforter has come! (447)[32]

As often in Baldwin, knowledge of context—both the song itself and its biblical basis—is crucial to full understanding. The song refers to the "Comforter" or "paraclete" in John 14, 15, and 16, spoken of just before Jesus's death, who is to continue Jesus's work when Jesus is no longer physically present.[33] The Comforter is sent to sustain the faithful in the darkness of this world, and to this extent the song is a general hymn of Christian hope, prophetic not because of its actual words but because of context—the exultation and terror of the singing group's travels and the community meeting in a country church outside Atlanta; the civil rights movement understood, as recent scholarship has resituated it, as a church-based prophetic movement.[34] But this is not all. Verses Baldwin does not quote, familiar to the audience which knows the song in full (447), promise not only a sustaining hope but the end of suffering: the "great King of kings, with healing in his wings, / To every captive soul a full deliverance brings" (13–14), a deliverance both from sin and implicitly from captivity in our world. The song recalls, as well, its sources in John, particularly Jesus's words that when the Comforter comes, he will "reprove the world of sin, and of righteousness, and of judgment. . . . / . . . because the prince of this world is judged" (John 16:8, 11). By implication, then, Arthur sings in part of a coming repudiation of the world's false righteousness and false judgment, and a condemnation of "the prince of this world," a formula that in common Christian use includes both the devil and the earthly powers that serve him.

Arthur's song stops short, however, of promising imminent redress. To speak of the Comforter, in John, is to give eschatological hope absolute urgency: the time of judgment, begun by Jesus's death, is now (D. A. Carson 562–63). But John does not speak of imminence. There is a parallel in Baldwin. Like Jesus's, Peanut's murder indicates that the "prince of this world" rules without control, and, as well, already stands judged. But whether that judgment can be brought to bear or, on the contrary, today's masters can persist indefinitely in arrogance and evil is left unclear.

Baldwin shows the initiation of an art promising overturn and a new world in a scene following these events by some months, after Arthur, leaving the South, has gone west and then to Canada, London, and Paris.[35] There, called on to sing, he responds with the Gospel song "Daniel Saw the Stone," which appears as an epigraph to Book One as well as at this point in the text.[36] This step in Arthur's development is not shown as a specific response to the events above; Arthur's only direct comment on them is to tell Hall, after a few days in Paris, that he must return, sooner rather than later, to the United States and the South (456). Rather, Arthur's embrace of an apocalyptic-eschatological theme appears as an artistic end of apprenticeship, a generational and generic shift in African American music, a response to his time, and a release of what is already within and around him. Baldwin conveys all this by bringing Arthur, with his French lover Guy, to a nightclub where he encounters an aging blues artist, Sonny Carr (501–13). Baldwin uses the mixed-race trio of U.S. musicians and the audience of French, European, black and white American, black

African, and north African aficionados to embody the world's turmoil and, in their precarious unity, its hope. Carr's first name creates a resonance with the Sonny of Baldwin's early story and with its affirmation of blues as a music of endurance and, tentatively, hope. The older singer's acquaintance long ago, as an already-mature artist, with a young Paul Montana—he recognizes Arthur because Arthur resembles Paul when young (513)—sets up a transfer of performing authority from the elders to the young. The shift is generic as well, as Carr performs a set of blues, folk, and convict work song standards—"Water Boy," "Jack of Diamonds," "See See Rider," "Take This Hammer," and "Yellow Dog Blues"—before bringing Arthur on stage and bidding him, "Sing 'Daniel'!" (511).

This call signifies a transition in the art needed to articulate the community's needs—from blues and songs of labor to Gospel and from enduring suffering to its apocalyptic end as the aim African American art points to. Finally, Arthur's response signifies the artist's function as a "vessel" (21): he reaches beyond performing intention into his memory, into the song's past transmission, and into the world around him calling for such a song. For, before Carr speaks, Arthur has been momentarily unable to think of any song at all, but at Carr's directive, "Still not certain of the words, Arthur opens his mouth, and the words come out!" (511):

> Daniel
> saw the stone
> that was hewed
> out the mountain, . . .
>
> Daniel
> saw the stone
> that was rolled
> into Babylon. . . .
>
> Jesus is the stone
> that was hewed out the mountain,
> tearing down
> the kingdom of this world! (511–12)

The song is a mainstay of apocalyptic Gospel singing, originating in some versions before 1907 and in Baldwin's before 1926. It derives from a core text in general apocalyptic thought, in which Daniel interprets Nebuchadnezzar's dream of a stone that smashes an idol of gold, silver, brass, iron, and clay—representing successive, degenerating kingdoms—and becomes a mountain filling the earth:

> And in the days of these kings shall the God of heaven set up a kingdom, which shall never be destroyed: and . . . it shall break in pieces and consume all these kingdoms, and it shall stand for ever.
>
> Forasmuch as thou sawest that the stone was cut out of the mountain without hands, and that it brake in pieces the iron, the brass, the clay, the silver, and the gold; the great God hath made known to the king what shall come to pass hereafter: and the dream is certain, and the interpretation thereof sure. (Dan. 2:44–45)

The story, with other texts in Daniel, inspired the tradition of the "Fifth Monarchy," God's kingdom that is to succeed all earthly empires.[37] The stone "cut out of the mountain without hands," signifying the spiritual force that overcomes tyranny and oppression, became the topic of an 1884 sermon by the famed Richmond Baptist minister John Jasper.[38] Baldwin's *The Fire Next Time* (1963) and Martin Luther King's "Dream" speech both allude to the phrase—for Baldwin, the generations of African Americans who have withstood persecution "were hewing out of the mountain of white supremacy the stone of their individuality" (*FNT* 100); King tells his hearers, "With this faith, we will be able to hew out of the mountain of despair a stone of hope" (233). Among modern theological commentators, John J. Collins notes that the statue's destruction signifies "the transcendent power of God to destroy all idols and the kingdoms that worship them" (97–98); Gerhard von Rad, with a more temporal emphasis, observes: "The main point is, of course, perfectly clear: with the terrible fourth kingdom [of iron and clay] into which the empire divides, world history has come to an end. The stone which is to be cut 'by no human hand' and which is to destroy the kingdom and itself to become a great mountain is an image of the kingdom of God that fills the whole earth" (*Old Testament Theology* 2:311–12). Baldwin has Arthur sing one traditional stanza, in which "Jesus is the stone" that tears down the kingdom, in the nightclub scene, and uses another in his epigraph, in which Daniel sees (foresees) the stone doing this. In either wording, the song extends John's "the prince of this world is judged" (16:11) to its outcome, the fall of the prince's power, promising an end to all tyrannic empires—then Babylon and Persia, now those of our age. The corollary, the advent of God's kingdom, is unspoken but plain to those who know Daniel.

Once Arthur sings solo, Carr and he, elder and youth, sing two songs together—"The End of My Journey" (also called "He'll Understand and Say Well Done") and "Another Building Not Made with Hands." These tell of the long work of witnessing for truth and God's acceptance of this work. The first looks to the day "when I come / to the end of my journey, / . . . weary of life, / and the battle is won"; the second gives God's assessment and then the singer's: "I'm pleased with what you've done, / and your race has been run" and, echoing Second Corinthians and varying Daniel: "I praise God, I have another building, / not made with hands!" (*JAMH* 512–13; see 2 Cor. 5:1). The songs accord recognition to prophets who are scorned or who simply live their whole lives without seeing what they prophesy. And their performance completes Arthur's selection as apocalyptic prophet-artist and his acceptance of that role from his artistic forebear; behind him and Carr hover the figures of Moses as well as Elijah, prophets who commissioned their own successors (Joshua and Elisha).[39]

This certainty that prophetic work is "well done" is necessarily acquired by faith or personal belief, whether in God or some vision of the future; we recall that those who by faith "obtained a good report" still "received not the promise" (Heb. 11:39–40). The verses in Second Corinthians that the last song alludes to speak of this issue. Paul says that "in this [house] we groan, earnestly desiring to be clothed upon with our house which is from heaven," words prophetic of Arthur's short life, before concluding, "For we walk by faith, not by sight" (2 Cor. 5:2, 7)—a capacity that Arthur is reaching for, that Sonny wills for him, and that Hall ascribes to the quartet members in youth (15), but that Arthur may not be able to sustain. So the two songs sung with Carr also foreshadow the chief crisis of Arthur's future life.[40]

Viewed over his whole career, Baldwin's representations of art and the artist develop from his call for a fine-grained mimetic art focused on African American life and manners, in his early essays on aesthetics; through a first statement of the prophetic art idea in "Sonny's Blues" and a view of art as the excavation of what lies buried in individual and community life, in *Another Country*; to a growing emphasis on the prophetic in art and an implied, and finally direct, expression of apocalyptic-eschatological ideas in art in the final novels. The prophetic conception of an art not chosen *by* the artist but *for* him or her, in a way analogous to how prophets are assumedly called by God, is most fully explored in *Just Above My Head*, and also most directly presented there. This work's sense of art as expressing the lives of "millions" and articulating a hoped-for justice "tearing down the kingdom of this world" is recognizably distant from Baldwin's starting point.

Yet there are constants. Baldwin's emphasis on African American community history and experience as a source of truth in art is one, whether expressed as the early essays' emphasis on African American "field of manners" and "ritual" ("MTG" 27); Sonny's "spare, flat statement" recalling all the lives before his ("SB" 140); the saxophonist's ability to tap into his own and the community's torment in *Another Country* (8–9); Leo's ability to play his crucial scene "for all the colored kids in the audience" and without betraying "the history which held me like a lover" (*TMHL* 433, 435); or Fonny's and Arthur's dedication to communal art. In each manifestation, the bases of art are social and communitarian, rooted in black Americans' experiences together over historical time; and, in all, art plunges us into the underlife of the individual and nation, finding, if it is true art, what is almost unbearable for the artist and his/her audience, yet must be made "part of the world's experience" (*AC* 112). Finally, the turn to prophetic and apocalyptic art does not negate individual, social, or artistic truth because to Baldwin it is plain beyond any speaking both that we *can* never be redeemed without a change down to our foundations as persons and a society, *and* that we have in us the capacity for this change—whether or not we can realize that capacity. But to understand these points fully, we must look at Baldwin's ideas of the body and of the city.

CHAPTER 3

The Apocalyptic Body

> And I look at my body, which is under sentence of death. It is lean, hard, and cold, the incarnation of a mystery. And I do not know what moves in this body, what this body is searching. It is trapped in my mirror as it is trapped in time and it hurries toward revelation.
>
> —*Giovanni's Room*

> For now we see through a glass, darkly; but then face to face: now I know in part; but then shall I know even as I am known.
>
> —First Corinthians 13:12

With the above words from *Giovanni's Room* (1956), part of a character's meditation at the novel's conclusion, Baldwin first broaches an idea of the apocalyptic body that will thread through all his later fiction and that stands alongside those of prophetic commissioning and prophetic art as a core of his thought. In Baldwin's work the body can be seen as apocalyptic in four related senses, involving the ideas of revelation of the hidden and of a coming new time as discussed earlier. First, it is an embodiment of the holy, whose deep nature becomes clear to each person in a process akin to revelation. This idea is central in the conclusion of *Giovanni's Room* and appears frequently in other works. Further, the body's love, specifically sexual love, in momentarily overcoming separateness and estrangement, provides a pre-vision of the combined eros and agape—bodily and personal love, public and selfless love—to be attained through an apocalypse of body and society. The body is apocalyptic, further, because it lives by need and impulse and not law. The casual and committed loves outside marriage experienced by many Baldwin characters—Gabriel and Esther, Richard and Elizabeth in *Go Tell It on the Mountain*, for example—defy social and religious authority, as do both casual and committed homosexual love, literally outside the law in most of the United States in Baldwin's time. The antinomianism these relations embody is implicit in New Testament teachings that Christ's law supersedes Moses's, but is held in check by Paul's view of self-restraint as part of Christ's law, one Baldwin rejects. Finally, the body is apocalyptic in that it will, or may, *undergo* an apocalypse; that is, at some unspecified time and in an unspecified way, people will become aware of and begin to live the life of the body—its muscles and fat, its organs, its smells, fluids, and secretions—as a manifestation of the sacred. For Baldwin, however, this apocalypse is not the outcome of the body's action alone, but part of a larger personal and public change. For alongside the body's holiness is its dishonoring—by law, custom, religious belief, other human bodies, one's own misguided belief—and alongside both is the social triangle of the body, commerce, and the police. All are stumbling blocks to making the body's apocalypse real.

These ideas radically oppose those of Baldwin's church background, with their downgrading of sex and bodily pleasure. Specifically, Baldwin opposes Holiness teachings on disciplining the body in preparation to receive the Spirit, implying that a holy spirit can enter our bodies as they are, or is inherent there. More generally he rejects the traditional Pauline teaching upholding conventional morality within the faith community (e.g., Rom. 6:1–2, 1 Cor. 3:16–17 and 6:9–20). In the broadest context, Baldwin's emphasis on the fleshly body's holiness rejects the traditional Western dualism of soul or spirit and body, as well as the specific Pauline view of the flesh as source of corruption for the body.[1] "[I]t seems to me," Baldwin said in his address to the World Council of Churches, "that the flesh and the spirit are one; it seems to me that when you mortify the one, you have mortified the other" ("WR" 755). In Baldwin, to counterpose soul or spirit to body is wrong and itself manifests the unholy. Putting the point another way, such a division separates body from *itself*: divides brain, ideas, beliefs, observation, memory, learning, veneration of others and of ethical models, from the body as need and desire, construed as "the flesh" and a source of contamination. To accept this division, Baldwin suggests, is to live voluntarily (or under social discipline) in chains.

In these respects, Baldwin may appear simply to upend the Holiness belief in bodily sanctity, retaining the conception while reversing its valence. Counterbalancing this idea, however, as often in Baldwin, is another, equally powerful: that we are *not* perfectible in sexualized sanctity, are limited and imperfect, and yet our lives and bodies are sacred as they are—a resonant phrase for him, we will see. Baldwin's sense of the ways we fall short of hopes and act treacherously and cruelly to ourselves and others is integral to his imagination. Hence, it is necessary to fashion an ethic of acceptance on the basis of good and bad conduct, not particular behaviors, that is part of what he means by accession to the kingdom.

These ideas Baldwin developed with increasing power and complexity from *Giovanni's Room* to *Just Above My Head*. Their expression in *Giovanni's Room* is relatively discreet—there are no direct homosexual descriptions, for example, in what seems a "paying of dues" for having the book received seriously in its time. But the essence of what follows in later works is present not just in the novel's ideas but in the oblique but unmistakable self-declaration that begins it, its dedication to a male—Lucien Happersberger—and accompanying quotation from Whitman (this novel's closest approach to an epigraph), "I am the man, I suffered, I was there." These inscriptions present the book as manifesting a life, and so the idea in the text, that its protagonist's sexual body is sacred—in fact, in some sense the body of Christ—is also a statement that a specific homosexual body in the real world is holy. This declaration is parallel in significance to what Marlon Ross observes about Baldwin's public appearances, that while adopting a generalized and heterosexualized African American voice, Baldwin nonetheless projected his own persona unmistakably in demeanor and body language, in what Ross calls "sissy heroics" (title; see especially 634). With *Giovanni's Room*'s publication, and with the public persona that it, as well as his public appearances, projects, Baldwin opened a space within literature for the apocalyptic body, one he enlarged in subsequent fiction until, in *Just Above My Head*, he broke down the walls around it and expansively inhabited the space he had created two decades before.

The Sacraments of the Body

The closing scene of *Giovanni's Room*, already mentioned, begins what will be Baldwin's frequent practice, presenting the body and its sexuality—especially but not only homosexuality—through sacral language. David, the protagonist and narrator, undertakes his meditation in circumstances that could not be more dramatic: viewed in his mirror, his body, under "sentence of death"—the common condition of every human body—replicates that of his ex-lover Giovanni, sentenced to die this morning. The reader understands that David is guilty, potentially, of two murders—of Giovanni, whom he has abandoned in terror of his own love and in futile pursuit of conventional normality, and of himself, his inner core and possibility of truly living, if he cannot somehow face and accept who he is.

David does accept himself, in a rumination mediated by Paul's words in First Corinthians, "When I was a child, I spake as a child, I understood as a child, I thought as a child: but when I became a man, I put away childish things" (13:11; *GR* 168). In literal meaning, Paul's words cut two ways—they can mean becoming a man in conventional senses, and have been so read in this passage (DeGout 428), or they can mean putting away early ideas or illusions. In David's use of the verse, he longs "to make this prophecy come true," wonders how his penis, or "sex," viewed in the mirror, "can be redeemed," understands that "the key to my salvation, which cannot save my body, is hidden in my flesh," and assesses that his nakedness is that "which I must hold sacred, though it be never so vile" (*GR* 168–69). David, then, believes that his flesh holds the key to salvation even if it cannot save itself—thus, the salvation is of his inner self—and that the key is to hold this flesh, his nakedness, "sacred." In context within the whole book, this must mean to do what David has refused to do until now, to accept and hold sacred his "insistent possibilities" (43). On condition that he do so, David implies, he can experience "the heavy grace of God, which has brought me to this place" and "can carry me out of it" (168–69). Acceptance, the meditation implies, will be painful, even unbearably so, both because of David's objective guilt in Giovanni's death and because of what David, and Baldwin, apparently see as the meaninglessness of much gay life (for example, 43). David's nakedness will have to be "scoured perpetually with the salt of my life" (169). But this harsh acceptance is acceptance nonetheless.[2]

Besides communicating his plot resolution, this meditation marks Baldwin's first direct use of scriptural and theological language to describe the body's capacity for transcendence. The terms David uses—*incarnation*, *mystery*, *revelation*, *prophecy*, *redeemed, salvation, sacred, grace*—are insistently sacramental, and they echo in presentations of sexuality elsewhere in this and other works. The most resonant of these terms in the present passage are *incarnation*, *mystery*, *revelation*, and *grace*. Incarnation is the process of the immaterial becoming material, and specifically, of Jesus's taking human form. *Mystery* and its plural, used twenty-seven times in the New Testament, usually signify what has been or is hidden, especially what God has hidden since the world's inception but now reveals: Paul says the believers "speak the wisdom of God in a mystery, even the hidden wisdom, which God ordained before the world unto our glory" (1 Cor. 2:7). (The most important contrary sense, in Revelation 17:5, is discussed later.) Baldwin implies, then, that David's body, and the mortal body in general, are material manifestations of God's hidden truth. (Indeed, since Jesus's birth as man is itself the incarnation of a mystery, so, the meditation implies, is David's homosexual body in some sense the body of Christ.) That hidden truth, clearly, is "what moves in this body, what this body is searching," but it is also the answers to these implied questions, and the body moves, as well, toward *revelation* of the mystery. This term implies apocalyptic truth, the unveiling of the hidden; and the truth unveiled is that the body—David's specifically—is "sacred" and can be redeemed through grace, freely given acceptance or mercy, here conditioned on David's being able to accept his body as holy.

"The heavy grace of God," used in David's conclusion, is a particularly resonant phrase, especially as Eric, in *Another Country*, will also refer to the grace needed to accept himself. David has shown little or no religious conviction through the book, apart from a polite response to his concierge (69). Moreover, despite this earlier presentation of David as a believer in some sense, he does not now seem to reach for a residual belief that has become crucial, but rather, to accept the sacred quality of his body and sexuality without a specifically religious meaning. In substance, the "heavy grace of God" seems to signify both a controlling force in David's life that has led him to his present calamity, but may lead him through it if accepted, and an inward capacity to accept this force that cannot be willed but may, with difficulty, be acceded to. Grace, then, as used here, is an interior process, not an external bestowal, yet, in other respects, is similar to that in Methodism and related theologies that believe grace confers the freedom to choose or reject salvation.[3] So for David grace is the ability, which he cannot will, to understand the inner truth of his life and possibly accept it. In this sense, despite Baldwin's overall lack of reference to a personal God, the "grace of God" refers for him to something real—a real quality of experience in some people's lives. The term, then, seems to allow

Baldwin to express a part of human experience not otherwise easily described, and it seems crucial for Baldwin's language to operate on this in-between level, neither specifically theistic nor simply secular.

Baldwin's use of Paul is additionally significant, and not only because this is First Corinthians' chapter on the supremacy of love (*agape*, "charity" in the unsatisfactory AV translation), which argues—pertinently to David—that "though I have all faith, so that I could remove mountains, and have not [love], I am nothing" (13:2). Besides this point, Paul's topic at this stage in his discourse is apocalyptic knowledge. The verse David quotes is part of a comparison of present imperfect knowledge to the full knowledge revealed at the eschaton, the world's culmination. "For we know in part, and we prophesy in part. / But when that which is perfect is come, that which is in part shall be done away," Paul writes in the verses preceding David's (9–10), and continues, in the verse following, "For now we see through a glass, darkly; but then face to face" (12). David's verse, then—which he recalls when in fact seeing "through a glass," that is, in a mirror—is not simply a comparison of early to adult knowledge but a step in Paul's comparison of indirect to direct knowledge of the divine. Both *face to face* and *mystery*, in fact, have revelatory meaning in Paul. The former points to the fact that "at the Eschaton, . . . we too shall know in [God's] way, with no more need for the kinds of mediation that the mirror illustrates" (Fee 649).[4] For Baldwin, who does not believe in a literal eschaton—though he does believe in its broader meaning, the coming of a new time—this direct, authoritative knowledge stems, in *Giovanni's Room* and elsewhere, from contemplation and direct experience of the body, what David sees in the mirror. Further, the substance of the knowledge is that the naked body is "sacred" and the "incarnation of a mystery." And the body, now "trapped" in the mirror and in time, "hurries toward revelation," as Paul's analogy signifies full knowledge to come. *Mystery*, in turn, besides the meanings already stated, refers to "a somewhat hidden world of apocalyptic reality" with its own "apocalyptic narrative in which the expected revelation of the heavenly Christ will overturn the structures of the world" (Martin 57). Baldwin's "incarnation of a mystery," then, suggests that realizing this mystery presupposes an apocalyptic overturn, though he does not stress this point in *Giovanni's Room*.

Use of a quasi-sacral vocabulary of sexuality only grows in later work. In *Another Country*, this vocabulary variously conveys the wonder, recovered innocence, and self-realization that sexual experience makes possible. Images of baptism/rebirth, mystery, and revelation describe Eric's sexual initiation at age sixteen, the start of his relationship with Yves two years before the novel's action, and eventually his brief affair with Vivaldo. In these episodes, "mystery" is used to denote characters' sexual natures, male and female bodies, and sexual communion (*AC* 204, 384, 385). In all three, water suggests the cleansing and symbolic rebirth of baptism. Eric and LeRoy, and later Eric and Yves, lie beside or above streams; after making love, Vivaldo and Eric feel the rain outside as a "blessing," a "wall between them and the world" (206, 222, 386). For his part, Vivaldo feels he has "fallen through a great hole in time, back to his innocence" and is now "clear, washed, and empty, waiting to be filled" (386). And Eric's first sex act, years earlier, had the force of revelation:

> What had always been hidden was to him, that day, revealed and it did not matter that, fifteen years later, he sat in an armchair, overlooking a foreign sea, still struggling to find the grace which would allow him to bear that revelation. For the meaning of revelation is that that which is revealed is true, and must be borne. (206)[5]

The characters' experiences in these episodes are basically secular. Eric's "revelation," for instance, comes from within, as an awareness of his profoundest nature, and so also the grace he seeks must come from himself. He must overcome the humiliation he feels from years of delivering oral sex in parks, on rooftops, in parked cars, in borrowed rooms (211, 260–61) and, like David in *Giovanni's Room*, he must accept what has always tormented him. He has done this in part by loving Yves, and learning to "love himself" so as to be worthy of Yves (215), yet he continues, in this meditation, to search for peace with himself. Vivaldo, in the later scene in which he and Eric make love, accepts a homosexual impulse that, previously, he has externalized as sexual violence (and retrospectively, a topic of "fascinated, even romantic, horror"); pushed away in Rufus; distanced as "a long time ago" with Harold (112, 69–70, 82, 315). In a psychically complex way, acknowledging this impulse lets him pass on from it to the heterosexualism he is bound to by deepest response. Further, accepting with Eric the closeness he feared with Rufus (342) allows him, in his and Ida's crisis later that day, to destroy the "distance" called pity and feel himself, "very nearly, in her body" (426). Yet these changes come not by will but by acceptance.[6] All this is what Baldwin describes with the word *grace*. Baldwin does not suggest that a God, in any identifiable way, is part of these processes, and yet his religious language is no mere ornament but suggests the deep, only partly controllable, power of sexual acts and truth, and the need for acceptance of both.

Baldwin's last two novels treat sexuality both mimetically and through extended applications of religious language to suggest varied states factually or symbolically comparable to elements of Christian deliverance. In describing Arthur's first full sexual experience with Crunch, at age sixteen in Atlanta during the Trumpets of Zion's southern tour, *Just Above My Head* employs graphic physical description, focused on the youths' feelings as well as their acts:

> He had never done this before. In the same way that he knew how Crunch feared to be despised—by him—he knew, too, that he, now, feared to be despised by Crunch. *Cocksucker.*
>
> Well. It was Crunch's cock, and so he sucked it; with all the love that was in him, and a moment came when he felt that love being trusted, and returned. (*JAMH* 211)

This literal description is intensified by interwoven Gospel lyrics:

> A friendly, a joyful movement began. *So high, you can't get over him.*
>
> Sweat from Arthur's forehead fell onto Crunch's belly.
>
> *So low*—and Crunch gasped as Arthur's mouth left his prick standing in the cold, cold air, as Arthur's tongue licked his sacred balls—*you can't get under him.* Arthur rose, again, to Crunch's lips. *So wide. You can't get around him. . . .*
>
> "Little fellow. Baby. Love."
>
> *You must come in at the door. . . .* (211–12)

"You Must Come in at the Door" is a Gospel standard, recorded in varied versions since 1926, initially referring to the door of Jesus's sheepfold and later, in the version Baldwin uses, to entry into Jesus or the Lamb himself. It is ultimately derived from John 10:1–9, the parable of the sheepfold, in which Jesus explains, "I am the door: by me if any man enter in, he shall be saved, and shall go in and out, and find pasture" (10:9), so the transference is legitimate.[7] Hall's reconstruction of his brother's experience, then, compares sexual union to union with the savior; the parts of Crunch's body to the parts of the sheepfold or the savior's body that the seeker cannot evade; and the lover's penis and semen to "the door." Similar song references lead to and follow this moment.[8]

Such descriptions partly draw on a much-discussed aspect of Gospel music and its derivatives, their underlying sexuality. Gospel singing often uses a highly sexualized delivery, while sublimating actual carnal sexuality; some secular singing by "crossover" Gospel artists like Sam Cooke and Marvin Gaye creates a sexualized aura exalted enough to feel, Gaye once said, "something like sanctified" (qtd. in Wolff et al. 262). More is at work than emotive equivalence, however. Besides sacralizing sexual feeling, Lee Edelman suggests, Baldwin's Gospel and sacral language of sexuality suggests real utopian possibilities, implying, in the Crunch-Arthur scene, a potential "healing of the divided psyche" based on "a trust, indeed, a faith, sufficient to withstand the world's reprobation" and phrased as a secularized version of "the language of religious surrender and redemption" (69).[9] Finally, Baldwin's uses of sacral language for sexual acts retain recognizable theological meanings. In *Beale Street*, for example, Tish feels Fonny's body as "sacred," their mixed semen and blood (she is a virgin) as an "anointing," one's lover's body as a "changing envelope which contains the gravest mystery of one's life," and, retrospectively, that in sex Fonny "rode . . . not so much into me as into a kingdom which lay just behind his eyes"; Tish's mother, Sharon, says of her later pregnancy, "This is sacrament" (*BS* 68, 35–36). Besides directly describing sexual union as sacred, Baldwin's language presents versions of David's recognizing the "mystery" of his body and of an inner kingdom "behind [the] eyes" recalling the "secret place" in *Another Country*—both suggesting an incarnation of the apocalyptic body. Additionally, "anointing"—in one sense, performed in ritual appointment to offices such as king, priest, or prophet—points toward what we will later see as Tish's symbolic identifications with Jesus's mother Mary and with Revelation's "woman clothed with the sun."[10]

Beyond experiential responses, Baldwin presents sexual union as able to create a partial, temporary break from oppressive reality into a zone of freedom, and this experience, at least by implication, offers a foretaste of a future freedom that will be available to all. When Arthur first kisses Guy during their brief affair in Paris, Robert Reid-Pharr observes, he is described as "trembling in a kind of paroxysm of liberty" (*JAMH* 479; *Once You Go Black* 109), an experience Reid-Pharr reads as an "escape" for Arthur from the memory of Peanut's murder and from constraints of identity, community, and tradition (108); the point is valid for Guy as well, whose Algerian ex-lover had to leave France. Further, as their affair continues, the lovers are described as "using themselves in defiance of murder, time, language, and continents" (*JAMH* 487)—they no longer simply allow their differences to drop from them, but engage with each other over and across these barriers. Lovemaking, then, becomes a way of at least psychically challenging the system of murders, in France, Algeria, and the United States, that shapes their world. And, moving toward climax, they feel a "sense of mysteries overturned and the sky exploding"

(487)—apocalyptic portents of the end of "mystery" as the veil of social power and tyranny (Rev. 17:5) and of this world's downfall.[11]

Baldwin, then, makes three large claims about the apocalyptic body. It has a liberating, though also coercive, power: we each must, if we can, accede to what is truest, and perhaps most frightening, in ourselves, in a process akin to theological grace; and if we do, we may experience a secular union comparable to divine union. Further, the apocalyptic body possesses a tangible and momentarily absolute freedom—freedom from surrounding circumstances, freedom to encounter and mesh with the body of another. Finally, sexual ecstasy and unification can provide a counter to the world's violence, a brief break into a union similar to the biblically promised new world.

This view of the sacramental body, particularly Baldwin's part-metaphoric, part-ontological use of terms like "mystery," "grace," and "revelation," implying unchosen truths that must be accepted, raises issues central to debates on Baldwin and sexuality. These debates, focused on *Giovanni's Room* but relevant to later fiction, have asked whether Baldwin treats sexuality as determinate (an "identity"), as a continuum, or as nondeterminate, and where in this spectrum he places the most emphasis. In recent discussions, a "queer" Baldwin anticipating current ideas of dissolving sexual categories probably predominates, though the best interpreters recognize ambiguity in Baldwin's handling of identity issues. The applicability of queer theory, we will see, is problematic in Baldwin; but the alternative is nothing so simple as a "sexual identity" but rather an idea of deeply determinate parts of personal identities that one must accept, or reject to one's detriment.

Starting from the fact of David and Giovanni's functional bisexuality, discussions of *Giovanni's Room* have argued, variously, that the novel presents gender fluidity or indeterminacy as a desirable model or, alternatively, that it promotes bisexuality in a vitiating compromise with prevailing social ideology. Brett Beemyn and Myriam J. A. Chancy, among others, believe the book seeks "to appreciate sexual and gender fluidity" (Beemyn 58) or that in belatedly identifying with Giovanni, David attains "an acceptance of self along indistinct and unfixed racial and gender lines" (Chancy 185). This view draws strength from Baldwin's differentiation between U.S. and European attitudes (David assumes he must ultimately choose one orientation or the other; Giovanni sees no problem in retaining both). Further, Giovanni's opposition to exclusive categories matches some of Baldwin's beliefs at least as stated later, such as his comments in a 1965 interview that "those terms, homosexual, bisexual, heterosexual are 20th-century terms which, for me, really have very little meaning," and that he has never "been able to discern exactly where the barriers were" (Mossman 54).[12] Alternatively, Keith Mitchell believes these characters' bisexuality shows that "Baldwin's philosophy of love and sexual desire" often uses bisexuality as an evasion of responsibility for homosexuality, an effort to gain "a precarious acceptance by keeping one foot in the realm of heterosexuality" (262). The point would apply to other novels as well, since Eric and Vivaldo (*Another Country*), Leo and Christopher (*Tell Me How Long*), and others are also bisexually capable.

Both views miss what seems a fundamental distinction in Baldwin between ontology and psychology—or, more broadly, human character. Paradoxically or not, Baldwin's relatively few ventures into theorizing about sexuality do present sexual potentiality as varied and fluid, and its categorization as a social construct, yet his reading of character and action suggests that individuals possess an inmost nature that, though often more restricted or determined than the full range of human potentiality, must be discovered and accepted, as the ideas of revelation and apocalyptic unveiling imply. In relation to *Giovanni's Room*, the shared assumption of both viewpoints just discussed—that Baldwin shows bisexuality or sexual indeterminacy as preferable to exclusive or preferential homosexuality—should be questioned. First, despite the book's harshly negative portrayal of the gay *milieu*,[13] some exclusively or preferentially homosexual characters act more charitably and forthrightly than the bisexual David and Giovanni. The café hustlers, for example, remain helpful to Giovanni when David abandons him; Jacques, seen by David as "despicable," is given the book's strongest speech favoring homosexual love, still stirring after sixty years—"love him and let him love you. Do you think anything else under heaven really matters?"—and acts toward David and Hella with beautiful scorn (147–48, 55, 57, 127–30). More basically, if *Giovanni's Room* indeed develops toward David's reluctant acknowledgment of a deep-seated homosexual character—however developed: Baldwin sketches a rather standard Freudian psychogenesis[14]—then the assumptions of critics attacking as well as affirming its pro-bisexualism are falsified, whether or not Baldwin approves abstractly of less fixed gender identifications; David's deepest impulses, which he must discover and accept rather than choose, are homosexual. In essence, then, the real point is what Mitchell says—David, at least, uses bisexualism to deny his deep nature—but, contrary to Mitchell's assumption, the novel works to criticize this stance. At the same time, Baldwin does seem to present, in Giovanni, the possibility of a more fundamental, less forced bisexualism.

Baldwin's later novels continue to emphasize deeply lodged psychic dispositions that must be understood and accepted. The indeterminacy of sexuality in a fundamental ontological sense *is* important in them, as exampled by the characters already mentioned as well as Hall Montana in *Just Above My Head*, who has engaged in homosexual liaisons of opportunity that he now regrets apparently because of their lack of feeling, but not their homosexuality as such (318).[15] Other characters in this novel are able, with struggle, to change sexual orientations, though at devastating cost. It is plausible to regard such episodes as prophetic of a freer, sexually less determinate world—in fact, Baldwin's heavenly city—and this idea, I think, does form part of Baldwin's utopian apocalypticism. But at the same time, except perhaps for Crunch in this novel, the later Baldwin does not present characters who feel bisexual or sexually polymorphous in their deepest being. Crunch, exceptionally, though previously heterosexual and apparently not attracted to other males, seems deeply in love with Arthur; he will barely manage to throttle this love, and only half-successfully. Baldwin may, then, posit a primary bisexualism or pluripotentiality in Crunch, one that, it will turn out, Crunch cannot accept psychically or socially.[16] Other characters respond most deeply in one way or the other: Eric, in *Another Country*, and Leo, in *Tell Me How Long*, move toward preferential homosexuality while Vivaldo and Hall reaffirm their heterosexuality; *Just Above My Head*'s protagonist, Arthur Montana, realizes from adolescence that he is a "sissy" (20). Since both Eric and Leo have been seen as examples of bisexuality or role indeterminacy (Corber 168; Kilpeläinen), it is worth noting that Eric is now moving toward a settled homosexual identification, after having thought, during his affair with Cass, "that perhaps here was my opportunity to change" (339). Leo's bisexuality, similarly, appears in context as part of a decades-long avoidance of his deepest self. Baldwin, then, apparently thinks that while an undifferentiated sexual potentiality belongs to everyone, each person responds most deeply in some particular way; and this response, for these characters, is not a choice but a "mystery" that must be "revealed" and, if possible, accepted through "grace" (*AC* 206).

Baldwin, in sum, overall follows the model of a plurality of sexual stances in society that are made up of varied deep and powerful sexual natures in individuals; he does not, as a main emphasis, anticipate late twentieth and early twenty-first century ideas of polymorphous sexuality. His brief discussion of whether homosexuality is "natural," in his 1954 essay on André Gide, "The Male Prison," suggests as much, even though superficially social-constructionist. Baldwin's examples of why it is useless to ask if homosexuality is natural—doing so is like asking "whether or not it was natural for St. Paul to suffer for the Gospel" and others ("MP" 232)—play off an unexpressed antithesis between biological nature and the actors' own given, ultimately unwilled "nature." In what is probably the latter sense, Baldwin refers twice to Gide's "nature" and "sexual nature" (231, 232). So, Baldwin suggests, "sexual nature" can be and perhaps usually is deep and unwilled, as Paul's voluntary suffering was in accord with his whole being. Baldwin's sexual utopianism, then, lies less in foreseeing a new, more uncategorized sexuality for everyone than in envisioning a multiplicity of sexual states in which people express their deepest selves and for which a reformed society can make room.

Among these states or unchosen preferences, Baldwin places an implied emphasis on those conventionally most despised, specifically the practice of cocksucking, and this emphasis can be related both to Ross's "sissy heroics" and to Baldwin's revision of Pauline teaching. Several of Baldwin's male characters are shown as engaging in this act preferentially and, especially, treating it as the expression of deepest love. Starting with John Grimes's fascination with Elisha's thighs that "moved terribly against the cloth of his suit," and with the bodies and penises of older schoolmates (*GT* 8, 11)—and noting a probable double entendre on Isaiah's "a man of unclean lips" (6:5)—we can see John as awakening to an attraction to other men's genitals. Eric, in his years of pickup sex, predominantly gives oral sex to heterosexually identified men (*AC* 211); Rufus's remembering "such pleasure as Eric gave, or got" (46), and Vivaldo's pulling Eric "to him through the ruined sheets" after sex (386)—clearly Eric's body has not been head to head with his—imply that Eric performs the same act with them.[17] Finally, Arthur expresses his burgeoning love for Crunch by sucking him off and, later, Jimmy memorializes his own love by recalling how he would "go down on" Arthur (*JAMH* 211–12, 576). For Baldwin, then, the sacraments of the body, in homosexual love, specifically focus on the acts considered most shameful and unmanly in heterosexual culture and hold them up as of greatest value, in a double application of defiant sissydom and of Baldwin's revisionary understanding of Paul's "things which are despised" and "our uncomely parts" (1 Cor. 1:28, 12:23).

Holiness, Imperfection, and Ethical Acceptance

Baldwin extends his uses of religious language in *Another Country* and later works to include the body's sacredness as it is—in its imperfect, partially blasphemed states—in a correction of Holiness emphasis on its sanctification; the importance of conduct and humility; and, finally, a broad ethical acceptance of given experience that is necessary for what Baldwin would see as true community. In *Another Country*, Reverend Foster speaks at Rufus Scott's funeral:

> I ain't going to try to judge him. That ain't for us to do. You know, a lot of people say that a man who takes his own life oughtn't to be buried in holy ground. I don't know nothing about that. All *I* know, God made every bit of ground I ever walked on and everything God made is *holy*. And don't none of us know what goes on in the heart of someone. . . . We got to pray that the Lord will receive him like we pray that the Lord's going to receive us. That's all. That's *all*. (121)

Rev. Foster speaks with the humbleness we think a minister should feel, and does so simply and directly, in contrast to Gabriel's highly rhetoricized sermons in *Go Tell It*. Since his role in the plot is brief (*AC* 120–23), it is easy to miss the fact that in these few words, he speaks the central lesson of Baldwin's novel.

The minister means only to answer the point about suicides by pointing out that all God's work is holy, as was Rufus, whatever his wrongs and sins; and the lesson he offers is of absolute humility: we pray for Rufus as we must for ourselves. That is all Rev. Foster can know, but the reader remembers that in his last hours, Rufus stood at the urinal in Benno's bar:

> [The men's room] smelled of thousands of travelers, oceans of piss, tons of bile and vomit and shit. He added his stream to the ocean, holding that most despised part of himself loosely between two fingers of one hand. . . . He looked at the horrible history splashed furiously on the walls. . . . *Suck my cock. I like to get whipped. I want a big stiff prick up my ass. Down with Jews. Kill the niggers. I suck cocks.*
>
> He washed his hands very carefully and dried them on the filthy roller towel and walked out into the bar. (83)

Rufus, then, confronted both the world's bottomless confusion and hate over sex and race, and his own self-contempt, before starting his last journey. And so the moment when he despises his penis reaches across time to Rev. Foster's unknowing answer. Baldwin, then, triangulates Rufus's last hours with his minister's elegy to make the fundamental point that the body and its sexuality are sacred, a point underlying everything else in *Another Country*.

Besides its direct meaning, this implied lesson contains a corrective to the core Holiness emphasis on disciplining the body with the aim of "entire extinction of the carnal mind" (qtd. in J. Peters 137), in efforts to achieve a state of sanctification—ideas, we know, with deep roots in John Wesley's theology and Pauline teaching. Attaching the idea of holiness to the "most despised part" of oneself implies that holiness may be attained—indeed, is inherent—without this disciplining, one most people are not committed or strong enough to practice. Therefore, it further corrects the arrogance that belief in one's own sanctity can allow, what John L. Peters sums up as Holiness doctrine's "Pharisaism," or "spiritual pride [and] self-righteousness" (186–87). It implies, instead, a humility inherent in the attitude to the body that it expresses: sexual organs are everyone's possession, what matters is the use made of them; Rufus's holiness exists despite his sullying it by cruelty and contempt, and his failure, after all, was not that he had sex with Eric or Leona but that—in another resonant use of this word—he "had despised Eric's manhood" while making use of his love (*AC* 46), and brutalized Leona while using hers. So, finally, this acceptance of the sexual connects with the humility expressed in Rev. Foster's "don't none of us know what goes on in the heart of someone": the body's holiness is inherent but can be self-traduced by the smallness and cruelty all are capable of.

These ideas—Rev. Foster's that what God made is holy, the consequent rejection of disciplining the body and of the traditional body-spirit dualism underlying that aim, the belief that imperfect beings are still, in themselves, holy, and finally, the resultant importance of conduct and humility—form a rough unity in Baldwin leading, in *Just Above My Head*, to an ethical conception of tolerance that is also a claim for all to enter the apocalyptic kingdom. This compound idea underpins a sermon by Julia and an imagined plea and declaration by Arthur that together provide the moral core of this novel as Rev. Foster's eulogy did in *Another Country*.

Julia's sermon is most specifically a repudiation of church hypocrisy and narrow-mindedness, particularly regarding the condemnation of bodily adornment and indulgence. More generally, the sermon suggests that all who act with respect for others find God's favor. Julia's last public act in the church, when she is not quite fourteen, it is recalled in present time about twenty-five years later (*JAMH* 38–44) and then recreated in Hall's narration (160–63). Its occasion was the funeral of Mother Bessie Green, whom her minister ordered shunned for having earrings.[18] Julia takes as her text "Set thine house in order," from Isaiah's words to King Hezekiah in illness (Isa. 38:1; *JAMH* 161), and develops the text as an extended metaphor: the dying believer scours the stove, pots, walls, washes the windows, cleans the mirror, all with time running low, and at last offers to remove her earrings, but asks God's aid to her trembling hands and blind eyes. God replies, "I see what you done with your kitchen. I see what you done with your stove. . . . I see how you scrubbed that mirror because you didn't want Me to be ashamed of you and so we could see each other face to face. You can come into my kingdom with your earrings *on*!" (163). Sermon and peroration develop a core ethical and theological idea: those who live truthfully and "order their houses" need not transform themselves to enter the kingdom but are accepted as they are. Though Julia was presumably not thinking in these terms at thirteen, the sermon's applicability to homosexuality and sex in general is obvious, and consonant with her broadmindedness as an adult. Finally, the sermon's core idea is echoed in words Hall imagines for Arthur late in the book: "Arthur had to pull himself to a place where he could say to Paul, his father, and to Hall, his brother, and to all the world, and to *his* Maker, *Take me as I am!*" (472).[19] Superficially but importantly a claim for acceptance of homosexuality, these words and Julia's sermon more deeply express that the body and its desires and needs are part, "as they are," of the apocalyptic kingdom.

Julia's sermon and Arthur's imagined plea complement the idea of the apocalyptic body through a broad opening out of ethical inclusiveness that encompasses both the ordinary human in his or her imperfection as against those self-conceived as having achieved "Christian perfection" (Mother Bessie against her minister) and the morally reprobate against the compromising and conventional (Arthur, as we will see, against Crunch). This inclusiveness also means that Mother Bessie's earrings—by implication, particular tastes, indulgences, sexual practices and obsessions—do not *matter*, if "the house is in order," that is, if those practicing them have lived without cruelty and exclusion. And this ethical standard, finally, in the sermon and in Arthur's imagined words, has the force of apocalyptic truth: Mother Bessie, her "mirror" cleaned, will see God "face to face," in Paul's metaphor for the knowledge gained at the eschaton, and Arthur, in Hall's imagination, will address God to his face.

Baldwin's ideas about the body's sacredness and the possibility of an apocalyptic body remain unclear in several ways. First, is Baldwin simply using sacramental language figuratively to capture the intensity of sexual experience, or to imply a real possibility of new forms of awareness and understanding? The latter is consistent with Baldwin's belief (for example, in *Another Country*) in communication, in breaking down barriers of defensive denial both between persons and in ourselves. It would seem that for Baldwin, the transcendence found briefly in sexual union is also possible through the difficult work of truth and acceptance in the relations of lovers and (we will see) of citizens, and that this is part of what he means by the force of social love. Yet, sexual immediacy and interpersonal honesty are obviously distinct, and the first needs to be led up to or followed by the second if it is to last, as the experiences of Vivaldo and Ida, Leo and Christopher, and other Baldwin pairings imply. With this caveat, it appears that Baldwin does mean we can reach a new way of apprehending the body, in which its demands will not be felt as impure, lower, or entrapping, but as parts of the sacredness of life. Yet it remains unclear how the state Baldwin figures as an apocalypse differs from the self-integration proposed, for example, by psychoanalytic theory—or by simple maturity and frankness between people—except that, for Baldwin the incorporation into maturation of psychic defeats and compromises, hopes forgone in accepting "reality," ought not, and in a reformed state of being need not, occur. It is unclear, further, how closely insistence on the sacral qualities of sexual experience meshes with the ethic of tolerance, which posits imperfection as its basis; the best answer may be simply that this is one of the points where Baldwin emphasizes two sides of one reality, in tension. Finally, of course, Baldwin does not specify how we are to make the body's apocalyptic state real in practice, but only indicates through his language of the body that doing so may somehow be possible.

More specifically, how strong or durable are the apocalyptic body's claims in the face of a repressive society? Breakthrough and release are momentary; social pressures and those of ingrained psychic structures are continuous. Hall's narration foreshadows that Arthur will bear these pressures better than his first lover:

> Arthur was stronger than Crunch: it is as simple, as dreadful, and as mysterious as that. . . . Crunch feared solitude, and was easily bewildered, he could not live without love. But Arthur could live on stones—he sought love everywhere, but he could live on stones. (*JAMH* 213)

Yet Arthur will have to struggle to maintain the opening of his true self that he experiences in Atlanta, and will be unable to do so fully.

Most basically, Baldwin's idea of the apocalyptic body raises questions about the relation between the psychic and social repression that make apocalypse necessary and their reflection in the strength of apocalyptic release. Self-suppression of bodily desire outside of social convention and adherence to religious strictures on bodily pleasure consume enormous amounts of psychic energy. They further require warding off attraction to others, by denying it or branding it wicked, and devaluing those who provoke the attraction, through prejudice, contempt, or hatred. The reversal of this inward projection of psychic energy—no longer repressing and silencing desire but directing it outward, letting it speak—is responsible for the explosive release embodied directly in orgasm, more broadly in the ecstatic recognition of one's desire and others' beauty that I am calling an apocalypse of the body. The force of release also comes from other, social weights on the soul: for Arthur, at the time of his initiation with Crunch, the "awful pain" of Dorothy Green, the young Memphis churchwoman he briefly flirts with (189); Crunch's pain in his mother's degradation (190); the South's menace in 1951 (197); and Arthur's knowledge that Crunch will soon be lost to Korea (203). Paradoxically, then, the force of apocalyptic release, a component of its fused biblical meanings, is conditioned on the strength of the repressive force it overcomes, seeming to suggest that in a hypothesized future when body is no longer self-divided, this release may no longer occur. Indeed, this outcome is possible; yet, biblically, the apocalyptic event is not an end but a gateway. Baldwin's treatment of apocalyptic oneness of the body also suggests that in a future reality, this oneness may occur as a continuing state, without need of repeated apocalyptic release, as the ordinary form of day-to-day living. But how this might occur is not made clear.

Dishonoring the Body

Besides his claims for a possible apocalypse of the body, Baldwin recognizes the many ways in which we dishonor the body, each a means of crushing down or evading its anarchic, utopian openness and mutuality and so helping maintain the world as it is. These can be summarized under the headings of direct dishonoring of the body by oppressors, dishonoring through cowardice abetted by adherence to religious or social law, and dishonoring through silence and invisibility, the outward conformance to this law. Together, these provide the many bitter defeats that fill Baldwin's pages alongside his portrayal of tentative victories.

Baldwin does not often use biblically-inflected language in describing these defeats—they belong definitionally to the world as it is, not as it might be, this language's focus in Baldwin. Instead, he traces character development naturalistically but often obliquely, requiring readers to fill in implied details. Especially in later works, this process often involves connecting widely separated episodes in the disrupted chronologies Baldwin comes to prefer. Portraits of defeat and loss grow in complexity and importance in these works, in which, alongside redemptive possibilities, an older Baldwin shows the immense damage we do to each other and ourselves in a world—he implies—that depends for its stability on our failures to be free.

Rapes, threatened rapes, and sexual humiliation by oppressors occur in several Baldwin novels. Deborah, in *Go Tell It on the Mountain*, is raped by a gang of whites (63). Fonny's friend Daniel, in *If Beale Street Could Talk*, is raped in prison and describes a prison gang-rape he witnessed; Fonny is thrown in solitary for resisting a rape attempt (145, 162). Julia in *Just Above My Head* suffers rape, continuing violation, and a near-fatal beating by her father Joel. These attacks aim to destroy the target's will and self-worth, and have this effect on Daniel, though Deborah is able to bear forward through Christian faith, Fonny by deepening his resistant rage (*BS* 162), and Julia by sheer inner strength (*JAMH* 284).[20]

Caleb Proudhammer, Leo's brother in *Tell Me How Long the Train's Been Gone*, provides a study of sexual and general prison torture and their lasting effects on personality. We learn of Caleb, seven years Leo's senior, through Leo's memories of his teens before his imprisonment, of his return from prison four years later, and of his religious conversion and personal transformation several years on. (In present time, Caleb appears only for a moment, in the novel's last paragraph.) At a southern prison farm after conviction on false robbery charges, Caleb is targeted by a white guard, Howell, after trying to insist on respectful treatment. Homosexual taunting is prominent in Howell's overall harassment: he asks Caleb, "Who the fuck do you think you are?" but also, "Nigger, if my balls was on your chin, where would my prick be?" (252–53). Later he speculates on the size of Caleb's penis and touches his backside, and still later asks, "Nigger, remember that question I asked you?" (236–38). Eventually, Caleb is broken and repeats, as Howell demands, "I ain't worth shit" (239).

These events help shape Caleb's later psychic transformation. Though actively heterosexual, Caleb has some homosexual impulses: in terror and despair after his return to New York, he clings to Leo in the bed they share, "terribly excited," and the two masturbate each other (210–11).[21] The next day, while telling Leo about Howell's taunt, Caleb goes out of his way to say, "If it came down on me like that, well, all right, I'd suck a cock, I know it, if I loved the cat, why the fuck not[?]" (233). The comment means nothing unless Caleb is telling Leo, who has just performed a sexual act with him, that homosexuality is all right because he, Caleb, has homosexual feelings as well. But his prison years have desolated Caleb—at one point he simply repeats, "Oh, what they did to me. Oh, what they did to me" (209). His sense of worthlessness intensified by racist treatment of their father (344) and later by his own unchecked murderous rage at betrayal by his white army buddy (398–403), Caleb seeks psychic coherence in religious belief and maintains it by building a rigid character structure in which his early gaiety and irreverence give way to arrogant self-righteousness. In the process, Caleb blocks his homosexual feelings, at least overtly; we hear no more of them, and he later contracts a conventional marriage (408–9, 483–84). Caleb, then, shows both the use of sexual terrorism by the rulers and the murderous effects of religiously based self-suppression.

Caleb's brother barely avoids his own secular self-suppression. In a long scene in Book Two of *Tell Me How Long*, a nineteen-year-old Leo and three white theater friends, all summering with the Actors Means Workshop in New Jersey, meet a slightly older black native of the town, Fowler, and his protégé visiting from Philadelphia, Matthew, a man a bit older than Leo, in a working-class pizzeria. When the pizzeria closes, the six drive to a bar in the black part of town, stay for a while, and return, and Leo ends by having sex with one of the theatre group, the more established actress Madeleine (*TMHL* 151–99). While driving to the black neighborhood, the group stops high above the river, a symbolic locale for immersion into the self and baptism into new life—another of Baldwin's many uses of water imagery to suggest these experiences. Above the faintly seen river, Leo feels a "sudden fear, as present as the running of the river, as nameless and as deep"; as the six reach their destination they again have "that terrifying bluff above the terrifying river" before them, but turn to park by the noisy bar, and Leo feels they have "crossed from death into what certainly sounded like life" (182, 187). It is, then, partly the possibility of a descending once more into black life that has unnerved Leo, a Harlem denizen struggling to leave Harlem and live and work among whites. His and his friends' labored jokes about color show how fraught this negotiation is (147, 149, 161–63), and its trickiness is underscored by the serious subject Matthew has been debating with Fowler, whether to join the Army for its benefits or the Merchant Marine, the frequent choice of dissenters during World War II (178). This issue puts Leo's verbal radicalism—he would "rather drop dead than fight for this miserable country" (178)—to the test. To become Matthew's friend would be to plunge into black life and politics, that is, into the "terrifying river." And this choice is a suddenly live possibility, since during the drive Matthew's "thigh was against my thigh" and Matthew, "with one great hand, lightly touched the back of my neck," while earlier, referring most directly to his career choices, Matthew has urged, "What a grown person does with his life is that person's business" (186, 187, 175).

Leo fails the test—turns from the river, returning across town to its white side. He sleeps both with Madeleine and with his far more serious white "sister," Barbara, and leaves New Jersey temporarily, avoiding Matthew's and Fowler's intentions to meet again (*TMHL* 194–95, 303). Later, when he and Barbara are finishing the summer in virtual quarantine in the white part of town, we learn that "Matthew had left town, we never saw Fowler again; I did not go to the Negro part of town anymore" (350). So the night of the river is an avoidance of Leo's sexual and racial deepest self, with lasting effect in his mature sense of a "blasphemed" beauty in himself "which I had never recognized and which I had, myself, destroyed" (73) and consequent damage to the bases of his art. Yet, the night he is with Madeleine, Leo wakes from a dream of sleeping "curled against Caleb, in our narrow bed," with his mother calling, "*Boy, do you know what time it is?*" (199–200). Baldwin uses this device to introduce Leo's memories of sex with Caleb, Caleb's prison experience and departure from New York, and his own sexual relationship, still at age fourteen, with an older Harlem racketeer (200–45). But the device is anything but arbitrary. The dream—in which his mother's words are a prophetic warning, and an implied reference to the novel's title—and the memories it stirs come on *this* night as admonishments and awakeners, so that Leo can to tell Barbara he is bisexual (she has guessed) and, more generally, is shaken from the complacency with which he might have descended farther into lies. Yet many years will pass before Leo overcomes this night's double denial and begins to live primarily as homosexual and, even later, to echo, in his love for Christopher, the chords of black radicalism that once sounded through Matthew.[22]

Others are less fortunate. Two characters in *Just Above My Head*, Sidney and Crunch, show the devastation resulting from internalizing religious and social law. Sidney, bartender at a Harlem bar Hall Montana patronizes, is an important minor character, significant for his eventual political and sexual choices. On first meeting, he responds to Hall extravagantly, smiling radiantly, his face seemingly "changing like a fountain of water spinning in the air," and striking Hall as "incredibly beautiful." Sidney describes Hall (and Hall's current girlfriend Martha) as a present that came when "I was so lonely" (*JAMH* 123–24, 138). For his part, Hall calls Sidney's friendship a "new love" (139). Thus, both men's unstated homoeroticism is in play. As they talk, Sidney says that he blames himself for a lot but can't change, so "I might as well keep on blaming Sidney. He's all I got" (138); we don't know if he is referring to homosexuality. When Baldwin picks up this narrative thread nearly three years later, on Hall's return from Korea, Sidney—now engaged to Martha—retains his old warmth, stroking Hall's cheek with the hand wearing a ring Hall has just given him (321). He is focused, however, on proselytizing Hall for the Black Nationalist beliefs he has adopted, similar to those of the Nation of Islam, and in doing so his metaphor is that black people can get nothing from the "devil and his papa," the white man, "if you don't bend over and spread them cheeks" (333). Presenting white domination as homosexual penetration, Sidney's new outlook externalizes his still-active homoeroticism as a temptation by the race enemy, ensuring that he will never acknowledge it. Whatever his political thinking, then, Sidney has adopted religious puritanism partly as a way of finding structure and, like Caleb in *Tell Me How Long*, avoiding the chaos of desire.[23] In effect, Sidney's abandonment of the idea that he is "all I got" has been his downfall.

Crunch in turn shows the consequences of choking off one's inner being in the effort to adapt to perceived reality. We learn early in the novel that Crunch eventually went insane—as Hall laconically explains, "One morning, fucking, he realized that the devil had got inside his woman, and was pulling on his prick, and he tried to beat the devil out of her" before being subdued by neighbors and later sent to an asylum (*JAMH* 37). We don't know why. Part of the answer must be external—"for years before he was carried away, [his] two front teeth were missing," kicked out by a black police officer in circumstances that Hall does not specify; Crunch never had them replaced because he "wanted black people to see what black people did to black people" (37). Part of Crunch's psychic collapse, however, is internal. After Crunch and Arthur have become lovers on their southern tour, after Crunch has made love to Julia (and just before telling Arthur of this), and while he is waiting for his draft notice, he asks what Arthur will do when he, Crunch, is gone. Arthur says he will wait for Crunch, and Crunch asks:

> "Arthur, what about . . . [o]ther people."
>
> "What other people?"
>
> "Arthur—have you ever had a girl? No, I guess you haven't."
>
> "What you talking about?"
>
> "It would be good for you to have a girl." (259–60)

As the scene continues, Arthur says he cares only for Crunch, and Crunch bursts out, "Well, you can't love me forever, man, you got to grow up" (260). We realize

Crunch is actually speaking to himself, as people giving advice often do: it is he who feels he "can't love [Arthur] forever" and must "grow up," classifying Arthur's and his homosexual acts as adolescent. Further, while Crunch's question about other people seems to mean forming relationships with them, it is openended and may also mean: what about their opinions? At least, it can mean this to Crunch, already thinking about "grow[ing] up."[24]

Only as Arthur sifts memories years later during his Paris visit do we learn how this scene played out on Crunch's return from Korea. Crunch then insisted that their love was "all over," that Arthur must "grow up, and realize what kind of world he was living in," and, further, that those whose opinions Arthur is ready to disregard "have the power of life and death, my friend. They can grind your ass to *powder*!" (*JAMH* 463). And Crunch pursued Julia (who did not return to him) searching, Hall surmises, for "some unassailable corroboration of his manhood" (463–64). Yet it was Crunch who could not stifle his passion, and inevitably

> the dam *did* break, more than once, during those flame-colored, awful months, nearly drowning them in the flood. And it was Crunch, at the absolute limit of his endurance, no longer able, simply, to contain it, who roughly pulled Arthur into his arms, sobbing and shaking, plowing home. . . . Yet, at the same time, the shadow lay between them still, the war was not over. . . . Eventually, each reconciliation was tinged by the inevitable nightmare of remorse and hostility which would follow it: then, the reconciliation itself became a nightmare. Crunch could say neither yes nor no, and it was Arthur, finally, who crawled away from Crunch. (464–65)

Crunch, then, struggled with himself to eliminate his deep-felt homosexual component and conform himself to the "kind of world he [Crunch] was living in," and, ultimately, succeeded in redirecting his sexuality. But what is suppressed persists as neurosis or psychosis, obsession or hallucination; Crunch's madness, narrated so early, is the end of a psychic history. We do not know what happens specifically, but something like his dishonored sexuality surfaces, in his mind, in the person of his girlfriend, "pulling on his prick," and must—again!—be beaten away in rage and despair. Completing Baldwin's narrative circle drives home the terrible cost of dishonoring the body in conformity to "the world."

A final form of dishonoring is silence, in outward adherence to religious or social law. Here dishonoring shifts from individuals to those around them, who—whether or not the individual is self-shamed by having to remain concealed—confer dishonor by making frankness impossible. A short list of those silenced in this way, temporarily or lastingly, would include John in *Go Tell It*, who struggles to tell Elisha "all that can never be said" (225); Matthew in *Tell Me How Long*, who flirts elaborately with a woman in the bar when, on the evidence, he is mainly interested in Leo (193, 194); and Arthur in *Just Above My Head*, who, Scott shows in detail, is silenced by the heterosexual assumptions behind his father's concern that he move past his friendship with Crunch and not "come to grief" (266; Scott 162–64). In a slightly different dynamic, social reticence keeps Hall from broaching the topic of Arthur's homosexuality until Arthur himself does so at twenty-six—though Hall does "dare" to say, not long before this, that "whatever makes you happy, that's what you supposed to do" (52–55, 560).[25]

Silencing in response to social norms is arguably embedded, as well, in the narrative structure of *If Beale Street Could Talk*: Ernestine, Tish's sister, is probably asexual or lesbian, but Tish, the narrator, shows no awareness that this may be so. Indeed, Tish and others in her affectional family are strongly homophobic, a point I suggest as part of Baldwin's characterization of their milieu.[26] The case for Ernestine's sexual nonconformity is inferential, arising from details and gaps in Tish's story. As narrated by Tish, Ernestine is twenty-three, unmarried, with no mention of a fiancé or boyfriend, present or past. As a child, she was vain in stereotypically feminine ways, posing in front of mirrors and curling her hair, but in adolescence became "tall and skinny," favoring slacks and tying her hair up, and began reading intensively; her face "became bonier and more private" and her "long narrow eyes darkened with whatever it was they were beginning to see" (*BS* 32–33). She is an intellectual of a Black Nationalist stripe—she avoids newspapers and movies because "I don't need no more of the white man's lying shit" (33). She works in a settlement house for children, and later, to make money for Fonny's defense, becomes part-time private secretary to an actress (107). Talking with her in a pickup bar, Tish realizes that the patrons "can only suppose that Ernestine and I are tired whores or a Lesbian couple, or both" (102). At the family conference at which Fonny asks to marry Tish, Ernestine responds to a joke on marriage by Sharon, saying "very quietly" that "I don't think I'm ever going to marry. Some people do, you know—Mama?—and some people don't." Sharon, "very steadily, and without moving," replies, "Well, I can understand that." Yet Ernestine adds that "sometimes you would *like* to belong to somebody" (74). In sum, Ernestine comports herself in several stereotypically masculine ways, can be taken as lesbian, and has evidently thought seriously before deciding she will probably not marry, while her mother must also have thought seriously about the matter before now, and wishes to reassure Ernestine that her choices will be honored. Sharon's response is, indeed, significant, showing that Ernestine's departure from the sexual norm is steady enough to be a matter for thought. Ernestine's further comment about sometimes wanting to belong to someone can refer either to relationships she hopes for, or to ones she has had but not spoken about. Yet Tish's narration discounts Ernestine altogether as an emotional being, neither wondering about nor referring to her inner life.

If in fact Ernestine is or may be affectionally lesbian, then the novel shows the effects of a culturally imposed silence: Ernestine, fiercely intelligent, dedicated to the common uplift, resourceful and decisive, can speak of this part of her life only in veiled hints. Tish, indeed, can hear Beale Street talk, but cannot hear her sister.

The possibility that Ernestine may be lesbian or asexual, but is not recognized as such by Tish, the narrator, has some impact on how the book is read. Several interpreters have argued that, through Tish, Baldwin constructs an idealized African American family, unconventional in structure (Fonny and Frank, his father, are effectively part of Tish's family rather than their own) but conventional in its devotion to the male and its general patriarchalism; and these values have been taken as Baldwin's own—at least, as ones he adopted for this novel. If, however, Ernestine is or may be lesbian while Tish is blind to this possibility—and to her mother's possible awareness of it—then the first part of the critical perception is accurate (Tish narrates according to a patriarchal ideal) but not the second. Instead, Tish's partial blindness into her sister's life would, as constructed by the author, critique the narrowness of that ideal. Additionally, the novel has sometimes been seen as a response to Eldridge Cleaver's attack on Baldwin's homosexuality in *Soul on Ice* (1968); Baldwin, in this view, wrote a novel without homosexual characters, centered on a black family that is militant, quasi-Nationalist, and homophobic as well, to show that he could surmount Cleaver's attack, see the black family without prejudices of his own, and keep his finger on the community's pulse. Indeed, *Beale Street* does all this but if, in addition, it includes a family member who may be homosexual, though closeted, it cannot accede to Cleaver's view of black militancy as exclusively heterosexual, or his larger belief that black homosexuality is a negative adaptation to white domination. Instead, Baldwin may critique Cleaver and African American patriarchalism in general by showing a black militant culture many of whose members evade awareness of homosexuality in their midst.[27]

Baldwin's attention to the varied ways in which the body is dishonored shows that he is no mere romanticist of sexuality. The terrorizing and then self-annihilation of Caleb's soul in *Tell Me How Long*, the waste of Leo's years, *Beale Street*'s silences, *Just Above My Head*'s terrible losses—some self-inflicted, all socially influenced—show the power of despair, doubt, cowardice, the overwhelming of self-belief by adherence to law and custom. All act as barriers to realization of the body's apocalyptic possibility.

The Body, Commerce, and the Police

A final set of blockades lies in the body's interactions with commerce and the police. In *Another Country* Baldwin comments in reference to Rufus, who is about to enter on the transaction, "In any of the world's cities, on a winter night, a boy can be bought for the price of a beer and a promise of warm blankets" (41). The determinants of this exchange, in Baldwin's presentations, radiate outward to the poverty and homelessness that make the boys available; to the boys' patrons, mainly of the middle and upper classes; to the race and national inequalities that increase class differences; and to the police and justice system that keep unequal power relations in place.[28]

Baldwin's novels mention a variety of commercial and quasi-commercial sex acts, heterosexual and homosexual. The former include standard brothel prostitution, presented in a relatively positive light, as in Elizabeth's childhood impressions about the "house" her father keeps, which incomprehension and love for her father paint in warm colors (*GT* 155), and, in *Tell Me How Long*, the Harlem brothel Caleb uses to meet his girlfriend Dolores, seen by ten-year-old Leo as a friendly, even familial place (55–56, 120–21). The world of male homosexual prostitution is colder. Its inhabitants include prostitutes proper, shown in *Giovanni's Room*'s café scene (50–62), a subculture consisting of the boys in fairly friendly rivalry for patrons, each with his own *copain* (boyfriend) at home, and with a certain loyalty to one another; and the patrons—here, Guillaume—who pay more with gifts and food than cash. As Aliyyah Abdur-Rahman notes, Baldwin does not show the scene as one of sexual depravity but "indicts social systems that grant protection and prestige to wealthy, powerful men in society without regard for the detriment they cause to those who exist on society's fringes" (484). But Abdur-Rahman exaggerates in saying that Jacques and Guillaume buy "sexual favors from young boys who are quite literally starved and then cast the boys back into the streets" (484). Not so helpless as this, the youths know the scene and handle their transactions with reasonable skill. Outside this milieu are those prostituting themselves from desperation, like Rufus, who cannot bear to go through with the bargain on this occasion but has before (*AC* 41–45, 48). Adjacent is the world of pickups, quick sex, and cruising—movie theater sex, usually presented as intensely degrading whether consummated or not (*AC* 3; *TMHL* 384); attempted pickups in mixed bars (*AC* 249); sex in public and semi-public places (*AC* 211, 260–61, 333). This sex is not commercial, though sometimes payment is extorted (*TMHL* 384), but can be called sex for barter—an exchange of offered goods and services. In Baldwin's portrayal, these acts are "rituals" enacted between straight-identified men and acknowledged homosexuals and are "joyless," occurring only in "the shameful dark" (*AC* 261, 211). Finally, there are the worlds of "kept" men and women—Giovanni by Guillaume, employed and provided a work permit in consequence of one sex act and badgered for more;[29] Ida by Ellis, provided with professional chances—and the rape and abuse of children (Julia by Joel).

Two common threads run through these examples. The first is imbalance of power. Economic power counts more than sexual power, especially if it coincides with race or national difference—Guillaume has greater power than Giovanni or the hustler Pierre, Ellis than Ida, Rufus's would-be white partner than Rufus. (This power can be lost, however; when Rufus pulls out of the bargain, his patron has no way to enforce it, and they part on more equal terms [44–45].) In turn, "masculine" roles and identification dominate over "nonmasculine," penetrator over penetrated, even across race lines—Leo has more power than the blond boy who sucks him off (*TMHL* 384), Rufus more than Eric, and Eric's "ignorant army" of one-time partners (*AC* 211) more than he, despite their panic and confusion. And, of course, male has more power than female and age than youth: Joel rapes and then dominates Julia. The second common thread is that always, in any breakdown of this system into violence, the more powerful is exculpated. Guillaume's reputation is posthumously burnished and his homosexuality hushed up (*GR* 150–51); Joel's version of Julia's beating, Paul Montana says, is "the one that got sold" (*JAMH* 307). Those who dishonor the bodies of others end with their public honor intact.

None of this could exist without the power relations in society and the enforcing power that keeps those relations intact. Baldwin shows these through a piece of symbolic topography in *Another Country*, as Eric and others pass through Washington Square Park after Ida's debut performance. The park, by night part of New York's homosexual world, recalls Eric's whole past life to him; successive waves of memory engulf him and, after each, “another humiliated Eric was left writhing on the sands” (261). Then his attention moves from memory to his surroundings, specifically to the groups of folk singers at the park’s center, a staple of its life in the 1950s. Eric senses that

> there was something very winning, very moving, about their unscrubbed, unlined faces, and their blankly shining, infantile eyes, and their untried, unhypocritical voices. They sang as though, by singing, they could bring about the codification and the immortality of innocence. Their listeners were of another circle, aimless, empty, and corrupt, and stood packed together in the stone fountain merely in order to be comforted or inflamed by the touch and the odor of human flesh. And the policemen, in the lamplight, circled around them all. (*AC* 261)

The night milieu, then, consists of three circles: the innocent, locked in an extended spiritual childhood, unhypocritical because yet untested; the corrupt, fluent in a corrupt world’s ways and with no alternative way to live; and the police, whose position on the outer circle suggests both the horizons of this world, which would have to be passed in order to live differently, and their function of keeping the inner circles and the whole structure in place. If the reference to innocence evokes the loss of Eden, the circles’ Dantean resonance implies that this world is hell—as elsewhere Baldwin sees New York as Sodom. The police function to maintain it as it is, as the official and quasiofficial prison sexual violations in *Tell Me How Long* and *Beale Street* also remind us.

In this world, those whose bodies are dishonored can, for Baldwin, not live with integrity by the world’s rules, but only by recognizing and honoring their dishonor in the world’s eyes. As Rufus is this novel’s embodiment of those who fail to do this, and live by the world’s judgments until they can do so no longer, so Eric is the emblem of those who find a zigzag path to honor. “He knew”—Eric reflects in the temporary Eden of his French garden—“that he had no honor which the world could recognize. His life, passions, trials, loves, were, at worst, filth, and, at best, disease in the eyes of the world, and crimes in the eyes of his countrymen.” There are, therefore, “no standards for him except those he could make for himself,” and he must “create his standards and make up his definitions as he went along” (*AC* 212–13). Baldwin’s echo of Paul’s “filth of the world” and “more abundant honour” (1 Cor. 4:13, 12:23–24) suggests that, like the apostles, Eric is potentially a bringer of the holy, but, like them, must live outside the world’s law, and must create for his body its own honor. To honor the apocalyptic body, then, for Baldwin, is to live in anarchic disregard of this world's judicial, religious, and social laws. It is, further, to live at cross-purposes to, or in concealment from, the third circle, of the police. And so there is a tenuous hope. This life of inward antinomianism, following self-created law rather than the world's, can—and does for Eric—lead to an inner integrity, and is even compatible with material success. But to move beyond these, Baldwin implies, will require that the apocalyptic body find a home in the apocalyptic city.

CHAPTER 4

The Apocalyptic City

There'll be no sorrow, no sadness
Just only complete gladness
But any day, I know, I know that I
Am a-going home.

—"Any Day Now," Sam Cooke, 1954

And God shall wipe away all tears from their eyes; and there shall be no more death, neither sorrow, nor crying, neither shall there be any more pain: for the former things are passed away.

—Revelation 21:4

A series of Baldwin works define an idea of broad human transformation over time through a social redemption creating a possible new society of love. This possibility generates Baldwin's implied idea of the apocalyptic city, one with a double valence. Baldwin's city is the contemporary one we now live in, and therefore one of injustice and oppression; yet it is seen as capable of redemptive transformation. Paralleling Baldwin's idea of the apocalyptic body, his city is apocalyptic in several ways. It contains within it the possibility of holiness, seeds of mostly unrealized personal and social love, and in rare moments prefigures a society of love. It is apocalyptic, too, because it is home to the outcast, the hated, the dishonored, whose lives hold the present city up to judgment and who may, one day, transform it and so enter into the kingdom. Finally, then, the city is apocalyptic because it may one day undergo an apocalypse—a revelatory fulfillment of its capacities in a new time—if the Christian eschatological pattern that still shapes Baldwin's secularized imagination is true.

The city is Baldwin's locale for this imagined change partly because, by upbringing and temperament, he is a novelist of the city. His imagination dwells there. His characters live, work, love, and die in cities; except in the recalled southern family history of *Go Tell It on the Mountain*, small town and country settings are interludes or steps on a path. And so the transformation Baldwin envisages will occur in the life of cities, revivifying their human relations. Behind these circumstantial reasons, however, the city is the scene of transformation in Baldwin's poetics because it is the endpoint of the four-part eschatological pattern just referred to.

That pattern leads from paradise through fall and redemption to the apocalyptic recovery of paradise in the heavenly city. As often observed, this Christian myth is not cyclic, as are Golden Age myths in many ancient cultures, but linear, because the fall from and return to paradise each occur once, at the beginning and end of Christian history, and because the foretold return is not to the place of origin but to a new place. Biblical history, as Maynard Mack puts it, "begins with a garden and ends with a city" (3).[1] This pattern provides a structuring principle for Baldwin's last four novels, my focus in this chapter.

The mythic pattern is found fairly fully in *Another Country*, whose title, some part titles, and, with some displacement, narrative order refer to it. With differing emphases, parts of the pattern are found in other works. And all four of the final novels build toward some prevision of the heavenly city's advent. These references to apocalyptic transformation, of course, are symbolic and visionary, not representational. Baldwin is interested not in dramatizing an imagined future but in showing processes possibly leading toward it, and in whether it is a real or illusory hope. In a parallel way, he does not depict an actual Edenic stage of existence—Eden in Christian myth lies far in the past—but shows imaginative or temporarily recovered Edenic states. The main dramatic actions of Baldwin's works, therefore, take place on the middle ground of fall and redemption, but point forward toward anticipated apocalypses.

These visionary depictions of possible progress toward apocalypse intersect in complex ways with the history of Baldwin's time and with his inheritance from African American church and social progress traditions. Because of its specific mid-1950s setting, *Another Country* is able to focus most fully on the basic motif. At the same time, this novel, completed in 1961, reflects some of the reformative moods of the early civil rights period, even while opening a window on racial resentment in ways that disturbed some early readers.[2] *Tell Me How Long the Train's Been Gone* speaks from its own seemingly preapocalyptic moment in the middle and late 1960s. And Baldwin's last two novels, *If Beale Street Could Talk* and *Just Above My Head*, respond in part to the nonarrival of this moment as of the early and later 1970s.

From the Garden to the City

Another Country (1962) ends with an enigmatic statement: Yves, landing at New York's Idlewild airport and passing customs, with his lover Eric waiting for him, proceeds into "that city which the people from heaven had made their home" (436). The sentence contains a double irony. First, Yves knows nothing of New York's divisions and hates, made plain through the preceding chapters; the city he is entering is far from a heavenly habitation. A deeper irony lies in Baldwin's suggestion in a later essay, *The Evidence of Things Not Seen*, that "the people from heaven" was Native Americans' term for the first European settlers (44), that is, conquerors and murderers. Yet despite both ironies, Baldwin's sentence fits within the framework created by structure, part-titles, epigraphs, and overall title to state the idea of a world genuinely remade.

Book Two of *Another Country*, "Any Day Now," begins in a garden—Eric's, at a rented house in the south of France (183). Despite this scene's own constituent ironies—the garden is in contemporary France and Eric is uneasy over his and Yves's impending departures for the United States—its Edenic qualities, felt in the sunlight, the murmur of flies and bees, the garden's affinities to Africa, and, of course, Yves's name, are real. As we come to know Eric, we realize that this Eden is temporary but earned, a brief return to humanity's "first condition" ("SB" 129) before proceeding on the difficult path of redemption. Books Two and Three of the novel, then, begin with a garden and end with a city, replicating the eschatological pattern already discussed. Moreover, since the Eden of myth is long ago and that beginning

Book Two is momentary, Book One can be placed within the pattern as well, tracing a descent from the conflicted beginning of Leona and Rufus's love into the absolute destruction of her madness and his suicide, then an ascent to ambiguous, partial deliverance in Ida and Vivaldo's lovemaking. So, Book One moves from fall to the opening of a chance for redemption. (Yet the basic Eden-fall-redemption pattern will repeat in Vivaldo and Ida's relationship.) Its title, "Easy Rider," and epigraph, both from W. C. Handy's "Yellow Dog Blues" (1919),[3] signal that Book One's musical genre is blues, always for Baldwin the music of pain and endurance. Gospel, the music of hope, emerges in Book One primarily at Rufus's funeral and during Ida and Vivaldo's walk to the Silenskis' party (122–23, 145–46), but becomes co-dominant with blues in Book Two (181, 253–56, 313, 431).

Gospel specifically contributes Book Two's title, "Any Day Now," most probably taken from the song of that title, recorded in 1954 by Sam Cooke in what Michael Eric Dyson calls "two and a half of the most sublime minutes of American song" ("Soul Stirrer" 572). Speaking of reunion with the Father in heaven, the song voices the hope of a world without pain:

> One of these mornings
> I'm a-going away
> Any day now
> I'm a-going to heaven to stay.
>
> I don't know how soon,
> Maybe morning, night, or noon
> But I'm going to see the Father
> And by his side to stand.
>
> There'll be no sorrow, no sadness
> Just only complete gladness
> But any day, I know, I know that I
> Am a-going home.
>
> Then I'll shout Hallelujah
> And your praises will name, a-a-a-a-h,
> But any day, I know, I know that I
> Am a-going home.[4]

So Book Two's title—for those who know its reference—states a general hope of salvation, but in the particular context of hope for an existence with "neither sorrow, nor . . . any pain," as promised at the close of Revelation (21:4). Book Three's title, "Toward Bethlehem," continues the pattern of references to Revelation, though indirectly—drawn from Yeats's "The Second Coming," it implies the question whether the advent Yeats's title promises will be of the Lamb or the Beast.[5] The accompanying epigraph continues this querying: "How with this rage shall beauty hold a plea, / Whose action is no stronger than a flower?" (Shakespeare, Sonnet 65, 3–4) is the issue Baldwin's idea of a New Jerusalem based on love must address.

The overall movements from destruction to tentative redemption in the book's action, and from Eden to apocalypse, garden to city, and blues to Gospel suggested in part-titles and epigraphs,[6] allow us to understand its title. In its great chapter on faith, the Epistle to the Hebrews defines the perspective of those it calls "strangers and pilgrims on the earth":

> These all died in faith, not having received the promises, but having seen them afar off, and were persuaded of them, and embraced them, and confessed that they were strangers and pilgrims on the earth.
>
> For they that say such things declare plainly that they seek a country.
>
> And truly, if they had been mindful of that country from whence they came out, they might have had opportunity to have returned.
>
> But now they desire a better country, that is, an heavenly: wherefore God is not ashamed to be called their God: for he hath prepared for them a city. (Heb. 11:13–16)

This passage most probably defines the "country" in Baldwin's title. If we secularize the passage, a crucial but partial step, we can say those it refers to seek not a better country among those in their time, but a new one that may exist someday. This secularization is vital but insufficient, since in Hebrews the country is not simply "better" but "heavenly," and, at the end of the eschatological history already referred to, is to come "down out of heaven" to exist on earth, in the city Hebrews says God has prepared (Rev. 21:2). The Hebrews writer, then, has defined the heavenly city that may exist on earth one day if the "promises" seen by faith are true. For Baldwin, these sacral tones are part of his meaning: though it will exist on earth and will be made, so far as we know, entirely by human effort, the city will retain the holiness of its biblical original, as, also, Baldwin's redeemed form of sexual relations will.

Baldwin replicates the bitblical text's rhetorical structure in his own. Hebrews 11 declares that the "strangers and pilgrims" desire a country, but not the one "from whence they came out" (13–15). The writer refers to Abraham, Sarah, Isaac, Jacob, and their descendants, who "came out" from their country at God's command (Gen. chaps. 12 and following). But Hebrews recasts the Genesis story, in which the promised country was Canaan, to present the patriarchs as prefiguring Jesus's followers in the time of the eschaton, seeking God's city (11:16). In parallel, several earlier passages in Baldwin's text suggest literal or figurative other countries in present society. Rufus wishes "to get on a boat and go someplace away from all these nowhere people, where a man could be treated like a man"; Cass naïvely asks Ida, "[T]here are other countries—have you ever thought of that?" (*AC* 68, 349). But the novel is not structured to imply anywhere else as a true refuge from the United States, the "miserable country" Ida wishes she could "grind to powder" and Cass herself realizes "isn't a country at all" (351, 406). Alternatively, Vivaldo at one point reflects that love is "a country he knew nothing about" (296), but the novel also does not present private love as an alternative or solution to public bigotry and violence—rather, we will see, it implies that private and public love can be fragile components of a solution. Baldwin's fictional structure, then, moves past these possibilities in a way paralleling the Hebrews writer's rhetorical arrangement. This structure reveals the deep pattern beneath the surface ironies of Baldwin's last sentence. If *Another Country* indeed refers to the "better" country of Hebrews 11:16, then, as Yves's and Eric's country of love exists in counterposition to the city of oppression, so it would also be possible, though difficult, to build on earth a future city of love. *Another Country* closes with this tentative hope.

Eden, Fall, and Redemption

The ideas of Eden, fall, and redemption do not appear in Baldwin's fiction in their scriptural senses. Rather, those senses—and the eschatological progression they imply—provide an imaginative underpinning for Baldwin's sensibility. In his fiction, people do decline from bright beginnings, and yet sometimes find their way to reconciliation with loss and to new hope. They experience both genuine and false states of simplicity and freedom, pass through the collapse or oppressive destruction of these states, and either become as corrupt and empty as the surrounding world or find some path to an equilibrium incorporating what they were, are, and may become. Further, these states embody a synecdoche between individuals and the world: what is possible for individuals prefigures, in Baldwin, what is possible or at least imaginable for society.

Baldwin's Eden is a serious idea, even if many of his references are ironic.[7] It is not an originary state from which humans declined, nor one of perfect goodness. His 1949 essay "Preservation of Innocence," about illusory innocence in U.S. fiction, defines the biblical Eden, metaphorically, as "a state of nature," not sinlessness ("PI" 596). In such a state, aggression and jealousy must exist alongside kindness and love. Hence, for Baldwin, Edenic states we may attain and lose, or be ripped from, are our only real Eden. Such states may belong to early youth, as for the child in "Sonny's Blues" who, sitting with his family in late afternoon light, "hopes that the hand which strokes his forehead will never stop" (115). They may lie in the discovery of sex, as for Tish and Fonny in *If Beale Street Could Talk*, or in the purity of vocational apprenticeship, as for Leo and Barbara in *Tell Me How Long the Train's Been Gone*, who call the decayed tenement where they first live "Paradise Alley" (*TMHL* 73). These states are evanescent: Barbara and Leo's yields to his refusal of experience, Tish and Fonny's is smashed by Fonny's arrest (*BS* 145), the child's will end when an adult turns on the light against the dusk outside, which is "what the old folks have been talking about" ("SB" 115). Eden, then, is tied to fall, replicating the biblical sequence in hours, weeks, or months.

Related to Baldwin's "Eden," but distinct, is his sense of innocence, a term he gives complex nuances. The word refers, first of all, to the simplicity of early life, not sinless but lacking knowledge and complexity. In "Come Out the Wilderness," Ruth remembers "the days of her innocence" in a southern town, poor but sheltered by her parents' love and their faith in God (205–6); John, in *Go Tell It*, recalls his "innocence and anger" (219). So, unlike Eden, a primary innocence has a defined locus in time. Beyond early life, "innocence" often signifies unwitting or willed refusal of awareness: Americans are "innocent" in that they destroy uncounted lives "and do not know it and do not want to know it" (*FNT* 5–6). Such an innocence is contrasted with, yet completed by, corruption: those who lose false innocence without a continuing vision of goodness become the "aimless, empty, and corrupt" who surround the singers in Washington Square Park (*AC* 261). Yet "innocence" in later life can also mean a continuation or recovery of simplicity through a basic receptive awareness that is not unknowing; in this sense Baldwin refers through Eric to a "terrifying innocence in Yves's face" in the moments before they make love (*AC* 222).

To attain this type of innocence in overall life, Baldwin suggests, we must both "remember" and "forget" Eden. To do either alone, David muses in *Giovanni's Room*, courts "madness," either through the "recurring death" of one's innocence or through "the hatred of innocence." It takes, he believes, "a hero to do both"—"remember" and "forget" simultaneously (*GR* 25). To do this, inferably, would mean giving up the expectation of experiencing Eden, coming to terms with the world of corruption, while retaining the early capacity for wonder and belief, the sense of other possibilities—in fact, of *Another Country*. This sense of possibility might be sensed in love, Baldwin's apocalyptic body, and in turn, the conviction of human possibility found in love might be felt in the social body, Paul's body of Christ and Baldwin's human community. But this possibility could not be realized in the social body today but only in the future—for Paul the eschaton, for Baldwin the relatively near human future. To retain or recover innocence in the social world, then, would be to imagine a different world; what is possible for two persons through love would become possible for the nation or world in future time. And redemption—the move from fall and corruption to unity and love—would open the way to such a future.

These are the possibilities Baldwin suggests in the love story of Ida and Vivaldo in *Another Country*, his most filled-out narrative of a path from innocence through fall to redemption. Vivaldo and Ida's affair follows and counterbalances Rufus and Leona's, which begins in racial hostility and obliviousness, devolves into brutality and self-abasement, and ends in her madness and his suicide.[8] Ida and Vivaldo's involvement begins in compensation—Vivaldo's for his neglect of Rufus, Ida's for a semi-prostitution revealed only later—and sparks into an uncertain love. Ida's initial hope is only "to go to bed with somebody that I *liked*" in contrast to the white men she has been trying to use as a ticket out of Harlem (*AC* 419–20). Ida is proud, suspicious of and a bit condescending to her "sweet boy" (419), and quick to take offense, but not at first hateful or vengeful toward him. In this fashion they enter the temporary Eden of their first lovemaking (171–79). But when we next see the couple, at and after Ida's Village singing debut—about three months later in the novel's chronology—they are enmeshed in petty racial warfare, not their first fight ("You *always* start it," Vivaldo claims), and Ida is already meeting Ellis behind Vivaldo's back (259–60, 261–62). Their quarrels, shown in Vivaldo's recollections, involve the unconscious race condescension that makes him wish to "do [his family] some good" by bringing Ida over, his appropriation of race language to attack her ("*house* nigger"), and, at bottom, his refusal to see social relations as they are rather than as he prefers—their being together, he says, changes the world "for me" (279, 262,

324). Ida generalizes Vivaldo as "white people" (262) and racializes all his flaws. In the end, it is Vivaldo who cries out that "suffering doesn't *have* a color," and pleads, "Can't we step out of this nightmare?" (417). This is an extraordinarily complex moment. Baldwin certainly does not mean black and white suffering are the same; Vivaldo's blindness has been to the difference. Yet it is true that suffering has no color. Baldwin is challenging us, as in his 1955 essay "Notes of a Native Son," to "hold in the mind forever two ideas which seemed to be in opposition" ("NNS" 84). But Vivaldo's truth cannot *become* true until it no longer masks difference; and so the two cannot step out from nightmare until he is ready, in Ida's repeated phrase, to "pay [his] dues" (*AC* 277, 325, 350). This phrase, for Baldwin, often signifies accepting the costs of one's actions,[9] but Ida's use is simpler. Her words, "You want to find out what's happening, baby, all you got to do is pay your dues!" (277) essentially mean he must open his eyes to reality—of her life, his, black and white life. Vivaldo does this, finally, under Ida's relentless pressure: it is she who insists, "Let me finish my story," who brings out the truth "because I'm trying to bring this whole awful thing to a halt. If that's possible," and who, at the last, when they cling together, is "stroking the innocence out of him" (417, 420, 431).

Vivaldo, then, has passed through a three-stage transition: momentary Eden, fall into discord, emergence to a tentative reconciliation and peace—a redemption—conditioned on shedding his innocence. Yet innocence, the core term in this final description, is not simply negative. It is both Vivaldo's most suspect attribute—leading him, time and again, to deny the race and sexual dynamics he is part of and taking advantage of—and also a saving grace, often his only one. We see this quality, in its most basic Baldwin meaning of simplicity and openness, in his initial appearance as an awkward post-adolescent who is all limbs (25); again as he walks with Ida to the Silenskis' party, "artlessly proud, in the shining, overt, male way" (142); again when he calls out Ida and Ellis on their snide homophobia (263). Vivaldo remains open to experience and his callowness includes a basic decency. If he is compromised by the innocence of obliviousness, this quality has not solidified, and his stubbornness as an artist, his joy in his renewed friendship with Eric, and above all his desperation not to lose Ida and his capacity, despite himself, to hear her out all guard against it. After making love with Eric, we recall, he feels carried "back to his innocence" (386), and the innocence of simplicity and receptivity remains with him as Ida helps him into adulthood.

Ida's arc is similar but more compressed. Her innocence lies partly in her early years, glimpsed though a recollection by Vivaldo and in her own narration

(137–41, 417–19), and partly in her long-past, now disregarded church background (145–46). This innocence shatters with Rufus's death. Toward the white world that she then enters she is never innocent, working to manipulate it by trading sex for advantage with higher-status white men and ultimately with Ellis (419–26). Doing so costs her far more than she gains. Yet her racial battles with Vivaldo only partly reflect her compromised position; they also show a determination to make him see, if possible, the truth about himself and her. And, as much as Vivaldo's naïve liberalism is a source of strength as well as weakness, Ida, at a deeper level than he, retains a cultural hope that shows in some of the Gospel and blues lyrics she sings:

> I woke up this morning with my mind
> Stayed on Jesus . . . (145–46)
>
> Trouble in mind, I'm blue,
> But I won't be blue always . . . (313)
>
> I'm pressing on . . . the upward way! (313)

Ida, then, undergoes a fall into falsity and near-despair. She is in danger of becoming, as the bassist at Small's Paradise calls her, a "black white man's whore" (425).[10] And yet, in fighting through self-disclosure "to bring this whole awful thing to a halt" (420), she brings both herself and Vivaldo to a kind of redemption. In this way, if anything can, the lovers' story answers the question in Book Three's epigraph.

These redemptions, in miniature, represent a national redemption, to which indeed they contribute in minute degree and for which they are in a small way necessary. Baldwin structures the contrasting stories of Rufus and Leona, and Vivaldo and Ida, so that they ask through synecdoche whether love, or even respect and awareness, are possible between the racial groups in the United States—that is, whether the nation can achieve redemption. The biblical issue behind this question is Ezekiel's: "But if the wicked will turn from all his sins . . . and do that which is lawful and right, he shall surely live" (18:21). If the nation can "turn" under pressure from African Americans, then, according to this tradition, the way will open for a breakthrough to righteousness. As Rufus and Leona's story answers the implied question in the negative, so Ida and Vivaldo's presents a conception of how the nation's groups, moving through and past their tangled histories and flawed psychology, could begin to understand each other. In Baldwin's account this beginning occurs primarily through African Americans insisting on the truth as they see it and white Americans opening themselves to experience—to revising their ideas about themselves, African Americans, and the United States, based on wider perception. The tenuous understanding these characters reach represents a possible new start, through synecdoche, for the United States.[11]

This guarded projection of a society brought closer to union is not Baldwin's alone. In immediate historical context, it belongs to the early period of the civil rights movement, from about 1957 to 1962, the years of the novel's completion. Sometimes forgotten, in contrasting this period with later struggles, is how expansive its hopes were, not merely for a change in the legal system, but for one in the social order and people's lives. Then, the Student Non-Violent Coordinating Committee's Statement of Purpose (1960) could define SNCC's goal as achieving "a social order of justice permeated by love" ("Statement"). This movement philosophy, in turn, built on long traditions. Decades before SNCC or Baldwin, Rev. Francis J. Grimké, in a 1919 Thanksgiving address, thanked God for "unmistakable evidences of a growing, ever-deepening interest of the race in its rights" while urging, "Whatever other races may do, or other individuals may do, let us make up our minds that we will serve the Lord, and that we will train our children to do the same. Linked with God; yielding ourselves in loving obedience to God, the gates of hell . . . will not be able to prevail against us; we will still be pressing on the upward way" (1:617–18). Grimké alludes to Jesus's "[U]pon this rock I will build my church; and the gates of hell shall not prevail against it" (Matt. 16:18), and his "upward way" echoes a popular hymn of the day, Johnson Oatman Jr.'s "Higher Ground" (1898). Grimké's and the SNCC statement's linked ideas find parallels in Baldwin: like Grimké, Baldwin draws on Joshua's "But as for me and my house, we will serve the Lord," a signature text in "Notes of a Native Son" (Josh. 24:15; "NNS" 83); Ida's "pressing on the upward way" (*AC* 313) uses the same hymn source as Grimké. Rather than direct influence, these echoes show the presence of a common culture, a dominant redemptive thread in African American prophetic religious tradition, whose political side I have elsewhere called "prophetic integrationism" because it envisions not submissive inclusion in the present United States but full citizenship in a country that—like Baldwin's—is to come.[12] The long final scene between Ida and Vivaldo (408–31) tries to show rigorously through character and plot how a reformation between individuals, and synecdochically in society, could occur—though there can be no assurance that either process will be lasting or reach its goal.

Though this scene is Baldwin's closing point for Vivaldo and Ida, the tentative redemption they achieve is a way-station, not an endpoint, in the eschatological pattern already discussed. In the novel's structure, this scene leads to the short final chapter on Yves's arrival, with its own ambiguous reference to the promised city. The link between Ida and Vivaldo's story and this promise is not made clear in narrative. Baldwin suggests a link, however, in an earlier, lightly comic passage in which Vivaldo, thoroughly stoned, lies on two friends' rooftop looking at the night sky:

> The sky looked, now, like a vast and friendly ocean, in which drowning was forbidden, and the stars seemed stationed there, like beacons. To what country did this ocean lead? For oceans always led to some great good place: hence, sailors, missionaries, saints, and Americans. (312)

The ironies are pungent—drowning is not forbidden, and "Americans" are for Baldwin a warning, not a promise. Yet, clearly, the passage is prefigurative; the "country" to which the ocean path may lead is that of the novel's title and the "city" of its final page. And, as Vivaldo looks up, above his head, he remembers Ida's voice singing: "Just above my head, / I hear music in the air. / And I really do believe / There's a God somewhere" (313). He falls asleep with Harold, whose sexual advance he has gently rebuffed, nestled with him, and awakes to find the sky "a great brass bowl above him"; Harold's hand is on his leg, and his friends Belle and Lorenzo lie "wrapped in [a] blanket, like two dirty children" (315). Despite the comic tonalities, this is a vision of universal peace, afforded to Vivaldo for a moment before he goes down again to the street, to Ida, and to the wars of love and jealousy.

Apocalyptic Cities

Each of Baldwin's last four novels offers, at some point, an evocation of the apocalyptic city: of a possible new city of redeemed life, of judgment on the oppressors' city, or of both. Twice these involve Baldwin's native city; once an outlier, San Francisco; and once the biblical representation of empire and oppression, Babylon. The implied ideas of social change are increasingly complex and problematic.

New York

Another Country, as just seen, moves toward the expansive prospect that, if its characters can reach a painful understanding, even love, then so may the nation overcome its parallel divisions and save itself. But the novel also presents a contrary vision of apocalyptic conflict without hope, centered on Rufus's final hours. As Rufus waits for the subway after leaving Benno's bar, he has a double vision, first of a train gone wild, its riders "turning on each other with all the accumulated fury of their blasphemed lives," then of a collapse in the tunnels, water "breaking like a wave over the heads of the people, filling their crying mouths, filling their eyes, their hair, tearing away their clothes and discovering the secrecy which only the water, by now, could use" (85). The imagery that has been so prominent in Baldwin—in John Grimes's descent into the self, in Eric's and other sexual baptisms—returns here in its formative meaning of primal chaos. Rufus is imagining a war of annihilation among the black and white people "chained together in time and in space, and by history," who surround him in the subway (86), as well as a snuffing out of their lives partly resulting from "secrecy," the lack of self-disclosure and self-knowledge Baldwin saw as typically American. Both visions also project outward, in the form of these real social possibilities, a semiapocalyptic hate Rufus feels powerless to act on. Rufus, then, is given to foresee apocalyptic destruction without the downfall of the imperial city and without revelation and renewal.

Baldwin qualifies this vision, however, providing Rufus a second, more ambiguous set of apocalyptic signs. As he walks onto the George Washington Bridge, the headlights on the parkway below seem "to be writing an endless message, writing with awful speed in an unreadable script," while "the city which had been so dark as he walked through it seemed to be on fire" (87). These are apocalyptic portents—of the opening of the book with seven seals (Rev. chaps. 5–8), and, especially, of the apocalyptic "day of the Lord" when "the elements shall melt with fervent heat, [and] the earth also and the works that are therein shall be burned up" (2 Pet. 3:10).[13] The signs would seem to confirm Rufus's intuition of an apocalypse of destruction; but the destroying force is now not water but fire, which in biblical context leads to renewal, when—Second Peter adds—"we, according to [God's] promise, look for new heavens and a new earth, wherein dwelleth righteousness" (3:13). Rufus, however, cannot read the signs in either register—the script he thinks he sees is unintelligible—and so his last seconds are dominated by water, that shaken onto his face by the locked seas within him and that lying below (87).

Conflicting apocalyptic portents, then, close Rufus's story. Yet, within *Another Country*'s structure, neither provides a defining vision. This vision, implied rather than specified, is not of near-term apocalyptic upheaval, but of redemption over time, with the mode of transition to the apocalyptic city not given. The novel's controlling mood is set by the description closing Ida and Vivaldo's chapter of fury, acceptance, and love: "The rain had ceased, in the black-blue sky a few stars were scattered, and the wind roughly jostled the clouds along" (431). The water that marked Rufus's terror and death yet also guarded Eric and Vivaldo (386) has receded, the stars have not fallen (Matt. 24:29, Mark 13:25). The natural world continues, with the time and the beginnings of awareness to make possible an apocalypse of love. And in it is the promise of love, as Ida, before sleeping, has listened to Mahalia Jackson's Gospel album *In the Upper Room* (431), with its repeating line, "In the upper room, with my Lord."[14]

San Francisco

The vision *Another Country* does not define—a combined apocalypse of destruction and rebirth—occupies the closing pages of *Tell Me How Long the Train's Been Gone*, whose present-time setting is San Francisco, the city of Leo's heart attack, recovery, and reemergence to life. Aside from Baldwin's having spent time in San Francisco and revised part of the book there (Weir 37–39, Leeming 283), the city is an apt scene for the visionary experience Baldwin places in it. More than many U.S. cities, San Francisco is an enclave of the middle class and rich, with the largely black and Latin working class its existence depends on found mainly in a few neighborhoods and in Oakland across the bay. There were, of course, plenty of poor people in San Francisco in the 1960s, as well as concentrations of beat, bohemian, and countercultural youth, but the former appear only by allusion and the latter in one description. The defining marks of *Tell Me How Long*'s San Francisco are its theaters, restaurants, and the glittering city itself seen from above.

To reach apocalyptic vision, Leo must, like Vivaldo, achieve a redemption, from the racial and sexual cowardice discussed earlier. But it is partial and the vision, too, escapes Leo's full understanding. The redemption is presented in snapshots rather than in detail. In approximate chronological order (differing from narrative order), they show us Leo waking with a "boy" the morning after a party; his meeting with and seduction by Christopher; his speaking appearance at a civil rights rally, when Christopher and some friends act as his security detail; and Christopher's brief affair with Barbara and return to Leo (*TMHL* 307–8, 442–52, 108–14, 473–76). These episodes, apparently occurring over several years, hint at Leo's turn to a more fully homosexual life and toward the immersion in black communal political life that he avoided as a youth.[15] The last episode, though it cannot be pinpointed chronologically, seems most recent and is the most crucial. Here, sorting through motives with Leo while Christopher is somewhere in the streets, Barbara avows that she wanted Christopher because "I was reaching backward for you—and for me. . . . He was you before our choices were made" (473). Barbara believes, too, that Christopher realized what she wished for, and, therefore, realized that love with Leo was possible (474); and she implies that accepting Leo's choice of Christopher has freed her to live for herself, though as Leo's soul-ally (475). Further, if Barbara is right about Christopher, then Leo, too, loves Christopher because he is "you before our choices were made"—racially and politically, Leo is partly embracing himself when young, partly embracing whom he would have then had he not flinched. He is not altering long-ago, irrevocable choices, but coming as close to undoing them as he, an older man, now can. All these outcomes lie behind Barbara's "sorrowful, gallant, mocking" toast, "Let us drink to the New Jerusalem," made that same night, before Christopher's return, in early dawn, "cold as sweating metal," to Leo's bed (475). Leo and Barbara have won, then, a kind of redemption, but, by implication, the heavenly city beyond it is not to be theirs.

Barbara's toast opens up the novel's final tableaus that look forward to that city's possible advent. These brief scenes (477–82) are Baldwin's fullest presentation of a directly apocalyptic prophetic vision. His treatment has both personal and cultural roots. It is a partial reconciliation with the once-rejected apocalypticism of his father and his own youth ("NNS" 63) and a partial embrace of the long African American church tradition of millennial-apocalyptic thinking (introduction, above), though that has usually stressed endurance through oppression over active rebellion. Finally, it is a response to the intellectual mood of the mid-1960s, when the world's structures of oppression seemed to many to be crumbling irreversibly, and the popular culture expressed quasi-apocalyptic ideas.[16]

The tableaus unfold in three short scenes, with a political epilogue, on Leo's last full night and day in San Francisco—the next evening, he flies with Christopher to New York and then, by himself, to Europe and back, these events occupying only a short final paragraph. The four scenes together, then, provide the book's concluding vision. In the night scenes, Christopher is Leo's guide, factually in that he and Leo's dresser Pete have scouted the places they will visit, spiritually in that he possesses the prophetic awareness to conduct Leo through experiences Leo will only partly comprehend. Baldwin first takes his characters to a top-end Chinese restaurant, where Leo takes in "the room, the people, the rise and fall, the steady turning, as of a wheel, of many voices, the laughter, the clink of glass and silver, the shining hair, the shining dresses, the rings and earrings," and reflects,

> Evil did not seem to exist here, or sorrow, or intolerable pain [and yet] [t]his groaning board was a heavy weight on the backs of many millions, whose groaning was not heard. Beneath this table, deep in the bowels of the earth, as far away as China, as close as the streets outside, an energy moved and gathered and it would, one day, overturn this table just as surely as the earth turned and the sun rose and set. (477)

"And where," Leo wonders in the words of a Gospel song, "will you be, when that first trumpet sounds?" He supplies the answer: "I want to be with Jesus, when that first trumpet sounds" (478): to side with this change, be it what it may.[17]

In the succeeding tableau Christopher and Leo, leaving the restaurant, stand "on a height, and San Francisco unfurled beneath us, at our feet, like a many-colored scroll." Reflecting on the years of dedication that have brought fame, Leo weighs simply enjoying his "work" and "those I loved," but believes this impossible for him:

> Indeed, I had conquered the city; but the city was stricken with the plague. Not in my lifetime would this plague end, and, now, all that I most valued, wine, talk, laughter, love, the embrace of a friend, the light in the eyes of a lover, . . . would have to be stolen, . . . for my own mortality was not more certain than the storm that was rising to engulf us all. (478)

The final tableau counters these: Christopher takes Leo to a mass music-dance scene, in a converted theater, with a deafening band and "hundreds and hundreds of boys and girls" standing, sitting, milling, and dancing. The music

> drove and drove, into the past—into the future. It sounded like an attempt to make a great hole in the world, and bring up what was buried. And the dancers seemed . . . with the music assaulting them like the last, last trumpet, to be dancing in their graveclothes, raised from the dead. [On wall screens] ectoplasmic figures and faces endlessly writhed, moving in and out of each other, in a tremendous sexual rhythm

> which made me think of nameless creatures blindly coupling in all the slime of the world, and at the bottom of the sea, and in the air we breathed, and in one's very body. (481–82)

The tableaus imagine the present world's corruption and oppression and their overturn, and picture this world, with its wealth and beauty—illusorily secure in the first scene—consumed by death. In the outdoor middle vision, Baldwin revisits John's hilltop experience in *Go Tell It on the Mountain*—now asserting the earthly city's certain end, left open in the earlier work.[18] He glances, as well, at Dr. Rieux's labor against contagion in Camus's *The Plague* (*La Peste*, 1947), itself a story of the struggle to save European culture; for Baldwin the death of present culture is sure and hope lies beyond. That hope appears, ambiguously, in the last tableau, which sees the decade's music as an attempt to make a "hole in the world"—as much of it was—and the youth culture as a version of sexual apocalypse, bringing orgasmic desire from "the bottom of the sea," John Grimes's place of chaos and sexual terror, groping through blind sex toward a barely imagined resurrection. By implication, the imagery of sexual contamination in this scene is one factor in the "plague" destroying the present world in the prior one.

This sequence of visions refers insistently to Revelation. The first tableau's diners evoke the wealth and commerce of Babylon at the moment of its destruction—indeed, Baldwin's sentence rhythms stay close to those of Revelation, which speaks of Babylon's "merchandise of gold, and silver, and precious stones, and pearls, and fine linen . . . and slaves, and souls of men" (18:12–13). The illusion that pain and sorrow cannot reach here recalls the Babylon Harlot's "I sit a queen . . . and shall see no sorrow" (Rev. 18:7). The trumpets in the first and third tableaus, and the city open like a scroll in the second, allude to Revelation's seven trumpets heralding catastrophes that will not bring repentance[19] and its vision of heaven departing "as a scroll when it is rolled together" (6:4). The plague vision, too, replicates those of Revelation (9:20, 11:6, 15:1, 21:9). Finally, the third tableau's bringing up of what was buried and its resurrected dancers echo Revelation 20:13, "And the sea gave up the dead which were in it; and death and hell delivered up the dead which were in them." Once understood, these allusions add structure to the three visions, guiding us through Revelation from the earthly empire in its arrogance and downfall to the coming of the Lamb's kingdom.

In the political epilogue mentioned above, during a drive the next afternoon from the waterfront ghetto of Hunter's Point across the Golden Gate into an unnamed fishing town, Christopher outlines what to him is the immediate corollary of this apocalyptic outlook: the black revolutionaries, he says, need guns. To Leo's response that he wants Christopher "to live," his lover counters with the questions, "Alone?" and "Walking over the bodies of the dead?" He will not separate himself, then, from his comrades in what is increasingly seen as a life or death struggle; and Christopher concludes, "If you don't want me to keep on going under the feet of horses, . . . then I think you got to agree that we need us some guns" (*TMHL* 482–83). In these sentences Baldwin pinpoints the thinking of many young black radicals and their supporters during the later 1960s and the start of the 1970s, when revolutionaries, black and white, viewed the United States government as the main enemy abroad and at home. Baldwin is true to the period's spirit in his 1972 tribute to two of them, George and Jonathan Jackson, joined "in the royal fellowship of death," in the apocalyptic closing paragraphs of *No Name in the Street* (197), and in fiction here.

But beyond evoking that era in Christopher's political stances, Baldwin does so in the visions to which Leo is witness. Leo is, in fact, "witnessing, not sharing," as he specifies of the third vision; after experiencing it he stands trying "to understand what was happening" (*TMHL* 481, 482). Aware of the coming destruction but not able to "share" apocalyptic hope, Leo is separated from the prophetic thinking of the young activists and only partly grasps it. But in the three visions, Baldwin captures the consciousness of that generation of radicals. As Leo believes his mortality is no surer than the rising storm, so they believed the stars in their courses were bringing a new way of living, whose nature could not be foreseen.[20]

New York Revisited

That this change did not take place is the most important determinant of the presentations of apocalypse in Baldwin's last two novels. The first of these, *If Beale Street Could Talk*, reflects its early 1970s social world in several ways. In part, in its woman-narrated, woman-centered focus, it responds to the then-emergent milieu of black radical feminism, not so much in reconsidering gender and patriarchy, issues it approaches conservatively (at least ostensibly), as in sharing some black feminist critiques of middle-class aspirations. *Beale Street*, for example, like Toni Morrison's *Sula* (published several months earlier, in late 1973), is structured around two families, one socially conventional and class-aspirant, the other socially disaffected. Far more important to the book's overall meaning, however, is its already-mentioned common ground with the political world of early-1970s black and white revolutionary thinking. *Beale Street* is the closest of Baldwin's novels in time and mood to *No Name in the Street* (1972), whose closing image of a new world "kicking in the belly of its mother, time" (196) it echoes symbolically (Scott 95–96). Baldwin avoids overtopicality, however—though the conjunctural mood is felt everywhere—by detaching the book from contemporaneous events and placing it, through part-titles and biblical parallels, in a long African American history and in a typology of change reaching back to Revelation.

The novel shows a society in which repressive institutions and practices wield near-total power, but also foresees a relatively rapidly approaching overturn, presented, in a new emphasis for Baldwin, as a long-term ripening of apocalyptic seeds. Tying these ideas together are the novel's two part-titles, "Troubled About My Soul" and "Zion." They come from the same source, the Gospel song "Troubled About My Soul":

> Lord, I'm troubled—troubled—trouble all about my soul
> Just as soon as my feet strike Zion, I won't be troubled no more.

The song has deep roots in African American tradition—it was reportedly sung by Negro prisoners in South Carolina's new death house in February 1931, a meaningful context for this book, and was field-recorded by Alan Lomax, also in South Carolina, in July 1937. Its use places the novel's events in a sequence from trouble to its end: for those who know the song, to say "Troubled about my soul" is to think, "Just as soon as my feet strike Zion, I won't be troubled no more."[21]

But the path to this state is not so easy to show fictionally. Baldwin's treatment of change in *If Beale Street Could Talk* builds on three ideas—the city, the child, and time—and contains built-in ambiguities. The city is New York, specifically Harlem. Lower Manhattan—the Village, Lower East Side, and the Tombs (Manhattan House of Detention, on Centre Street)—is viewed from a Harlem perspective, in contrast to *Another Country*'s downtown focus. Harlem is where the Hunt and Rivers families live; Tish's memories provide glimpses of its "Sunday morning street" and of Fonny as a child losing a tooth there; family conferences take place there; characters return from work to its sustaining streets (*BS* 17–18, 10, 35–40 and 51–63, 32). But downtown is murderous. Nothing in *Another Country* parallels the trio with which Baldwin exemplifies New York's structure of power: Officer Bell, the legal system on the street, with his casual racism, casual lasciviousness, and eyes "that look only into the eyes of the conquered victim" (115, 145, 143); the Tombs, that system's arm of power, where Fonny thinks, "*Motherfuckers. You won't hang me*" (162); and the District Attorney's office, the system's directing intelligence and the executive power of the state, which holds witnesses incommunicado, arranges for them to drop from sight, manipulates trial dates (75, 105, 155). These represent, by synecdoche, the society for which they are enforcers.

New York, however, is not only itself, but falls under twin biblical signs: Sodom and Zion. Sodom, we recall, becomes an implied identity for the city through Tish's voicing of her baby's imagined question, "*Is there not one righteous among them?*" (163). The question asks if there is any reason to exempt New York, and by extension the United States, from judgment and destruction. Assuming "them" to mean whites, with African Americans as the "sojourners" represented biblically by Lot's family, the answer may seem obvious. Yet Baldwin shows more than one "righteous" among the whites: Hayward, Fonny's lawyer, a conventional practitioner gradually drawn into a deep and genuine commitment; Levy, the landlord who rents to Tish and Fonny because "he dug people who loved each other"; the Spaniards at the restaurant Tish and Fonny frequent (106; 111–12; 47–50, 117–20, 162). The perhaps surprising inference is that the United States, or its white population, will be spared utter destruction.

The implications of "Zion," Baldwin's title for the novel's brief second section, are richer. In evangelical tradition, Zion refers broadly to God's righteous kingdom, as in the Gospel source above. In this sense, Lynn Orilla Scott sees Zion in *Beale Street* as implying "the messianic promise of a future ideal community" (88). In many biblical uses, Zion is synonymous with Jerusalem as God's chosen place. Yet Zion's sons and daughters sin against God and the city is brought low in punishment, then "redeemed with judgment" (Isa. 1:20–21, 27). Zion, then—especially in the "Davidic-Zion" strand of prophecy that places special emphasis on the city—is both the righteous kingdom that is prophecy's goal, and the restored seat of justice and glory that will follow exile and punishment.[22] In its most far-reaching uses, in messianic chapters of Isaiah, Zion signifies a broadly apocalyptic national resurrection and the birth of a new world: "Awake and sing, ye that dwell in dust," the nation is told, "for thy dew is as the dew of herbs, and the earth shall cast out the dead"; and, "as soon as Zion travailed, she brought forth her children" (Isa. 26:19, 66:8). These images of resurrection and birth become part of Revelation, which takes up the theme of the woman in labor. Baldwin's use of "Zion" as part-title and controlling metaphor thus signifies future recompense for those who "dwell in dust" and the "righteous" who have aided them.

This sense of "Zion" becomes the frame for Baldwin's second major apocalyptic symbol, Tish's labor and the birth of her child. The nine months of the child's gestation, referred to throughout the narrative and in its final paragraph, coupled with the significance of birth as a "transformation" (102) and references to apocalyptic change in the closing pages, present the birth as an apocalyptic event, symbolically the start of a culminating transformation in world history. Scott notes that the novel's epigraph, "Mary, Mary, / What you going to name / That pretty little baby?" identifies Tish with Mary, and that so far as the novel "retells the Christ story, it imparts an apocalyptic view of human events and a vision of salvation" (94, 97). There is a more direct apocalyptic context as well. Tish's labor identifies her with Revelation's central redemptive symbol, the "woman clothed with the sun," who "being with child cried, travailing in birth, and pained to be delivered" (12:2–3). Confronted by a dragon seeking to "devour her child," the woman gives birth to an infant destined "to rule all nations with a rod of iron," who is "caught up unto God," while the woman herself is hidden from the dragon (Rev. 12:4–6). This vision adapts the image of Zion's birth labor in Isaiah 66, incorporating Jewish messianic prophecy into Christian apocalypticism. Elisabeth Schüssler Fiorenza comments:

> [John's] vision of the woman in labor pains alludes to Israel-Zion seen in Isaiah . . . as a mother awaiting the delivery of the messianic age. . . . The "birth of the Messiah" refers here not to the historical birth of Jesus but to his exaltation and enthronement as the "firstborn of the dead" and as "the beginning of the new creation." God has prevented the dragon from devouring the child. (80–81)[23]

Beale Street's use of this symbol promises specifically, then, that Tish and her child will be safe from the dragon; less directly, that the kingdom is at hand.

In addition to this parallel, Baldwin fuses Tish's labor with the culminating event in Revolution's second half, the general resurrection. In the visionary moment of *Beale Street*'s final sentence, during her labor, Tish seems to hear the baby "from far away, but coming nearer," as it "cries and cries and cries and cries and cries and cries and cries and cries, cries like it means to wake the dead" (166). Tish's ninefold repetition replicates the months of gestation, and the child's assumed purpose of waking the dead ties its birth to the earth's casting out of the dead in Isaiah 26 and the general resurrection in Revelation 20.[24] In fusing messianic birth with apocalyptic resurrection, Baldwin follows the line of thinking that believes the decisive apocalyptic time "is not just imminent but actually here and that humans are agents in bringing it about" (Rowland, "Revelation" 713). Baldwin's fusion, additionally, resolves an ambiguity between the resurrection imagery in Isaiah, in which the dead wake as part of an apocalyptic rebirth—"Awake and sing," above—and in Revelation, in which the seas and hell give up the dead to be "judged every man according to their works" (20:13). Because Tish's child, by its cries, stirs others to "wake," Baldwin's image favors Isaiah's view that the wakened themselves will live a new existence.

Baldwin's use of time further complicates an already complex presentation. A term used repetitively throughout the text, time has multiple meanings. Most simply, it is the factual months of Tish's pregnancy: "The baby wants out. Fonny wants out. And we are going to make it: in time" (135). The same nine months are those of redemption for Fonny, with a meaning new in *Beale Street*: sure in his racial allegiance, unlike the young Leo, Fonny is transformed from victim to fighter, who has "leaped from the promontory of despair" and is "fighting for his life" (162). Simultaneously, the time of the pregnancy, through Tish's equation of the end of the nine months with the waking of the dead, becomes apocalyptic time—time whose endpoint is an abrupt discontinuity: the baby begins to live, the dead wake to life. Finally, Baldwin superimposes on these a sense of time as the ordinary passing of life in a world of pain, the world we live in all our lives until apocalyptic time begins. This is inevitably, for most people, time that brings mixed joy and suffering, leads toward dissolution, and involves struggles over time—for a better life for oneself, one's children, one's people. "Somewhere, in time," Tish muses, "Fonny and I had met: somewhere, in time, we had loved. . . . Somewhere in time he looked about him, knowing that he was being lied to, in time, with the connivance of time" (79). And so—condensed into an iconic episode of oppression and resistance—time in *Beale Street* is not only factual and apocalyptic, but the long historical time of African American experience.

In this way, while continuing to expect an apocalyptic birth, Baldwin moves away from *Tell Me How Long*'s fairly immediate apocalyptic expectations and back to the emphasis on historically developed African American culture that marked his earlier works. In doing so, Baldwin also turns toward the tradition in African American prophetic thinking that views the race's history through figural parallels with Exodus, the wilderness march, and the immense "arch" of biblical time from the ancestors to Canaan (von Rad, *Old Testament Theology* 1:134). Those influenced by this tradition, we know, routinely posited generations or longer as the time over which African Americans would win equality. Yet Baldwin's turn back to the idea of long historical time is only partial, since his controlling images remain an onrushing apocalyptic time and a birth that wakes the dead.

Baldwin works to conceptualize the relation of historical to apocalyptic time in an early meditation by Tish, one of his most important discussions of historical experience and change. At a family gathering, just before Tish reveals her pregnancy, her sister Ernestine puts on a Ray Charles recording:

> I listened to the music and the sounds from the streets and Daddy's hand rested lightly on my hair. And everything seemed connected—the street sounds, and Ray's voice and his piano and my Daddy's hand and my sister's silhouette and the sounds and the lights coming from the kitchen. It was as though we were a picture, trapped in time: this had been happening for hundreds of years, people sitting in a room, waiting for dinner, and listening to the blues. And it was as though, out of these elements, this patience, my Daddy's touch, the sounds of my mother in the kitchen, the way the light fell, the way the music continued beneath everything, the movement of Ernestine's head as she lit a cigarette, the movement of her hand as she dropped the match into the ashtray, the blurred human voices rising from the street, out of this rage and a steady, somehow triumphant sorrow, my baby was slowly being formed. (*BS* 35)

"Steady, somehow triumphant sorrow" is almost a definition of the blues and, at least in part, life as persistence through hardship and loss. Expressing these qualities, the blues necessarily stands in tension with the Gospel promises of *Beale Street*'s epigraph and part-titles and the apocalyptic tone of its conclusion. Tish's meditation looks back on a history that was "triumphant" partly because people were not beaten into the ground, "kept on keeping on" as the saying goes; even more, because of an *attitude*, a half-rueful, half-joyful acceptance of human imperfection. But for Baldwin, speaking through Tish on the final page, this advance through time has an end point; the music, the street sounds, Fonny's struggle create the baby, and so lead to an apocalyptic discontinuity, a symbolic break into new existence. In this way, Tish's meditation creates an imaginative resolution to the tension between ordinary and apocalyptic time.

But not a necessary resolution. *If Beale Street Could Talk* responds to its particular historical juncture—the years since *Tell Me How Long*'s publication in 1968, even since *No Name in the Street* (1972). In the interval, the colossal hopes and energies of the 1960s had partly lost force and partly been smashed, but—as Baldwin would view matters—superficial legal changes had altered life on the ground not at all. Baldwin, through Tish, imagines that decades, even centuries, of sorrow and effort will mature into a new birth, an upheaval in time. But this is not necessarily true, and was not true historically. Put another way, the baby as the outcome of the elements in Tish's reverie is necessary, but its apocalyptic character is not. It was equally possible—and true historically—that black people, others disinherited by the empire, and their allies among the righteous, would "keep on keeping on" through time, without any decisive change; and in this case, the imaginative perspective of *Beale Street* would not be adequate. *Just Above My Head* starts from this reality.

Babylon

The central fact of *Just Above My Head*, never directly mentioned in the text, is the postponement of the apocalyptic overturn the prophetic artist heralds. This overturn is directed at Babylon, the biblical locale Baldwin uses in place of the U.S. cities he has made apocalyptic symbols in prior works. The novel's central evocation of apocalyptic hope, we know, is Arthur's song "Daniel," which imagines the stone in Nebuchadnezzar's dream rolling into Babylon, "tearing down / the kingdom of this world!" (512); and singing the song signifies Arthur's commissioning as prophetic witness to its vision. The scene's placement at the close of Book Four, the novel's longest unit, covering the hopes and losses of the civil rights years, seems to make it thematically summative; and its reference to Babylon gains resonance from the use of this name in some revolutionary writings of the period to refer to the present United States.[25] Yet in the novel's mid-1970s present, some sixteen years after this scene,[26] "Babylon's" power is fully intact. This paradox shapes the novel's presentation of social reformation and raises basic questions about the possibility of change, explored in my next chapter.

Babylon is the biblical name for the principle of empire and domination. In the Book of Daniel, nominally set during the Exile but composed centuries later in the era of Greek domination, Babylon is the first of the four successive kingdoms, generally taken as Babylon, Media, Persia, and Macedonian Greece, that Daniel fictively predicts will hold sway until God's kingdom arrives (Dan. 2:37–44).[27] The kingdoms also represent imperial domination over minorities—in Daniel 7–12, first of all the Jews in the Greek cosmopolis. In Revelation, written under Roman rule,

Babylon is retained as the name for the oppressing power, now representing false religion in league with imperial dominion. Virtually all interpreters have accepted that the name refers symbolically to Rome, but the substitution, connecting John's prophecy with Daniel's, has its own force: Babylon appears as the principle or essence that Rome represents historically. This principle—of national and world domination by a society fusing deceptive ideas (Rev. 17:5) and repressive state power (the beast in Revelation chaps. 13–20), with the addition of almost limitless moral blindness in the majority population—is roughly what Baldwin saw in the contemporary United States, as references throughout *Just Above My Head* testify. In the novel, the power of empire, represented by the Korean War and southern segregation, reaches down into the smallest human relations, destroying or maiming all it touches: the Trumpets of Zion quartet, Hall tells us early on, "didn't get too far before the hammer of Korea smashed it" (*JAMH* 31), and the war's legacy touches the surviving quartet members to the present day.[28]

Hall's narration evokes this seemingly limitless power in vignettes and descriptive phrases bridging the pre-civil rights and civil rights eras and mainly focusing on the South, where that power was most direct and brutal. (In this Harlem-centered book, we get few scenes set in New York outside Harlem or in other northern cities, so that the South comes to stand for the whole white United States.) Birmingham around 1951, to a minor character, Sister Dorothy Green, is like the biblical city where God "knows he won't find one righteous man" (184). Years later, when Hall and Arthur return South following Peanut's disappearance, it seems, Hall says, "as though the landscape awaited the scalding purification of the latter rain" (534).[29] These same scenes are thrice called "apocalyptic," but in the sense of unrelenting battle, not imminent transformation (51, 521, 562). Jimmy's greeting to the brothers in the Florida town where they find him doing movement work—"Welcome to the slaughter, children" (50, 538)—inverts the meaning of the chapter following Nebuchadnezzar's dream in Daniel, the story of the "burning fiery furnace" (Dan. 3:6–28): those in the furnace have no mysterious guardian, nor do they necessarily emerge unscathed, but endure the fire alone, in terror, and sometimes to the death.

Harlem offers only ambiguous succor. There, for Crunch and Arthur, back from the South probably in 1951, the streets are "full, vivid, with people, children, sound—it was as though they were moving through an element which held them up, sustained them, and protected them" (254). But in a later scene, Baldwin finishes a panoramic street description by focusing on a boy sitting still at the end of a bar, whose "forehead sloped back into a tangle of black hair which had not been combed in days" and whose eyes "were black with wonder" (333). Baldwin gives no information on this person's desolation, but we realize that Harlem resides within Babylon, if partly a refuge from it.

Babylon's temporal power appears unshaken in the book's present, the mid-1970s. Hall now lives in a semi-suburban Bronx neighborhood and Julia in a similar Yonkers area; Hall's children seem accepted at school. But Hall's street is lined with "exiled trees," the route to Julia's house lies through a "placid and terrifying" landscape where a car ahead flaunts, "AMERICA: LOVE IT OR LEAVE IT," and Arthur, visiting Hall sometime in these years, wonders "what goes on behind all these careful shutters. It *can't* be—*nothing*. But . . . it sure don't seem to be *something*" (17, 23, 25, 18). Hall for his part jokes, "We couldn't all make it to Canada. Some of us had to stop here" (18). The implication is that "here" is not a free country and that if life is better than in the past, there is no real prospect of ongoing change. These characters, in sum, live African American middle-class lives in the wake of the civil rights movement: not free though freer, half-integrated into a sterile American prosperity against which Julia's African-accented clothes and true African décor (25, 27) seem an inoculation. *Just Above My Head*, then, is premised on the fact that the near-term hope of a world rebirth recorded in Baldwin's two prior novels, and seemingly promised in Arthur's song, has not come.

This fact, though shown elliptically, is one dimension of Baldwin's assessment of apocalypse in *Just Above My Head*. A second lies in two ideas that may seem unrelated or contrasted to it: long-term, cross-generational effort for family and community advance, what may be called a traditional black strategy for freedom, and, additionally, black people's embattled status as Americans. Neither is a new emphasis. The first returns to the "unspoken recognition of shared experience" addressed in "Many Thousands Gone" ("MTG" 27) and continues *Beale Street*'s stress on long time. Cultural or temperamental hope, emphasis on advancement across generations, and racial self-reliance all play a part in this portrayal of communal striving.

So, the day after Christmas, most likely in 1950, Hall descends into streets "bleak with the price of the promise to be kept," a promise brightly visible in "the 'do-rag' brothers, and the barbershops, the women, the girls, the children," who are all, in Hall's view, poisoned by unmet hopes, and yet "something in the poisoned marrow of the bone perpetually calculated and achieved the antidote" (*JAMH* 148). The community's life, Hall implies, somehow turns bitterness into wary hope. One variant of this embittered optimism—that of freedom in the spirit—emerges when a waitress says she doesn't care much for the kingdoms "up yonder" and "down here," but that "we *got* a kingdom. We just got to move on *in* it" (319).

The dominant variant, however, appears in an exchange involving Hall's parents, Florence and Paul, as well as Peanut, possibly around the fall of 1955.[30] Peanut, politically radical like most younger characters in this book, derides the declaration of desegregation some time earlier in Washington, D.C., where he has been living. Whites, he protests, "got the *gall* to claim to be giving us something they didn't never have the right to take away" (299). Paul and Florence respond, variously, that desegregation "don't mean I want to eat with white people. It just makes life a little easier" (Florence); "We didn't wait for white people to have a change of heart, or change their laws, or anything, in order to be responsible for each other" (Paul); "You've got to depend on yourself. . . . [I]t was a good thing they changed the law, but we can't wait for that!" (Florence; 299–300). Paul, significantly, says that while he was "a kind of half-assed Garveyite" when young, "we're here now and we can't go nowhere else" (300), a point meshing with Hall's dislike of Sidney and Martha's embrace of an organization similar to the Nation of Islam, in slightly later scenes (329–30, 332–35). These characters voice an idea of African American advance lying between nationalism or separatism and a narrow integrationism calling just for lowering racial barriers; they speak for racial effort aimed at gaining and keeping maximum leverage and staying, as a community, "on the upward way" (Grimké). This outlook, and the real history it points to, more centrally than characters' individual stories, occupy the ground of redemption in *Just Above My Head*'s version of the eschatological paradigm.

Yoked with the idea of advancing over time in the United States is the issue of African Americans' identity—one Paul Montana touches on in the exchange just quoted. Again this is old ground for Baldwin, as his statement of the race's "*blood* relationship" with whites in "Many Thousands Gone" ("MTG" 32) and his hope to "achieve our country" in *The Fire Next Time* (105) show. But Baldwin's tenor here differs sharply from that in earlier fiction, where Sharon in *Beale Street* could exclaim, "Who*ever* discovered America *deserved* to be dragged home, in chains, to die" (156). In this and similar references,[31] Baldwin's characters express an attitude to the United States' role in the world; here, he is after something more basic, African Americans' underlying, partly involuntary, partly willed self-identification. Baldwin provides a meditation for Arthur on this matter as he sits with Guy in a Paris street café:

> If Guy is saying he does not like being a Frenchman, what would he think of Arthur if Arthur proclaimed that he did not like being a black American? And, indeed, for the very first time, and almost certainly because he is sitting on this unknown avenue, he puts the two words together *black American* and hears, at once, the very crescendo of contradiction and the unanswering and unanswerable thunder and truth of history—which is nothing more and nothing less than the beating of his own heart, his song. In many ways, he does not like being a black American, or being black, or being American, or being Arthur. . . . However: here he is. . . . (*JAMH* 492–93)

Arthur's first point is plain: for black people to call themselves American in a country that at best half-accepts them is a contradiction. The "thunder and truth of history" may at first seem to underscore this point, but Baldwin's sentence structure places the two ideas in opposition, and the truth is "unanswering and unanswerable"— it provides no resolution to the contradiction and yet is absolutely undeniable. So Arthur's point is that he is indeed a *black American*, with all the contradictions the term implies. Further, Arthur, like most of us—especially in oppressed groups—does not like many things about himself, yet they are who he is. And if the "thunder and truth" are given by two hundred years of history, as undeniable as one's ancestors and life events, so also, as part of a contradictory reality, are they voluntary, given by the beating of Arthur's heart, itself part of that history.[32]

The other side of Baldwin's phrase, of course, is that Arthur is a *black* American, and the adjective implies a history of its own—including, paradoxically or not, the history of becoming American—as well as a culture. Arthur is a Gospel singer; his songs—"his song" in his rumination—are part of a distinct culture with meaning for the whole world but originating in and reflecting African Americans' particular experiences. So Baldwin, like Ellison a little earlier, sees African Americans as a group with a double existence, American and African American at the same time.

Baldwin writes a confirming but complicating scene when Julia, who has earlier moved to live in the Ivory Coast, lunching with Hall after returning, explains her responses as an African American in West Africa. A black person from the United States meeting African villagers, she tells Hall, doesn't "know a damn thing about any single day they've spent on earth . . . you know more about the Mississippi cracker, even though you hate him and you know he hates you." So, like Arthur, and others such as Langston Hughes before him,[33] Julia cannot be other than American. Yet, when Hall asks about being "back," Julia says she is "glad to be back. But—that's the question they asked me over there. And they weren't wrong." To be looked on, she says, "not merely as yourself, but as part of something other, older, vaster," begins "to make: sense" (550–51, 555, 556). Julia's words, acknowledging that some part of herself is indeed "African," reflect African Americans' growing recognition of Africanness in the book's period and are a necessary corrective to Hall's over-simple question. Yet, slightly earlier in this scene, Hall has felt the contrast between himself and the once-European Jews sitting near him in the Russian Tea Room: "*they* were homeless; I was home" (554). Out of these materials Baldwin stitches a complex intellectual construct, incorporating an idea of an African "home" within the reality of the United States as "home" and, as well, of an exile in the United States that is not exile *from* Africa so much as exile *in* one's home.[34]

Baldwin's construct signifies his characters' only partly willed adherence to traditions going back to the early nineteenth century, when Africans in the United States—partly in response to white efforts to sponsor "colonization," or resettlement of free Negroes in Africa—began to define themselves as Americans. The 1827 statement against "colonization" by Richard Allen, founding bishop of the A.M.E. Church, asserting, "This land which we have watered with our *tears* and *our blood*, is now our *mother country*, and we are well satisfied to stay where wisdom abounds, and the gospel is free" ("Letter"), can stand as a milepost of this intellectual shift. Allen, like others before and after him, pointed to the role Africans played in building the wealth of the United States and the resulting right to share equally—"We have *tilled* the ground and made fortunes for thousands, and still they are not weary of our services"; but his statement is most significant for stating the idea of the new "*mother country*" as principle. This belief in turn implied—in Henry Highland Garnet's grandiloquent 1848 phrase—"that this republic, and this continent, are to be the theatre in which the great drama of our triumphant Destiny is to be enacted" (25). Never uncontested, this remained the dominant viewpoint, one with close ties both to the reformative prophetic stance mentioned earlier—the ideas of conquering rights in the United States, with God's aid, through African Americans' own efforts—and, obviously, to the perspective that anticipated a generations-long road to equality.[35]

The two issues discussed so far—the eclipse of the book's apocalypticism and its simultaneous presentation of a long-term ameliorationist perspective—may seem to show Baldwin as artistically incoherent: he seems to offer the second stance as a corrective while not fully admitting that the first has failed. In fact, though conventional thinking contrasts these ideas, the novel does not allow a counterposition. Baldwin does not, on one side, view apocalyptic-regenerative belief as an aberration, as many did who reassessed the 1960s in hindsight; nor, on the other, does he present the cross-generational perspective as a substitute or a preferred strategy, continuing after the apocalyptic moment of the 1960s. Rather, by spacing the scenes involving this strategy throughout the narrative building up to Arthur's experience in Paris, the novel implies that the black strategy for freedom itself led up to the millennial-apocalyptic hopes that soared then. Indeed, Arthur's café reflection on identity in history occurs earlier on the evening when he will sing "Daniel," just days before he will return to the United States and the South: the moments are fused, not distinct. Further, present-time episodes neither explicitly repudiate nor reaffirm the prospects of millennial justice, while also not showing a clearcut continuation of the longer ameliorative effort. Rather, as already seen, the characters seem stuck in a somewhat improved world offering no clear path forward.

The reasons are fundamental. The conversation among Peanut and Florence and Paul Montana certainly proposes that African Americans have always striven for communal and family betterment. Yet the debates about integration, communal improvement, and opposed nationalist ideas represented in this and other dialogues belong to a specific time of ferment, when change was at hand and it seemed worthwhile to dispute its direction. Outside of such a period, on the street level that counts for Baldwin, these debates fall off. In consequence, in the novel's recent past—Arthur's last years—and its present, there is an absence both of civil rights activity and of debate over civil rights objectives. So if Baldwin does not present the apocalyptic city as a present-time possibility, neither does he suggest that patient ameliorative work can take its place.

The central intellectual problem in *Just Above My Head*'s presentation of Babylon and its fall, it becomes clear, is the status of the apocalyptic upheaval the narrative seems to promise. It is possible to read the novel's present-time sections, with chronologically earlier episodes, as meaning the apocalyptic goal was empty; African Americans have made their modest advances by maximizing a tenuous hold in society, at the cost of enormous losses, and the idea of destroying "the kingdom of this world" was fantasy. But, for the reasons just given, the ameliorative perspective does not substitute for the apocalyptic one in any simple way. Alternatively, presenting both viewpoints may mean it is necessary to retain both. But in this case, their relationship is not fully clear, and it is also unclear how apocalyptic vision can be maintained when the social rebellion and hopes for justice that nourished it have dissipated, as in Baldwin's and the novel's present time. Yet again, the novel might imply holding on until a new time of struggle; but there is no clear statement of this idea. Finally, these issues also pose the question of how to evaluate the prophetic certitude of the Paris club scene, now apparently shown as hollow. In these ways, Baldwin's text calls into question its own centering ideas of breakthrough to a new world and the efficacy of prophecy.

A City of Love?

Baldwin's novels after *Another Country* may seem to move progressively farther from the idea of a city of love. Leo's vision of a rising energy that would "one day, overturn this table" of the privileged, *Beale Street*'s evocations of resistant hate and the dead waking, and Guy's wish in parting from Arthur for "a deluge in America. That would please me very much" may appear to hope for an apocalypse of vengeance with no balancing hope for a world of love (*TMHL* 477; *BS* 162, 166; *JAMH* 514). This darker tone probably reflects two factors. One is the seventeen years between *Another Country* (1962) and *Just Above My Head* (1979). Those years, in the United States, began with the lunch-counter sit-ins and freedom rides, went on to mass protests and rebellions, climaxed in assassinations, shootouts, attacks on police, and police ambushes of black revolutionaries, and ended with the eclipse of an independent black radical movement and with what Baldwin would regard as an illusion that the civil rights agenda had been satisfied. Baldwin, then, in his later works, increasingly took account of the ruthlessness of "Babylon" and its agents. The second factor is the violent and bloody imagery of Revelation itself, especially when considered in relation to a society whose agents act as just outlined. Revelation's vision of judgment includes, for example, the call for birds to "eat the flesh of kings, and the flesh of captains, and the flesh of mighty men" (19:18). Such evocations, Christopher Rowland argues, are purposefully "iconoclastic and disturbing." A vision limited to love and inclusion, Rowland contends, risks "baptizing the status quo of this world's injustice, as the kings, magnates, and captains ride into the kingdom on the tide of the love of God. That sentimentality is ruthlessly challenged by the apocalyptic vision" ("Revelation" 701). Baldwin's idea of the middle ground between present society and the heavenly city—the ground of justice and cleansing—seems to react to recent history in the light of this biblical hermeneutic.

Nonetheless, the novels after *Another Country* do continue, though with less assurance, to project a society of love. They do so partly in continuing to affirm interracial understanding and sometimes love. Barbara and Leo's twenty-year comradeship in *Tell Me How Long* and the acts of those I call "the righteous" in *Beale Street* point to the possibility of this kind of understanding. Baldwin explores this issue most explicitly in Guy's dialogue with Arthur in *Just Above My Head*, occurring—like Arthur's meditation on being black and American—in the café earlier on the evening when Arthur sings "Daniel." Here, Arthur challenges Guy with some racial typing: Europeans, he charges, whatever their differences, unite in calling him "nigger" (*JAMH* 494). Guy's lengthy reply covers several issues and forms a coherent argument. For Guy "sympathy" between black and white, which Arthur has caustically dismissed, is indeed necessary—"there is no other hope." Further, while Arthur's general point about Europe may be true, he, Guy, is incapable of calling Arthur "nigger," and, in turn, Arthur "will never abandon anyone you love" (495–96). Finally, and of utmost importance, Arthur is not a "victim," but has been "the object of a conspiracy—and the conspiracy has failed" (496). Black life and culture, Guy implies, have withstood the effort to destroy them and will play their part in forming the world's new shape. So to Arthur's fatalism about universal bigotry, Guy opposes the possibility for individuals to break from cultural imperatives, with the easily ridiculed "sympathy" playing its part, and he argues that the world's cultural future remains up for grabs. This conversation's effects ripple through later events. Guy, responding to Arthur's need "to give himself to someone who needs to give himself to Arthur" (459), acts as a catalyst to Arthur's later ability to give himself to Jimmy. Equally, by developing and deepening their friendship, the tentative understanding Arthur reaches with Guy—a former French soldier who hates French colonialism and a devotee of a jazz-inflected French antiracist culture—leads forward to the nightclub scene in which Arthur is able to respond to the multiracial and multinational trio and audience and achieve his vision of the Fifth Monarchy. So far as that scene prefigures the city that will rise in place of Babylon, that city will be, as Gospel tradition has said, of "every nation."[36]

Ultimately, however, the idea of a city of love is validated only partly by the possibility of love between the races and predominantly by that of love among the oppressed, the world's great majority. If *they* cannot build a community of love, none can exist. Love is not only the content of the city, but love among the oppressed is part of the road to it, as John Grimes's visionary experience of suffering in *Go Tell It on the Mountain* suggests. This point perhaps lies behind *Just Above My Head*'s attention to the long tradition of community advancement. The same point may underlie the novel's repeated use of vignettes of Harlem's streets and bars (56–57, 148, 332–33), as well as of the mutual self-help and mutuality in struggle in southern churches and communities before and during the civil rights era (179–80, 400–1, 434–35). In one instance, Hall imagines Arthur's first view of these churches, at age sixteen, about 1951:

> He has no way of recognizing the wide, low church basement [where church sisters are serving lunch]. He does not know what it cost—the blood that bought it, the pain and sweat and danger which built it, the passion that holds it up.... He sees, but does not see, the swollen ankles, the flat feet, the swift, gnarling fingers, serving the deacons, repudiating the helpless condition, refusing, with a laugh, despair. (179–80)

Such sketched scenes bear the narrative weight of suggesting a communitarianism in struggle that can stand as our present promise of the City. Indeed, such scenes prefigure the nation's future, if it can overcome its exclusionary past and present. As it is possible that the momentary apocalypse of sexual love can, in a freer future, become a daily apocalypse of *agape*, so a besieged community's vibrancy and defensive solidarity may, in a renewed society, become the bread of all. The scenes showing this kind of community life provide, in effect, *Just Above My Head*'s glimpses of a future *civitas*.

Balancing the potential city of love, however, is the present one of embattled love, self-destruction, violence ratified, and despair—whose name, Babylon, we know. So, the boy at the bar bears his burden alone, Joel is believed, Crunch keeps his teeth unreplaced to show "what black people did to black people" (*JAMH* 37). The terrible costs of destruction within the community, with the blows rained on it by the larger society and state, form one half of *Just Above My Head*'s vision. In conjunction with the novel's portrayal of community and its prospect, or dream, of a new world, these evils raise the same questions as apocalypse's deferral about the possibility of new life and the conflicting claims of prophecy and doubt.

CHAPTER 5

Prophecy and Doubt

Hurry down sunshine, see what tomorrow brings
The sun went down, tomorrow brought us rain.
—"Hurry Down Sunshine," *Just Above My Head*

Oh, my loving brother, when the world's on fire
Don't you want God's bosom to be your pillow
Hide me over in the Rock of Ages
Rock of Ages cleft for me.
—"When the World's on Fire," *Just Above My Head*

In his last novel, Baldwin responds to the eclipse of the civil rights era's utopian hopes by taking as his subject the competing claims of prophecy and doubt. To explore these claims, he reexamines the premises of his fiction, the ideas of the apocalyptic body and city and of prophetic art, each of which receives its fullest exposition in *Just Above My Head* yet is also systematically questioned through plot and commentary. As his vehicle for this dual focus Baldwin uses the narrative structure he has created for this work, a double-voiced narration in which Arthur

Montana's story is told by the more worldly and skeptical Hall, who expresses his own outlook alongside Arthur's, allowing both to speak in contention.

This contrast depends in part on a further one, between *Just Above My Head*'s past time, the pre-civil rights and civil rights eras that occupy most of its length, and its post-civil rights era present, which shapes the novel though mentioned only intermittently. In its past-time narrative, *Just Above My Head* represents Baldwin's elegy for characters who, profane and human, yet "walked by faith" (15). The phrase echoes Paul's words on the apostolic life, "for we walk by faith, not by sight" (2 Cor. 5:7) and so evokes, through these characters, the epoch in African American culture when its members lived at least in part by prophetic hope. In contrast, through Arthur's later crisis of belief—what Baldwin, in early notes, called "the failure of Good News"—and the surviving characters' lives in the 1970s, the novel pictures this era's passing into a quiescent period when sweeping hopes of justice seem no longer relevant.[1] In such a time, Robert Reid-Pharr suggests in a deeply-felt commentary, African Americans have learned, or strive, "to forget the bloody injustices that have been done them and thus to re-member, to reproduce a world that, if not more just, is at least a bit more comfortable" (*Once You Go Black* 118).

Ultimately, Baldwin's narrator, even while recognizing something like Reid-Pharr's "forgetting" in his own life, does not accept such a stance as adequate to the past and present. Hall, a complex artist-narrator in his own right, instead adopts an implied aesthetic of tragic awareness. Yet, in fidelity to those he portrays, he allows Arthur's contrasting (perhaps abandoned) prophetic-apocalyptic consciousness to speak on its own and to reenter the novel through its final dream sequence. Each of these stances, moreover, is associated with an artistic genre—blues and Gospel, respectively—so that, self-reflexively, the novel also meditates on the claims of distinct artistic modes for representing our time and our future. The contrast between these perspectives—rather than the validity of either—is, I argue, Baldwin's basic point. Through its overall structure and its dream-conclusion, *Just Above My Head* confronts readers with the need to choose between hope and skepticism, even while recognizing the intellectual validity of both.

Besides its specifics, this view of *Just Above My Head* challenges still-frequent perceptions of an artistic decline in Baldwin's later work. If this novel has been seen, even by so astute a critic as Caryl Phillips, as "excessively rhetorical, structurally confusing, and lacking in coherent characterization" (244), that and similar judgments partly reflect its discursive style, but more a failure to enter its cultural world or to perceive the way in which, in a decade that saw previous certainties collapse, Baldwin set himself to reassess basics. Contrary to the thesis of decline, this novel's ability to mobilize opposed character viewpoints and worldviews in a sustained double-voiced narration, to reexamine its author's basic aesthetic and social assumptions, and to raise issues as fundamental as the possibility or impossibility of social reformation marks it as a culminating work of formal mastery and intellectual power.

Double-Voiced Narration

Reflecting these complex purposes, *Just Above My Head* is Baldwin's most complex fictional structure. It has the largest number of important characters; it employs an intricately associative version of Baldwin's favored present time–past time–return to present time structure, with a hard-to-follow, sometimes inconsistent chronology and other narrative contradictions.[2] Most significantly, it tells its story through a narrator, Hall Montana, who is a deeply complex, factually unreliable, sometimes self-serving, and necessarily inventive craftsman. Hall's role is basic to Baldwin's purpose. Rather than as essentially unreliable, Baldwin has constructed Hall as an imperfect narrator, self-deluded about important points yet aware of his own limitations, struggling to record the truth and, in working to dramatize a distinct viewpoint alongside his own, functioning as artistic arranger of Baldwin's dual perspective.

Hall's text is rife with events that Hall avoids telling, promises to cover but doesn't, or narrates in a self-protecting way.[3] Yet, centrally for Baldwin's presentation, Hall is aware of and emphasizes the malleability of memory, his own included. Late in the text, he comments, "The burden—the role—of memory is to clarify the event, to make it useful, even, to make it bearable. But memory is, also, what the imagination makes, or has made, of the event, and the more dreadful the event, the more likely it is that the memory will distort, or efface it" (554). Though specifically about another character, the statement applies to Hall as well: his narration is filled with hedges—"But, if I do [remember], I remember very dimly"; "on Judgment Day, I won't know what I can say I *know* about anybody else's life, including Arthur's"; "So maybe my memory is playing tricks on me" (38, 311, 384)—that show he is fully aware of the approximating he does as narrator.[4]

Several interpreters have noted that Hall's narration is unreliable but have not adequately dealt with the scope of its unreliability or his own awareness of it. These commentaries argue either that Hall's narration embodies Baldwin's evasiveness on crucial issues (Clark 57–59) or that Baldwin presents an inferable counternarrative behind the façade of Hall's. Scott, for instance, asks that we "separate the story that Hall wishes to tell from the one that emerges over the course of the novel, which is the one that Baldwin has told" (143). Focusing on homophobia, Scott argues that Hall severely underplays its effect on Arthur, particularly as felt from his family. "Throughout the text," Scott observes, "Hall works hard to minimize, even conceal, not Arthur's homosexuality itself, but the effects of homophobia on Arthur's life and the extent to which Arthur's alienation from his family is deeply connected to the silence imposed by attitudes to homosexuality," including Hall's own discomfort with the subject (167). While partly valid as concerns this topic, however, Scott's approach is less applicable to the novel as a whole, which rests largely on the believability of Hall's account, and in which, further, Hall uses his own fallibility to relativize his assessment of events.

In Baldwin's construction of Hall's narration we can infer two purposes, one artistic and one substantive. The first is to call attention to narrative art's very artfulness. Baldwin repeatedly offers examples of this aspect of Hall's art. In one instance, near the conclusion of Book One, Hall describes Arthur in a Harlem bar, looking out over the bar as if "seeing something for the first time." Hall adds that he himself had his back to the bar (though he scanned it on entering) and "could not see what he [Arthur] was seeing," and then, with a preliminary "Well," describes those at the bar in detail—the "gray-haired man, with the yellow teeth," the "tall boy in the corduroy pants, who . . . seemed to be a friend of the bartender's," and several more, as well as their interactions (56–57). Hall, then, is telling us his description is part memory and part art, creation through imagination; much is implicitly a genre scene that might have been observed anywhere in the Harlem of that time, supplementing whatever Hall may actually remember.

So far, Baldwin is making the point that narration consists of just such acts of invention. His artist-narrator is using his overall knowledge to reconstruct and, as needed, supplement his memory, in scenes inferably meeting his deep sense of truth. The issue of truth is thus thrown back at readers: specific mistakes by the narrator do not invalidate the whole of his account, but only render it an approximation, while readers must use *their* deep sense of truth to affirm or deny the narrator's. This point about narrative art is certainly not unique. In a comparable moment in *The Human Stain*, Philip Roth's narrator, the novelist Nathan Zuckerman, explains his use of invention involving one character: "How do I know she knew? I don't. . . . For better or worse, I can only do what everyone does who thinks that they know. I imagine. I am forced to imagine. It happens to be what I do for a living. It is my job" (213). Zuckerman, then, avows his use of conjecture, but also claims for his narrative the authority of imaginative coherence, and additionally, claims vocational authority—"It is my job." Hall's use of an inconsistent, partly refutable narration forgoes both claims (unlike Zuckerman, Hall is not a professional writer). Baldwin, as creator of Hall's narration, thus makes a claim more sweeping than Roth's: his narrative lacks, or, rather, repeatedly undercuts, the authority conveyed by mimetic convention and depends for its authority on the artist-narrator's largest imagination of reality and the readers' assent to that imagination as plausible.

Beyond this artistic-vocational point, however, Baldwin's care that Hall narrate a story containing acknowledged gaps and inventions has the thematic purpose of establishing that other truths besides Hall's are possible. Baldwin's creation of Hall's narration as conjectural, moreover, goes beyond any specific issue (such as homophobia) to involve the central story of Arthur's personal and artistic rise, his artistic dedication and its purposes, and his decline, and establishes that Hall's imaginative construction of this story is only an approximation. The point applies, of course, to the meanings Hall reads from the story as well as to its details. Hall's evaluations of the story both project his own ideas and, as views of someone who does not claim full knowledge, also implicitly forgo the claim of full narrative authority. In this way Baldwin constructs, in Hall, a narrative consciousness that assesses the events of Arthur's life—and the prophetic and apocalyptic ideas his life has centered on—skeptically, and yet is aware of the provisional, challengeable nature of its own judgments.

Differences between Hall's view of reality and Arthur's begin with basic beliefs. Hall is a religious skeptic, with views akin to Baldwin's own. Hall believes that the "energy called divine is really human need, translated"; that God is something "we have created"; and that "it [apparently, theistic belief] was all a lie, from top to bottom: and since we had built it, only we could dare it down" (334–35). These views both echo and differ from Baldwin's that God is a human "creation" and that humans "expand and transform" God's nature in their own repeated "act[s] of creation" ("PI" 596, "WR" 755). Hall and Baldwin agree on God's human origins, but Hall is more assertive about his atheism, less ready than Baldwin to see value in speculation about God. Hall, however, is respectful toward Arthur's religious feelings; he imagines, for example, that Arthur and Jimmy confess their love for each other "in the hearing of men, and in the sight of God" (562), viewing the lovers' declaration in their own religious terms, though presumably he would not accept these terms himself. Hall and Arthur, then, respectively embody the analytical and deconstructive, and the synthetic and reconstitutive aspects of Baldwin's sense of a human-fashioned God. In fact, Hall's God-as-human-construct and Arthur's God who witnesses his love for Jimmy are both human constructs. Hall, however, remains antipathetic to theistic belief and his apparent preference is for humans to do without God.

Hall, additionally, in subtle ways, shows skepticism toward the underlying aim of Arthur's prophetic vocation, to inspire belief in a possible new world beyond "Babylon." Hall is a political radical who hates the Korean War before he goes to it, who sums up afterward, "It was bitter to see that you were part of a country that didn't give a fuck about you, or anybody else," and who, in the present, decades after the Supreme Court's "All deliberate speed" order in 1955, interprets it as designating "the time needed to outwit, contain—and demoralize—the niggers" (*JAMH* 136, 381, 430). And he loves his brother desperately and will do anything, go anywhere, to help him in *his* mission. But Hall shows little confidence that injustice is transient, as a prophetic outlook must assume—as, for example, Francis Grimké shows in assuring his hearers that with trust in God and effort over time, the "gates of hell" will yield (1:618).[5] Grimké, of course, was of an earlier era; Hall's outlook represents a post-civil rights era awareness of the limited changes gained after enormous effort and costs. This mood does not devalue the prophetic moods of earlier decades, but has not found its own key to hope.

More broadly still, while honoring Arthur's effort, Hall places his and others' lives under the lens of a human experience that never changes basically: "Yesterday, we were the children, Ruth and I and Julia: we're the old folks now, and this is what will happen to Tony and Odessa, please God be willing"; "I have wondered, more than once, why I started it [the book we are reading], but—I know why. . . . It is an attempt to face both love and death" (27, 517). This recognition of time, loss, and continuity from generation to generation, true and moving, also implies the emptiness of eschatological claims: life goes on, is lost and renewed, in times past, now, and times to come. What we hope for our lives is that they pass through to completion with some joy and without too much pain, and we hope the same for our children and theirs—with some gains in status or comfort over the generations. For most people, indeed—though they may hope for heaven—questions of social redemption, a new world, seldom arise or seem real, except, significantly, when the whole society stirs, as in the 1960s.

Hall's preconceptions, like Arthur's, have biblical roots, though different ones. Arthur's sources of artistic inspiration lie in the Old Testament Prophets, or

"Nevi'im," and the Gospels and apocalyptic writings of the New Testament; Hall's standpoint is, roughly, that of the biblical "Writings," or "Ketuvim," the group of books dealing with life as lived today (Job, Psalms, Proverbs, Ecclesiastes, Song of Solomon, and others). Rather than focusing on warnings to the nation or on a future society of righteousness and justice, these concern conduct in a "timeless present" (Sweeney, *The Prophetic Literature* 18); each deals with some aspect of ongoing social, individual, or religious life in a society not seen, within them, as subject to basic change. The difference in perspective, Marvin Sweeney argues, is amplified by the Christian Old Testament's placing the prophetic books at its end, after the Writings, in apparent transition to the New Testament's eschatological framework (in the Jewish Tanak, the prophecies precede the Writings, so that they seem to show disruption and then restoration of Israel's ordered relation with God). While the Ketuvim do record doubts—even despair—about God's purposes, life's ordered quality dominates.[6] Among these texts, Hall's tale of a life cut short amid confusion and despair resonates most with Job, whose "Man that is born of a woman is of few days, and full of trouble" (14:1) echoes, we have seen, in Baldwin's artistic vocabulary. Baldwin, we recall, saw life as tragic because death must come, because "one day, for each of us, the sun will go down for the last, last time" (*FNT* 91). Hall shares this idea—"one day, one's shit will hit the earth an hour or so before one joins it, or, maybe, less" (*JAMH* 16)—though balancing it with hope for his children's futures. So there is a strong tragic element in Hall's outlook, further discussed below.

Hall's outlook has, as well, like Arthur's, a characteristic artistic form: for Arthur, Gospel, this novel's dominant music genre, and for Hall the blues. Baldwin, we know, saw blues as the music of those "disasters which can be summed up under the arbitrary heading 'Facts of Life.'" Blues in this sense is closely related to tragedy: it becomes the attitude allowing us to live through the painful or tragic, "ride with it" ("UB" 57, 59).[7] Hall, then, creates a juxtaposition between Arthur's world outlook and his, each with its own biblical affinities and associated artistic genre.

This same comparison of worldviews is implied in Baldwin's title, when placed in text context and traced to its sources. The book title is usually explained as referring to the identically titled Gospel song, whose lyrics several sources give as:

Just above my head
I hear music in the air
And I really do believe
There's a God somewhere.

These words seem to signify hope, and have been glossed, for example, as expressing a "leap of faith in a God who is intuited, but who seems always absent" or as capturing the difficult "struggle of all four major characters to become reconciled with their experience" (Lynch, "Just Above My Head" 293; Scott 169). As the lyrics are not used in the novel, commentators trace them either to standard sources or to Vivaldo's memory of Ida singing them in *Another Country* (313).[8] Yet uses of the title phrase in the later novel defy salvational readings. It appears four times: in Hall's early dream of his bedroom ceiling descending as if "to crush me" and hanging "not more than two inches, just above my head"; twice in Hall's following waking meditation on the sky that "will be there forever, just above my head," when he is beneath "that darker sky, the earth" (15); and at the moment of Arthur's death, when the stairs where he has fallen seem to be "staring down at him from the ceiling, just above his head" (15, 15, 582). So in narrative context the phrase refers not to God's presence or any "music in the air," but to the measureless power of death. Yet, nonetheless, the Gospel lyrics exist and Baldwin expects his readers to "hear" them—in fact, hear "music in the air"—in counterpoint to their narrative uses.[9]

These points make a look at the lyrics' appearance in *Another Country* useful. They occur in Vivaldo's recollection of Ida's singing, but Vivaldo pauses as he remembers: "But was it *music* in the air, or *trouble* in the air?" (*AC* 313). The answer, of course, is that Ida most likely has sung both. The latter phrase, not found in standard printed versions of the song, is prominent in one of its most memorable recordings, Sister Rosetta Tharpe's duet with Marie Knight, "Up Above My Head," which reached number 6 on the "race charts" in 1948 (Visser 32). Baldwin may be thinking of this version, despite differences, or may know the "trouble" lyrics independently. In Tharpe and Knight's version, also with a slightly differing refrain, the singers first "hear music in the air," then "see trouble in the air," and, in the third stanza, hear both (parentheses show the words of the second voice, Tharpe's in this stanza):

Up above my head (Up above my head)
    I hear music in the air (I hear trouble in the air)
Up above my head (Oh up above my head)
    I hear music in the air (I hear trouble in the air)
Up above my head (Oooh-oooh-oooh-ohh)
    I hear music in the air (Ohh-ohh-wa-ohh-wa-ohh)

> And I really do believe (I really do believe)
>
> There's a heaven somewhere (—heaven somewhere)
>
> (Tharpe, Knight)

Tharpe and Knight's lyrics, containing their own echo of Job 14, pose the question whether "music" or "trouble" dominates in our lives. Indeed, the juxtaposition of "trouble" and "music" incorporates the standpoint of blues into Gospel thematics but also reminds us that Gospel is blues experience infused with hope. Standing alongside the lyric of consolation—"music in the air"—the "trouble" lyric points to an ambiguity in prophecy itself, which promises an end to trouble yet also may warn of trouble ahead. Emphasizing this possibility, Tharpe and Knight's duet closes with both singers again seeing "trouble in the air," though still believing there is a "heaven somewhere."[10] The lyrics Baldwin apparently refers to in *Another Country*, then, juxtapose two views of our possibilities—one of hope and one that the "trouble" of present life, and perhaps trouble to come if we seek better, may prove more durable than hope, though this very possibility, in the song, is a reason to believe.

Returning to *Just Above My Head*, we can understand its title in a way informed by *Another Country*. For those familiar with the song's versions, the title connotes a double presence of both "music" and "trouble" above our heads. The title phrase, then, implies the novel's central issue, the hope implied by prophecy and the countervailing doubt provoked by continued suffering, and points indirectly to Baldwin's systematic questioning of all he has told us in this and prior works.

Questioning the Apocalyptic Body

Just Above My Head's portrayal of homosexual love, Baldwin's most extensive treatment of sexuality as sacramental union, is from another viewpoint a study of the effects of internalized self-oppression and the difficulty of maintaining a redeemed consciousness in an unredeemed world. These problems are seen through Crunch and Arthur's concurrent stories. In Crunch's life, we have already seen, they are felt in his equation of maturity with heterosexuality, his inability to recognize (much less integrate) homosexual capabilities in an overall mature individuality, and eventually his psychotic collapse. Arthur's development incorporates self-oppressive ideas less centrally—he is never in real doubt about his homosexuality—through an internalized sense of social norms and so of his own strangeness; isolation from family and others; and later, when in a stable adult homosexual relationship, renewed self-doubt during the last phase of his life. But he accommodates these pressures more successfully than Crunch, and for long keeps them at bay.

Assessing Baldwin's questioning of the apocalyptic body requires distinguishing three factors. Two are complementary: the relative evanescence of Arthur's experience of sacral love—ecstatic interludes that could hardly be sustained at full intensity over a lifetime—and, with this, his varying experiences of love over his life, including the weight of external and internalized homophobia. These factors correspond to the dramas of personal redemption or corruption in other Baldwin novels. Finally, we must assess the residue of utopian possibility that cannot be accommodated fully in present society.

Arthur's experiences of sacral love come rarely. Though the steps are presented in hints and out of order, and his fourteen years with Jimmy are barely covered, we learn that Arthur's intimations of a sacramental sexuality begin in his first love at sixteen and that, twenty-three years later, he dies weighed down in part by resurgent homophobic self-doubt. Arthur and Crunch's early bliss lasts only two or three months.[11] Even before they are separated by Crunch's posting to Korea, Crunch has begun pulling back, though the end of their idyll, for Arthur, is postponed until the terrible year following Crunch's return. It would be easy, then, to regard the couple's ecstasy as mere first love, if not for the weight of sacramental and apocalyptic imagery Baldwin places on it, which seems to signify true possibilities of an altered way to live. There is, apparently, a similarly blissful period, also signaled by sacramental language, as Arthur starts life with Jimmy, about nine years later—Hall's apartment, where the two spend much time that winter, becomes "a kind of joyful tabernacle" (*JAMH* 558).[12] Arthur's affair with Guy has some of these same qualities. Between these times, after the end of his life with Crunch at about nineteen, Arthur is involved in casual pickups at least when on tour with Hall (21), and presumably in New York as well. Hall draws a curtain over Arthur's later years with Jimmy, but from some hints and the fact that they have quarreled and Arthur has gone on alone to London on the day of his death (522, 580), we realize the truth of both halves of Jimmy's summation, "That wasn't no easy scene, our love, but we *did* hang in there, baby, for almost fourteen years" (577).

From the beginning, Arthur faces and must overcome socially constructed, internalized negations of his sexuality. His first kiss with Crunch quickly gives way to "terror" (194), which comes, significantly, not when he is alone with Crunch, but at breakfast with others. The question that makes sweat pour down his back,

"Is this my life?" occurs to him in this company and is an internalization of the non-existence of *his* existence in their eyes. Later, in New York, he will yearn for Crunch's "broken-down, filthy, miraculous room"—it refigures Giovanni's, which David feels as entrapping (*GR* 84–88)—where "only he and Crunch knew what wonders had taken place" (*JAMH* 269). For the homosexual, Baldwin suggests, the sure sense of naturalness found in private space erodes in public space, when thinking by social rules. This public liminality of homosexuality in heterosexual society impacts Arthur, as well, in his and Crunch's need to dissemble their love (194, 192) and, once Crunch is overseas, when Arthur feels that "for the first time in his life, he had something to hide" from his parents, and cannot ask Paul, his father, what he longs to: "What's happening to me?" (264, 267). Though later he will live more openly, at least among intimates, these questions—"Is this my life?" and "What's happening to me?"—resonate with a socially induced sense of his existence as strange and unnatural. Internalized as a feeling of monstrosity, this sense holds Arthur back from Jimmy at a crucial early point in their friendship, though Jimmy is making an obvious play for him: "The boy before him was suddenly sacred, causing Arthur to feel gross, ugly, and clumsy" (470; see 465–72).

The relation between this sense of perverseness and the church culture within which Arthur sings for most of his career is interpretively problematic. At a late point in his trajectory, judgments from this quarter apparently wound Arthur deeply—Hall refers to "spiteful people whose tongues so lacerated" Arthur after his shift in repertory, and Jimmy recalls "when people started talking about us, the way they did, you remember" (6, 575). At the end of his life, Hall believes, Arthur still feels "he will never be released from the judgment, or the terror, in his own eyes," internally marshals "the paraphernalia of the Judgment Day, selects the judges," and wants to "state his case," though, Hall comments, he can be "released from the judgment only by dropping the case" (579). This assessment, in particular, seems to suggest that relentless external and internalized religious homophobia is central in Arthur's downfall.

The supposition requires qualification. First, Hall's scriptural allusions ("the Judgment Day" and others) do not refer literally to God's judgments or even the Gospel community's; the panel of "judges" Arthur is selecting, we will see, is broader and secular—the musical ancestors of his art. Hall's statement does not even refer primarily to Arthur's feelings about his homosexuality, but to a broader sense of dishonor, though homosexuality must be involved in part, as the repetition of "terror" indicates (194, 579).[13] Second, the Gospel and Pentecostal publics themselves, several sources attest,[14] are paradoxically latitudinarian toward sexual and other practices they condemn, when practiced silently by community servants. The gibe by Bumps Blackwell, one of Sam Cooke's mentors, about the Gospel backlash against Cooke, "[Preachers] can be homosexuals, they can drink whiskey, they can do all kinds of sinful things, but they can't sing a pop song" (Wolff et al. 121), points to this latitudinarianism and suggests that the community may have targeted Arthur's perceived artistic apostasy as much as his sexuality.

Most fundamentally, we recall that at a crucial point in his development, Arthur, in Hall's account, "had to pull himself to a place where he could say . . . to all the world, and to *his* Maker, *Take me as I am!*" (472). Though Hall is summarizing a gradual development, narrative sequence implies that Arthur gains this confidence through his affair with Guy and the start of his relationship with Jimmy, which follow soon after. So if, indeed, Arthur eventually loses confidence in his sexuality and its compatibility with his idea of God, this must reflect both acceptance of "the world's" image of God and, also, Arthur's loss of belief in the new world of love that seemed to make his imagined declaration possible. Arthur's internally homophobic erosion of self-acceptance, in sum, derives partly from the loss of prophetic-apocalyptic assurance that is this chapter's main theme.

Both the inability of a consecrated love to sustain itself in a hostile society and the failure of its healing impact affect Arthur through Crunch as well. Arthur's first lover's rejection of their love centers on the core issues of homosexuality as immature and society's judgments as supreme (266, 463). This rejection's effect on Arthur's sense of worth, not spelled out in the text, is felt in the fact that for years he does not quite get over Crunch's absence, hoping "for a long time that Crunch will come to visit him, even, perhaps, come to stay" in the loft he begins renting sometime after their days together (571).[15] Even more, and inferably with the weight of finality, Crunch's later mental collapse bears down on Arthur. It is when Crunch is taken away, Hall judges in a passage I will return to, that the balance of Arthur's life "began to shift into that despair which was to kill him" (213). This shift, we should note, is not only, or even mainly, a matter of internalizing homophobic self-judgment. Rather, Hall implies that the destruction of those he loves in and by a malignant society, and perhaps his own inability to prevent this outcome, help turn Arthur toward "despair."

Sacral love, then, in *Just Above My Head*, cannot exert a lasting healing force amid stronger social negatives. Here, Baldwin revises an implied pattern in earlier work. As both early and recent interpreters have noted, in *Another Country* Eric's love acts as such a force toward Yves, Cass, and Vivaldo.[16] The two characters Eric cannot aid, significantly, are African American and non–middle class. One is LeRoy, his lover in adolescence, who can awaken, trouble, and ultimately heal Eric but, himself trapped in the marginal and dangerous role of a "bad" African American in a small southern town, must part from him. The second is Rufus, whose settled heterosexual identification, and class and racial sense of Eric's whiteness, let him offer Eric sex while "despis[ing]" him (*AC* 46), but who cannot integrate or even consciously recognize his homosexual feelings. Baldwin, then, is aware in *Another Country* that homosexual love by itself cannot heal across social (class, racial) barriers; lasting change requires the tortuous social squaring of accounts we see between Vivaldo and Ida. *Just Above My Head*, however, adds a bitter codicil: homosexual love also cannot heal across gender-identification lines within the same race and class. Crunch, like Rufus, has formed a primary heterosexual identification before his homosexual relationship—he, of the four youthful companions, "made out best with 'the ladies': his term," while in later years he feels "*like something hanging on the other edge of a prick*" (*JAMH* 86), and he will settle back into these roles after his affairs with Arthur and Julia. Crunch can offer Arthur love in the unfamiliar setting of the South but cannot long maintain this love against tacit social expectations in Harlem, his own "public space." Arthur's answering love is incapable, in the long run, of reversing this pattern, of saving Crunch, or of solacing his desolation in a destructive world. So, Baldwin's reassessment of earlier work implies, the apocalyptic body cannot accomplish a lasting transformation, a greater wholeness and recognition of what is potential in the body, within a murderous society's precincts, but only—if at all—in the apocalyptic city.

Arthur, then, cannot fully fend off a "corrosive, internalized homophobia" (Scott 160), or what Hall calls "the double weight of the judgment without and the judgment within" (249), that bears down through his whole life (see also Edelman 69). Yet Scott is wrong to find in this factor the effective explanation for Arthur's deterioration as a whole (160–67), both because she does not account for the impact of the social quiescence of the 1970s or the influence of Arthur's musical choices, and, additionally, because she exaggerates the impact of homophobia as such. Hall, we recall, assesses Arthur as "stronger than Crunch. . . . Arthur could live on stones" (213). In adulthood, with more sexual experience, Arthur's retrospective weighing of his time with Crunch—in a reflection Hall writes for him during his Paris trip—is balanced and clear-headed: "He did not know if he had been lucky or unlucky in his first love. The question did not make much sense. It could be said that he had been lucky, and Crunch had *not* been, but the reasons for that were more mysterious than luck" (463). The person making such a judgment, we can infer, has lived through and surmounted sorrow and loneliness, and is not torn apart by self-doubt and negation. For much of his fourteen years with Jimmy, Arthur is "happy. There is no other way to put it. I saw my brother happy, for the first time in our lives" (557). In the context of his maturation and his long relationship with Jimmy, internalized homophobia does not appear as the central, causal factor behind Arthur's personal decline but, rather, as a weight he bears, at some times with difficulty and at some with grace, until other factors combine their weight with its own.

Just Above My Head's presentation and critique of the apocalyptic body, then, show that sexual love's anticipatory experiences of a new existence remain transient, as should not surprise us in a male- and heterosexual-dominant society. It is not true, in Baldwin's pages, that such a society's judgments inexorably crush those they weigh on. Yet the ability to withstand such judgments must turn in part on a sense of the world as opening toward more freedom or as closed and stagnant. So Baldwin suggests both that the ability to live fully in the body's holiness depends on the transition to a new society, and, more immediately, that the possible falseness of this social hope also may mean hopes to achieve the body's full freedom are mistaken.

Questioning the Apocalyptic City

Besides those about sacral love, *Just Above My Head* raises questions about its own apparent social vision. That redemption, redress for injury, and justice in society as a whole are real possibilities attainable through social action has been a core Baldwin assumption since *Another Country*. *Just Above My Head* highlights the possibility of such a reformation in its extended focus on the civil rights movement and its evocation of Babylon's fall, but also questions that possibility.

This questioning occurs through the novel's projection of difference between its present and past time, including events between the two times that are mentioned in passing but shape the characters' present lives, and through Hall's emphases in narration. The most important background event is the ebb of the social movements that dominated the novel's long fourth section (*JAMH* 285–514). Historically, the sixteen or so years covered by the novel's last section (515–84) saw, first, the climax of radical and revolutionary mass agitation in the late 1960s (omitted in Baldwin's text) and, then, the dying down of mass civil rights and radical activity in the United States between about 1970 and 1975, along with the decline of the period's international radical cultures. In the book's only direct reference to this history, displaced chronologically to the movement's height, during the southern tour when Peanut will be killed, Hall suggests a massive collapse of hope and commitment:

> And when the dream was slaughtered, and all that love and labor seemed to have come to nothing, we scattered: it was not a time to compare notes. We had no notes to compare. We knew where we had been, what we had tried to do, who had cracked, gone mad, died, or been murdered around us. We scattered, each into his or her own silence. It was in the astounded eyes of the children that we realized, had to face, how immensely we had been feared, despised, and betrayed. Each had, with speed, to put himself together again as best he could, and begin again. Everything was gone, but the children: children allow no time for tears. (419)

Hall's meaning, allowing for overstatement, is clear. He refers first of all to the assassinations of the 1960s—of King, evoked by the single word "dream"; Medgar Evers and Malcolm X of Baldwin's acquaintance; Fred Hampton and Mark Clark, and more. Further, in saying that "all that love and labor seemed to have gone for nothing," Hall points to the period's larger "dream," beyond legal changes, of "a social order of justice permeated by love" (SNCC, "Statement"), as well as that time's even more sweeping hopes for a freeing of "Babylon's" captives. In Hall's implied analysis, the dominant unjust society has been reconstituted, on a somewhat altered power basis, at the cost of the overarching aspiration for justice. This retrospective assessment goes beyond the novel's perspective of communal striving over long time to suggest that "Daniel's" hope of "tearing down / the kingdom of this world!" either was never possible or has been sidelined for an entire historical era, leaving it for Hall and others to pass on its memory.

This passage provides a key to the focus of Book Five. The civil rights movement, which bulked large throughout Book Four, quickly disappears as a live force in Book Five. Though most of the events occur soon after those of Book Four, and within the most active civil rights years, they are viewed retrospectively from a present framing perspective (517–24, 574–84) within which Hall's narration shifts to emphasizing characters' individual lives, as if in response to his own statement about people having to put themselves together. The major events are Hall's meeting his future wife Ruth, the commencement of Arthur and Jimmy's love, Hall and

Julia's reconciliation following Julia's return from Ivory Coast, and an overview of Jimmy and Arthur's early years together.[17] These events are told with an accent on ascent toward personal happiness: Hall walks home after his reunion lunch with Julia, for example, "scarcely believing that I could be so happy, or so free. Nothing, after all, had been lost. We were going to live" (557). Conversely, Hall avoids, as long as possible, telling about Arthur's downward path, saying he has "tried, every which-a-way, not to go there" (569). Like his parsing of the Movement's last period, Hall's narrative focus in this closing section is counter-apocalyptic, implying, without stating, that life consists (when we are lucky) of small gains of stability and contentment, not large-scale steps toward righteousness.

Since Hall is writing from a present in which he, his family, Julia, and Jimmy are survivors working to reconstruct their happiness, it is appropriate to ask if his narration reflects the selective memory that Reid-Pharr discusses as its central idea. Reid-Pharr believes *Just Above My Head* is a "hopeful" work because the survivors' lives manifest the ability to "forget" and "re-member," creating for themselves the "world that, if not more just, is at least a bit more comfortable" already referred to (*Once You Go Black* 118). Reid-Pharr views this ability as exemplifying basic qualities of general American and African American life. The very shallowness of Americans' historical awareness, he argues, creates "the incredible luxury of forgetting and thus of choosing a course different from the bloody past." More specifically, Reid-Pharr pinpoints a capacity for disengaging and moving on as basic to the race's life, noting that "generations of Black Americans, faced continually with communal exploitation and personal insult," have "told one another to 'forget it'" (103, 104). Reid-Pharr seems, then, to link the ability to "forget" to abandonment of the utopia of a "just" world in favor of a "more comfortable" one.

Reid-Pharr's summation does capture one essential element of *Just Above My Head*. Hall, in present time, is "forgetting" in precisely Reid-Pharr's sense—not factually, but in present life attitudes. His summary of his long-ago thoughts on himself and Julia, for example, "Nothing, after all, had been lost," even though containing a terrible narrative irony—Arthur's loss then lay unknowably ahead—also embodies an essential psychic trait: we must think so, to move forward. More broadly, Hall is ready, if reluctantly, to live in the "more comfortable" time he has survived into. And yet, Reid-Pharr's perspective misses both an essential part of Hall's outlook and the essence of his art. Psychologically and politically, Hall is too angry at the waste of life, and hates the United States too much, and, artistically, he is too much under compulsion by a vision of truth, to perform the act of forgetting Reid-Pharr assigns.

His not doing so is constitutive of Baldwin's text. *Just Above My Head* is a book of loss, beginning in anguish and ending in tears. Its griefs and terrors are partly those of life as such (Paul's too-early death, Hall's awareness of middle age and vanishing time) and partly those of a murderous society. In present time, of the Trumpets of Zion members, two are dead, one insane, and one, Red, an ex-con and addict (31–33). Additionally, Peanut's grandmother, setting off to look for him after his disappearance, collapsed and died while leaving her apartment (452); Red's mother, who found her, retreated, old at fifty, to Tennessee (452); Arthur and Hall's mother Florence shuns New York because "it robbed her of her son" (6). More remotely, Amy Miller, Julia's mother, died long ago, partly a casualty of her own religious and gender beliefs (163–67); Martha and Sidney lived on, self-crippled by theirs; Joel assumedly survives somewhere, heart corrupt. These are the dead and living dead in Hall's narrative, and his narrative is our source of knowledge: a source, then, of memory, not forgetting. Indeed, Hall's chosen role is as preserver of memory for "the children," as he implies in the passage above and states later (518); as transmitter of memory he is "not reconciled" (518)—to the present, its costs, even in some sense the life he has reconstituted.

Hall's need to transmit memory corresponds to the characters' need. Two questions from his children spark the novel's journey into past time, Tony's "What was my uncle—Arthur—like?" and Odessa's "Who's Red?" after Julia reports her chance meeting with that character (27, 30, 32). Odessa's question leads, circuitously, to Julia's bringing out her Trumpets of Zion photographs, and from there the gates of memory open. Without both personal and communal memory, Baldwin implies, the present, if "comfortable," is incomplete, leaving the non-rememberer in a shadow world. And so Hall's pursuit of memory constructs the book we are reading and prevents consolidation of the narrative on the basis of forgetting.

Further, since the deaths and losses are so terrible, their knowledge prevents an easy conclusion that the present world is good, or as good as a world could be. Inclusion of the communal past is decisive here. A parent's early death, one's own aging, even a brother's self-driven death—balanced by one's own survival and one's children's burgeoning lives—can belong to a narrative of mixed joy and sorrow, essentially unchanging over time; the murder of a civil rights worker and the death in grief of his grandmother can belong to this same narrative only if one affirms—as indeed many would—that exclusionary and brutal structures of power are permanent parts of human life, changing in who oppresses whom but never in essence. Whether or not this is so is the unspoken question behind Baldwin's apocalypticism.

Underlining the novel's questions about the permanence of unjust social power, ancillary details about two characters show this power intact and active in the period between the close of the main narrative and Hall's present time. Red, we know, became addicted in Korea (31, 425), smashed up, Hall's summary implies, by the United States as a power system—he "was thrown into prison for a crime he hadn't committed, then was thrown into the army, and then his ass was hustled to Korea, and he got hooked, as one of the more esteemed American lyricists would put it, over there" (31, referring to George M. Cohan, "Over There," 1917). Red is absent from most of the book's second half, and unmentioned after Arthur's "past seems to drop from him like a heavy illusion" during his encounter with Guy (479), so he works as an emblem of the reshaping of memory that creates the present. But his reappearance in present time, narratively at the start of the book—when we learn through Julia that he has served more than one term for armed robbery, that his wife and children have left him, and that he is on methadone and working with street children (32)—reminds us that "Babylon" persists and continues grinding up those it has ground up many times before.

In a more multi-sided example of this pattern, Hall speaks of the effect of Crunch's insanity on Arthur, in a foreshadowing statement partly quoted earlier, placed at the brightest moment of the couple's first love: "When, many years later, Crunch was dragged, howling, away from us, with that dreadful space in his mouth where his teeth had been, the sands in Arthur's life began to shift into that despair which was to kill him" (213). This moment in Crunch's life, we know, involves his denied homosexual component and his repeated need to beat it down. But it also involves the gap in his mouth, that is, the rage and hate growing from battery by a law officer who was himself a live emblem of the failure to transform society—a black cop serving Babylon, Arthur might say. It involves, too, the failure of a sustaining love among Babylon's prisoners: in Crunch's words, "*White man couldn't* touch *us, if we'd just learn to love each other!*" (37). So Crunch's disintegration partly shows the lasting effect of the restabilization of American power, as well as the failure to somehow rise above that loss with strength to live and oppose; it shows, too, that these events, refracted in Crunch's destruction, play some role in Arthur's crisis, remaining in blood and memory whether recognized or not.[18]

Hall's is, then, a complex, not simple, view of the passion for justice that animated his characters. His overall sensibility, in Book Five and earlier, is counter-apocalyptic, seeing life as cyclic and essentially unchanging, implicitly akin to the world of the biblical Ketuvim. More specifically, his account of the movement's end (429) implies that the struggle for substantive justice has been lost for an entire historical period, and perhaps was never a real possibility. Simultaneously, however, Hall insists on telling his readers of the monstrous waste of lives and hope that is part of his timeless world, that led from the movement's end to this present time, and that continues unabated in it. So Hall reemphasizes the pain that prompted prophetic vision, even while implying his own tragic vision.

Hall is able to do this because of the task he has set himself as artist, which differs from his personal philosophy. That task is, at its simplest, to memorialize his brother. But he cannot do this without also memorializing those Arthur knew, loved, and worked with, their times, their hope of a new life, and that hope's failure. And in telling this story, Hall is driven by a compulsion to truth no less coercive than the prophet's. In this sense, his art is like the prophetic and does what may be called holy work: "My hand is on the Gospel plow, and I wouldn't take nothing for my journey now" (519).[19] Such, roughly, are Hall's personal and artistic visions, which shape his shaping of Arthur's story.

Questioning Prophetic Art

Prophetic art is the third key Baldwin idea that *Just Above My Head* casts into doubt. The doubt is based both on the difficulty of holding to prophetic consciousness in a changed time and, more fundamentally, on questions about the power and efficacy of this kind of art. Baldwin raises these issues through the plot device of having Arthur, sometime in his later career, develop as a "crossover" artist who moves from Gospel and Gospel-inflected music to classic and contemporary jazz and pop, sometimes called "the standards," as his core repertory. Arthur's new focus, Baldwin implies, is a music of light feeling and irony, with a more surface, detached style and a primarily personal focus.

The costs of this shift are monumental. Not at once but in the course of years, Arthur's musical direction takes him further and further not just from Gospel but also from the prophetic art of his early career. The text's scant but definite evidence is that this musical shift leads to a gradual sapping of Arthur's belief in his own worth as an artist, as a community voice, and, ultimately, as the herald of a new world he had once felt himself to be—a "Trumpet of Zion."

Not simply an arbitrary style choice, Arthur's evolution can be contextualized within the historical changes already referred to. The apparent absence, in Arthur's later singing, of scenes like that in the Paris club (501–13) and the prevalence of major arena dates (23) reflect both his star status and, in part, a social shift in the music scene from the turbulence and hope of the 1960s toward the less impassioned 1970s. Baldwin provides no clear chronology, so Arthur's turn may begin either with or before this shift, but, overall, it is in line with the times as well as with career ambitions.

The signposts to Arthur's road are fairly clear when traced. We learn early that at some point Arthur "branched out from gospel," and that as a result, "people in the church . . . turned against him" (6). Later, Hall mentions that around the time of his Paris trip, Arthur "was already being pressured to 'branch out' from Gospel," and "was warily considering this" (453). Finally, at a later point, apparently when Arthur has been with Jimmy for some years, the two discuss the matter, significantly after a day's rehearsing when Arthur assesses, "I feel like we moving [in preparing the song]. But sometimes, I don't know—I'm not sure—I know where." At Jimmy's suggestion, they try a tentative version of a 1945 jazz-pop classic, Buddy Johnson's "Since I Fell for You" (566–68). The stylistic change-up is clear, particularly as the song the two were rehearsing, Johnson Oatman Jr.'s "Lift Him Up" (1903), is an evocation of redemptive sacrifice with a social outreach message positing Jesus's example as the way to "reach the masses, men of every birth."[20]

Baldwin's account draws in part on the experiences of such singers as Rosetta Tharpe, Sam Cooke, Donny Hathaway, Marvin Gaye, and Aretha Franklin, who began as church singers but "crossed over" to or made their careers in mainline club and concert performance. Some, notably Tharpe and Cooke, were known (at least in legend) for suffering the kind of blowback from Gospel audiences that Hall mentions for Arthur. Louis Gallien generalizes about Cooke, Hathaway, and Gaye that "being members of Holiness-Pentecostal churches made it almost impossible to simultaneously integrate secular and gospel careers" (133). Additionally, several of the male artists, especially Gaye, were torn between the ideal of "sanctified" life and their strong sexuality; some, too, again notably Gaye, practiced the eroticizing of Gospel lyrics and "sanctifying" of secular love lyrics noted earlier—further points of contact with Baldwin's portrayal. Even Arthur's commercial billing, devised by Hall, "The Soul Emperor" (22), recalls Gaye and Franklin, "Prince of Soul" and "Queen of Soul" respectively.[21]

While these parallels inform Baldwin's story, some of these artists, specifically Cooke and Gaye, moved toward rather than away from a socially conscious art over their careers—in the same period, the mid-1960s to early 1970s, indicated as that of Arthur's decline. Cooke's posthumously released "A Change Is Gonna Come" (1964), a major hit still widely known today, and Gaye's song and concept album *What's Going On?*, released in 1971 and performed worldwide, provide examples. So, a "crossover" aesthetic and accompanying star status did not by themselves mean a turn from musical idealism. These artists, moreover, did not necessarily lose the Gospel sense of acting as "vessels" (*JAMH* 21); decades later, Smokey Robinson recalled that while working on *What's Going On?* Gaye told him, "Smoke, this album is being written by God, and I'm just the instrument that he's writing it through" (Robinson; also qtd. in Gallien 127). Baldwin, in contrast, provides Arthur with lyrics from standards and newer hits dealing with personal love and loss—from "Since I Fell for You," the final lines, "I guess I'll never see the light / I get the blues most every night, / Since I fell for you," and, from Arthur's last performance, of "Feelin' Alright" (1968), by Dave Mason, "Boy, / you sure took / me / for one big ride" and "Lord knows, / I've got to stop believing / in all your lies" (568, 578–79).[22] Arthur, then, has not compromised his art by "branching out" from Gospel as such, but—in distinction to at least some real crossover artists of his period—is a prophetic-apocalyptic artist who, at a certain point, turns from the prophetic in art.

By his last months, not only is Arthur's career in decline (3), but, Hall believes, "he hated what he was doing" (522). The comment is open-ended, applying in part to Arthur's quarrelsomeness, drinking, drug use, and cultivation of and by "creepy people" (523), but may refer as well to where he has come musically. Jimmy, at least, in present time two years later, feels, "It wasn't him singing, anymore. . . . That's what he felt, I know. You [Hall] do, too. But he couldn't go back, either" (49). While Jimmy's first comment takes in Arthur's whole situation, "he couldn't go back" most probably means he could not reverse his musical evolution. In turn, a loss of belief in his own musical integrity may lie behind Arthur's catastrophic last performance, when, "certain that Jimmy was ashamed of him, and that he should have been ashamed of him," and "drunk, stoned" besides, Arthur suffers a near-total breakdown of artistic control, singing "Feelin' Alright," which he has always handled "as a funky, light, blues-ballad," as personal lament, losing command of the style and tone and, almost, the beat, and barely finishing (578–79). Sometime in these final months, apparently, comes the moment Hall tells earlier as foreshadowing, "when Arthur would cry out, weeping briny tears, *Look! What they done to my song!*" (250). "They" may refer to the agents or producers who initially "pressured" Arthur to move beyond Gospel (453)—that is, to commercial interests in music—or to the "creepy" people Arthur has been hanging with. Beyond these meanings, however, it must refer to Arthur himself, what *he* has done to his song—he, in the last analysis, chose his artistic path. So his tears, most probably, are not just for his behavior and his weakened artistic discipline, but for the loss of the musician he began as.[23]

Some such sense would seem to underpin Jimmy's assessment of Arthur's predicament in his final monologue, which makes three important statements about music and the music world. First, reflecting on his and Arthur's homosexuality and whether homosexuality is "psychological," Jimmy asks, "If that was true, how could we sing, how could we know that . . . *we* are the song we sing?" (575–76). Then, after a pause, Jimmy moves to the points noted earlier on the artist's "song"—that it "does not belong to the singer" but, rather, the "singer is found by the song," whose sound "is the sound of millions and millions" (576). Last, apparently referring to music executives and publicists—"it's absolute bullshit, you know, when they are defending how they make their money" (577)—he sums up:

> Arthur got hurt, trapped, lost, somewhere in there. I had to deal with some of his old friends, lovers, leeches, from Paris to London to Amsterdam, to Copenhagen: all Arthur wanted was for the people who had *made* the music, from God knows who, to Satchmo, Mr. Jelly-Lord, Bessie, Mahalia, Miles, Ray, Trane, his *daddy*, and *you*, too, mother-fucker, *you*! It was only when he got scared about what *they might think of what he'd done to their song*—*our* song—that he really started to be uptight about our love. (577)

In these linked comments Jimmy is partly saying what Arthur has said already: the singer must "make a confession" emotionally if not explicitly (52). So, shame over homosexuality, a running idea in Jimmy's monologue, can stanch the source of the song. However, this is unlikely to be the sole cause of Arthur's shame, if only because some Jimmy mentions, such as Bessie Smith and Mahalia Jackson, were thought or known to be homosexual or bisexual.[24] Equally, turning from the springs of one's most intense musical expression—for Arthur, its redemptive purpose—can itself undermine a sense of truth to one's inner self, and so sap the ability to lay oneself open in music. We can now see Arthur's evolution as mixed, a combination of shame at abandoning his deepest inspiration and of resurgent sexual self-doubt that both feeds and stems from artistic impasse. We can further recognize that while Jimmy's words about the song are not directly meant as criticism, the sequence of his monologue links them to those about Arthur's final phase and so implies a critique: they state an ideal in music that Arthur has lost touch with, becoming "lost," "somewhere," amid compromised art and commercial music production. Finally, we can assess Jimmy's list of those Arthur feared to shame. It begins with "God knows who," the griot or slave singer who created the song, and includes the lineage of those, from Armstrong to Coltrane, who were not necessarily all prophetic artists but created a black *sound*, one that refracted, with artistic integrity and depth, the community's past and the possibilities of its future.[25] This communal tradition, roughly, is what Jimmy means by "*our* song." Arthur's prophetic art has been part of it, and his failure to be true to it is central to his shame. Readers will think of Arthur's moment of exaltation in Paris, when he and Sonny Carr concluded their medley with part of "Another Building Not Made with Hands":

> I'm pleased with what you've done,
> and your race has been won . . . (513)

This is the commendation—from the music's fathers and mothers, not from heaven—that Arthur believes he has forfeited.

This sketched artistic history implies a critique of prophetic art—rather than just of Arthur's turn from it—because of the purposes with which Arthur is shown to have developed his art and the circumstances in which he tried to follow its requirements. The purposes become clear in two short passages placed before and just after Crunch is drafted and sent to Korea:

> My brother, turning sixteen then, was alone, and in torment, and in love. He sang, he had to sing, as though music could really accomplish the miracle of making the walls come tumbling down. He sang: as Julia abandoned her ministry, Arthur began to discover his. But the song which transformed others failed to transform him. (222–23)

> He was singing for Crunch—to keep Crunch safe, and to bring Crunch back, and he was singing for me, to keep *me* safe and to bring me back: he was singing to hold up the world. There entered his voice then, therefore, a mightily moving, lonely sweetness and the people were transfigured and transfixed: he sang to their love and their worry; he sang to their hope. With his song, and standing before the people, he made his confession at the throne of mercy, and knew himself, then, as his voice issued from him, to be redeemed, in the hands of a power greater than any on the earth. His love was his confession, his testimony was his song. (267)

The latter passage shows one of the few moments of full unity in Arthur's life, and exemplifies the nature of his art. His confession—its terms implying Arthur's religious belief, yet broad enough to represent Hall's "human need, translated" (335)—is of love, love of Crunch (and so sexual love) and Hall. This confession connects him to those whose love he sings to, whose brothers, lovers, sisters, parents, children are also in Korea, or on the street, or simply making their way through life, and this connection gives him the ability to make the Gospel message real for them. And Arthur, who must know that his song alone cannot bring anyone home, much less "hold up the world," presumably does believe that all whom he sings to can, and perhaps that God can, and that his voice joins him with them. More than this, in the earlier description he sings with a conviction tantamount to believing—Hall skeptically inserts "as though"—that his song can act as Israel's trumpets did at Jericho, in the story African American tradition has read as signifying entry to the promised country.

There are two warnings in these descriptions, one direct and one implied. The first is Hall's foreshadowing assessment, "But the song which transformed others failed to transform him" (223), referring most immediately to Arthur's pain over Crunch's affair with Julia but also to his later disorientation and shame: he will not find the peace to overcome these tribulations. Hall may, as well, refer to the faith or sureness of better to come that the song should impart to its hearers, which Arthur will not sustain to the end. In essence, this issue tests whether the prophet can long "walk by faith" (2 Cor. 5:7; *JAMH* 15). Baldwin arranges events so that by the time of his Paris performance, Arthur's faith has already been tested severely. Peanut and his grandmother are dead, Red a junkie, his mother gone; only Crunch's full catastrophe lies ahead. Arthur's response in Paris, we know, is to deepen and extend his commitment by accepting the mantle Sonny Carr offers. At this moment, too, Arthur experiences unity—with Carr, his musical elder and prophetic commissioner, and with his multinational audience, whose dream, for a moment in the 1960s, is his. Ultimately, however, these decisions lead back to the same test, in modified form, as time passes without clear signs of a change in the world, and even more as the oppositional energies that in Paris may have seemed limitless weaken and dissipate. Arthur's words to Jimmy at their rehearsal session, "We moving. But sometimes . . . I'm not sure—I know where" (566), would seem to show a sense of purposelessness in his path so far, a sense that what was to be inspirational has become routine, that can be related to this shift in the times. This sense generates a need for a new artistic direction that is simultaneously a move toward a less prophetic art and an accommodation to the world's transition between periods.

The hidden issue in Hall's description, "the song which transformed others failed to transform him," lies in the assumption behind its first half and is also presented by the movement's rise and ebb. Prophetic art has been based on the idea that art can transmit a spark to its hearers that touches something essential—a need or possibility of standing forth, as the earth's despised, to effectuate a new beauty and honor. The waning of oppositional movements suggests that these needs may not be fundamental, or may stand alongside others just as fundamental; people may on some level long for transformation, yet also—in other moods, or after exhausting effort—yearn for some advantage in a hard world and hope to get on with their lives. If so, prophetic art would touch not their very core, but one emotion among many, would be ancillary and not essential, a component or even accidental aspect of a striving among the people that surges and recedes for its own reasons, first welcoming and then ignoring the prophetic message. Unlike the issue of prophetic steadfastness, this possibility challenges the rationale for prophetic art frontally.

Hall, then, questions both the possibility of a new world and the idea of an art that awakens its hearers to this possibility. And, through Hall, Baldwin questions his own lifelong presentation of an art that reveals hidden reality ("unveiling") and can awake to new life those degraded in their bodies and social being. The history of the 1940s to 1970s through which his characters have passed, Baldwin implies, provides the most severe possible test of this idea of art.

Yet, simultaneously, Baldwin's picture of Arthur's disintegration shows the enormous cost of abandoning such an art. The prophetic artist is sustained through life's inevitable suffering by a sense of exalted purpose. And—Jimmy's list of musical forebears implies—this sense of purpose, whether valid in reality or not, is part of communal history and the race's roots, forming its own "long line" reaching to us from the past ("SB" 140), and constituting part of the baseline of the race's life. Without connection to this impulse in black life, Baldwin suggests, the black artist risks losing touch with the sources of genuine art. Further, beyond the matter of personal cost, Baldwin has suggested that prophetic and apocalyptic art spring from the deep reality of injustice and exclusion—both in the United States and over historical time—that the prophetic view, but not the tragic, believes may yield to a future state of justice. So to turn from this art means also to give up the "dream" of justice that created it—in a real way, Daniel's dream of the stone cut out of the mountain—and Baldwin's tale asks us to consider the costs of this abandonment too.

Rain and Fire

At the close of *Just Above My Head*'s action, three ideas seem possible about how to live and make art in a period of restabilization. One would be to embrace the limited changes achieved in the novel's present while accepting that society remains unjust and can be changed only incrementally—essentially, the response of Reid-Pharr's "forgetting" and "re-membering." There is much to be said for this idea. Aside from reflecting how most people process memory to validate current reality, it provides, as Reid-Pharr notes, a way of living in the present while assuming an open, nondetermined future. Yet this response has its own costs. Its closure of historical memory creates a lack of full knowledge in present time, as Hall's children's questions imply; and its flattened landscape of possibility may be only part of what human society is capable of. While Reid-Pharr does not indicate what kind of art his approach would entail (other than this novel itself, in his reading), surely it would lead to the art of feeling and irony that Arthur tried to practice.

A second response would be some version of Hall's tragically-inflected counter-apocalypticism, which would accept, as Hall now does, a future based on private and not large-scale social effort. But in social ideas, as already seen, Hall is "not reconciled" (518) to the new time's combination of important but partial gains with continuing inequality and injustice. In part this may be because he cannot now see how to leave his children an existence more fundamentally just than the present one, and yet knows that the fallen lived for more than this. Hall has assumed a mission of remembering and honoring them, but imagines no way of resuming what they began. This complex of partly contradictory attitudes would generate, in art, an equally complex approach that, we will see, is partly represented in the structure of Hall's narrative.

A third possible response to such a time, of course, would be to continue asserting the value of prophetic ideas and art, and the possibility of overall reformation at some future time. Arthur is the character most associated with prophetic thinking, but the little we know of his recent outlook suggests an ebbing of belief. From the early scene in which he takes down Hall's neighbors and neighborhood (17–18), we know Arthur hates and despises the present reality with which Hall has partly come to terms: "I know," he tells Hall, "that you think I ain't never satisfied with nothing, and—I guess—that's true. In a way." And he adds, "[T]his place *sucks*. With a straw," and, "You ever look into the faces of these people? Oh, baby. Shit. How did *that* happen?" (17–18). And Hall mentions that the day's fading colors "turned to fire in [Arthur's] glass," as if it were a small cauldron of apocalyptic light. We realize, nonetheless, that Arthur sees no way out of present reality: "Oh, baby. Shit. How did *that* happen?" These ambiguous responses, however, tell us little of how Arthur, had he survived into the book's present, would then have viewed prophecy and apocalypse—as valid ways to understand the world, no longer valid, or never valid. And, even if Arthur's own art had not taken a different direction, we do not know what forms a prophetic-apocalyptic art might take in such a period, if, indeed, it were not to harden into a museum of classic performance styles.

Rather than resolving the tensions among these viewpoints, Baldwin allows the major ideas he has held in balance to speak in a final dream scene (582–84) that is simultaneously a portrayal of Hall's sorrow and a prophetic vision Hall cannot fully interpret. Dreams and dream-visions are a prophetic mode important in some biblical contexts, particularly in Daniel, in some sense a governing text for this novel: both Daniel 2, discussed earlier, and the related account of the four kingdoms as beasts from the sea, in Daniel 7, are dream interpretations. Hall's dream, however, represents not an angelic revelation but what his unconscious mind is aware of that his conscious thought cannot assimilate fully, and offers, in place of authoritative interpretation, two song texts and a final comment.

In the dream, Hall, Julia, Jimmy, Ruth, and Arthur (restored by Hall's wish) stand on a country porch, sheltered from rain that hides them from view from the road. The children, younger than their current ages, are also present. The group has come outside in response to a voice—"Oh, children! Come, look here! Look over yonder!"—and they see Florence making her way up the road under the pounding rain, and next to her Amy, helping her hold up Martha, then Sidney and Joel, aiding each other, and a little later Paul. All these figures are associated, for Hall, with the long-ago Christmas day and evening, probably in 1950, that was a high point of the family's love (103–44). Paul and Florence bear gifts that Arthur gave then—Paul a silver acorn locket then given to Hall, "*to protect you*," and Florence a mother-of-pearl comb that flashes in the rain "like lightning flashes, or the pillar of cloud, by day" (582–83; 105–6). The dream is filled with signs of prophecy's futility. The locket does not protect Paul from the rain (582), and despite the comb's prophetic affinities

(Exod. 13:21 and following) Florence cautions against prophecy: when Arthur asks Hall, "Shall we tell them? What's up the road?" she sends "a warning, exasperated look," while Arthur's voice (we assume) confides, "Brother, I'm going away, to leave you" (583) This first dream scene, in which present-day characters (and Arthur) look on those from the past, compresses into one vision the novel's backward look over its decades-long span and the difference in eras this span represents. The succeeding scene, with the family group safe in the house, the children in bed, the past characters gone, poses the novel's main issue in a repetition of Arthur's question, "Shall we tell them? What's up the road?" The question "torments me [Hall], like a song I once heard Arthur sing, and can't now, in my dream, for the life of me, remember" (583)—and the dream moves to the songs and its conclusion, when Hall responds, "No, they'll find out what's up the road, ain't nothing up the road but us, man," and wakes, his pillow "wet with tears" (584).[26]

Arthur's question is in essence about the need for prophecy: shall we "tell them" what will come, in our time, and, so far as we can, in time to come? The two songs signify possible answers. The rain—dream manifestation of the tears that must already be wetting Hall's cheeks—evokes the first, "Hurry Down Sunshine," by Mary Fix and Will Shade (1927). The song lyric, "Hurry down, / sunshine, / see what tomorrow brings. . . . / The sun went down, / tomorrow brought us rain" (583–84), captures the universal experience of hope and disillusionment, of sorrow and "trouble" in life: "Hurry down sunshine," we say, anticipating "what tomorrow brings," only to find that "tomorrow brought us rain."[27] The genre, of course, is blues, Baldwin's music of pain, sorrow, and laughter.

This song, however, is not one Hall has heard Arthur sing (583). It is, therefore, Hall's song; what gives the story meaning in Hall's own eyes. But Hall cannot process Arthur's repeated question, in reality his own, until he hears the song Arthur sang, or one like it, and now he remembers "the beginning of a song I used to love to hear Arthur sing," evoked by Hall's sleeping consciousness of his pillow as the first was by his tears. The verses—from Arthur's time of faith and sureness—are part of "Fire Song," or "When the World's on Fire" (1928), a Gospel standard: "Oh, my loving brother, when the world's on fire, don't you want God's bosom to be your pillow?" (584).[28] These lyrics directly communicate an apocalyptic belief—the world is on fire—and so the song represents, for Hall's dreaming mind, Arthur's alternative to his own skepticism. In his sleep, Hall is able to read Arthur's song in his own way, as embodying a hope he cannot share, and his response frees him to wake and acknowledge his tears.

Hall's words are his answer to the book's central issue: prophecy is useless and redundant, for what is to come is much like what has passed; we are what is "up the road," and our children's lives after ours, not any transformed world. The questioning of all elements of Baldwin's belief system that has marked this novel, then, comes together in Hall's words. Hall's statement provides, as well, an explanation in the language of dream for why he has constructed his narrative as he has, with the movement's end and the novel's present time reduced to scattered references and his protagonist's downward slide all but excluded. Hall has organized his narration so as not to tell "what's up the road," except in hints. But this must mean that, telling the story of characters who "walked by faith" (15), Hall has not wanted to say directly that their faith meant nothing. He avoids saying so, we can infer, not simply or even mainly from psychic denial, but because he recognizes the value of lives lived with hope for the world's future and a larger scope than personal happiness alone. Recognizing this value does not mean the hopes were true. Hall, in fact, believes they were false, but still builds his story around them. Moreover, since the song he remembers for Arthur emerges from his own memory, at some deep level he must hold its truth open as a possibility, even while not accepting this possibility consciously. Indeed, his phrase, "a song I used to love to hear Arthur sing" (584), testifies to his investment in this vision.[29] Hall, then, is a divided character, whose experience leads him to deny transcendent hope but who does not want to advocate a life without it, and this division is why he answers Arthur's question (and constructs his story) as he does.

These points bring Hall's pivotal role in Baldwin's tale into focus. We know already that Hall's purpose in highlighting gaps and approximations in his own narration is to suggest that views of reality besides his may be possible. We know, further, that Hall's vision as *artist* is to include these alternative views in his narrative structure, and so allow contention between opposed ideas of reality. But these, I have argued, are Baldwin's purposes. Hall, then, is Baldwin's crucial creation: Hall's role as a tragic artistic sensibility who is simultaneously true to the lives he has described makes possible the balance between tragic and prophetic consciousness that is Baldwin's design for this book. And so Hall the artist represents a crucial aspect of his creator—Baldwin as mimetic artist, dramatizing clashing worldviews.

Yet Hall does not represent Baldwin as a whole, for he does not embody Baldwin the prophetic artist, who—at the simplest level—is more aware than Hall of the roots and meaning of Arthur's song. The song, then, requires a prophetic interpretation to balance Hall's, one unstated in the text but implied by biblical and Gospel contexts. The song derives from the main New Testament source for the idea of the world's end in fire, the Second Epistle General of Peter, which states that the heavens and earth are "reserved unto fire against the day of judgment," when "the elements shall melt with fervent heat, the earth also and the works that are therein shall be burnt up" (3:7, 10). According to Daniel J. Harrington's commentary, this theme "is not found elsewhere in the NT [New Testament]" (287).[30] This passage, therefore, is the song's source. In fact, the two are generally associated. "The World on Fire," a sermon on this passage by W. A. Criswell, longtime pastor of First Baptist Church, Dallas, and a major figure in southern Baptist history, after urging that apocalypse is a cleansing fire to be hoped for, rather than physical destruction, moves to its conclusion by mentioning a group of seminarians singing the lyrics Hall remembers, and inviting the congregation, "Did you ever hear that? Could you sing it with me? Let's try" (Criswell).[31]

The discussion in Second Peter involves *Just Above My Head*'s core opposition, between prophecy and doubt. Composed not by the apostle to whom it is attributed but most likely by a late first-century writer, Second Peter is concerned with the delay in the "parousia," or triumphant return of Christ, which Jesus's followers had generally expected to occur before the dying-out of the apostolic generation.[32] The letter cautions against "false teachers" or "scoffers" (2 Pet. 2:1, 3:3) who it says arose at this time and, among other points, rejected the promise of apocalyptic transformation by asserting that "since the fathers fell asleep, all things continue as they were from the beginning of the creation" (3:4)—broadly, what Hall assumes about the persistence of joy and pain through time. Second Peter contests the "scoffers'" claim in a two-part argument: their assumption is false and so, therefore, is their conclusion.

> [By God's word] the world that then was, being overflowed by water, perished.
>
> But the heavens and the earth, which are now, by the same word are kept in store, reserved unto fire against the day of judgment. . . . (2 Pet. 3:6–7)

The writer argues that the world has not been unchanged "from the beginning of the creation" but has undergone fundamental change before, in the Flood, and will again. So the verses are relevant to the idea of a renewed world that has guided much of Baldwin's work, and to Hall's challenge to that idea. Additionally, the passage is notable as the origin of the "prophecy, re-created from the Bible in song by a slave," that became the title of Baldwin's most famed work (*FNT* 105–6). That prophecy is inextricably associated with Second Peter, whose words have "found a firm place in Christian consciousness ('the fire next time')," as Harrington notes (287). Arthur's song, then, reminds the knowing reader of Baldwin's past use of apocalyptic reference as it makes its own point that the world is on fire and that it is right and true to expect its transformation. Since Hall's words challenge this belief ("nothing up the road but us, man"), Baldwin's tacit self-reference admits that not just Arthur's but his own artistic perspectives may have been mistaken. And yet this possibility is not his fundamental point.

By the novel's end, Baldwin has, though indirectly, made the cause of Arthur's decline essentially clear: a catastrophic loss of inner confidence and direction, related to the incompatibility of his prior eschatological-apocalyptic outlook with the temper of the new time, and involving abandonment of his prophetic stance in art, loss of a clear redemptive hope, and renewed sexual self-doubt. By contrast, Baldwin leaves unresolved the contention between worldviews that Arthur's history, the novel's juxtaposition of eras, and Hall's commentaries all imply. Indeed, he reintroduces the eschatological-apocalyptic view inherent in the story as an alternative to Hall's, through Hall's sleeping memory of Arthur's time of faith.

In his presentation of opposed perspectives in tension, Baldwin speaks in and from a 1970s moment in which the possibility of transformation seems to have gone out of the world's life. Though we cannot be sure, he seems to understand that this shift is not to be transient, and, in fact, it has lasted into our own time. Baldwin's unique contribution, however, is to respond not by restating (or, alternatively, renouncing) his prior, established view that a basic restructuring of society, whether reformative or revolutionary, is possible and likely. Rather, Baldwin speaks to this moment by admitting to the fullest the possibility that hopes for justice, and his own artistic practice, have been empty, but also presenting the need for such hopes and such an art, and the counterposed possibility that they are true. In doing so, Baldwin responds to what has been seen as a basic quality of the Old Testament literature. In periods of catastrophic defeat, Jon D. Levenson argues, the Hebrew writers did reaffirm God's promises, but not so as to obscure the voices of doubt. Rather, in such moments, "To acknowledge the grounds for doubting . . . itself becomes a religious act" (24).[33] So too for Baldwin—but in his secularized prophecy, there is no word of God, only alternative possibilities that humans must discern and choose between.

Just Above My Head, then, finally works not as lament and memorial, nor even as artistic self-questioning, but as a presentation of choices, one that fulfills Baldwin's role as prophetic artist, for the choices are real and fundamental. Nor would it help

Baldwin's case to privilege one over the other narratively. For, always, individuals and social groups must decide between ways of seeing and living, based on their experiences, the ideas of their times, their driving moral and practical needs. What Baldwin has done as prophetic artist is to clarify the stakes—the costs and implications of each choice. His prophetic message is that in our own lives and time, we each must decide if rain will or can give way to renewing fire.

CONCLUSION

Baldwin's Prophetic Art Today

To teach Baldwin in the second decade of our century is to entangle students in the nation's past and their own present. Their responses attest to his continuing ability to touch readers' sense of deep American reality. Baldwin's daring in raising homosexuality as a serious topic in literature, both in *Giovanni's Room* in 1956 and on the more profound level of *Just Above My Head* in 1979, strikes today's sexually ecumenical readers as inspiringly ahead of its time—sometimes still unsettlingly so, as in its mixing of sacred and sexual language. Baldwin's complex characterizations, particularly in *Just Above My Head*—which includes characters who are flawed and damaged yet self-healing (Julia) and, on the other side, who lose the balance between hope and despair (Arthur)—impress readers used to characters in literature less contradictory than themselves. And his ability to illuminate the back stairways of U.S. democracy—the criminal justice system, the bloody South—as well as the rich plenitude of Harlem's streets touches deep chords of recognition, discomfort, or both at once.

These responses also indirectly make the case for Baldwin's late fiction that has been a running theme of this study. These readers respond to Baldwin's contemporaneity in subject matter, complexity of structure and ideas, evolution of a hybrid colloquial and formal narrative voice, and rootedness in Harlem—all greatest in the late fiction. Finally, the best student readers open up to Baldwin's prophetic content, his vision of the heavenly city, as well as his knowledge of this vision's possible falseness, also a feature of his late work.

Such responses can serve as points of reference for Baldwin's present relevance. But we must turn to the novels themselves to assess the prophetic significance today of each of his major ideas—of attainable transformations in bodily-sexual and political-social life, and of art that shows both human possibilities and limitations. And we must do so, also, to answer the question implicitly posed by the preceding chapter: on balance and in sum, how does Baldwin weight the claims of prophecy and doubt?

Identity and Sexuality

Baldwin's view of sexuality, unquestionably radical for its time, has become the critically most discussed aspect of his fiction, although very largely on the basis of early work. One way to approach the present-day value of Baldwin's treatment is through an evaluation contrary to my own, Matt Brim's in *James Baldwin and the Queer Imagination* (2014). Brim adopts what might be awkwardly called a slightly-post-queer theory standpoint. By this I mean that Brim utilizes the categories of recent queer theory, notably the distinction between "identity" and "queer" or "non-identity," but also questions their adequacy. Brim points to the importance of "paradox" in jumbling and partly dissolving binary oppositions (5), but still affirms the importance of these oppositions, notably the one just mentioned. Brim writes about *Go Tell It on the Mountain*, and Baldwin's treatment of homosexual desire generally:

> I will draw [a line] between "gay" and "queer" in a variety of ways in this book, where the former seems the sign of normative oppression (i.e., identity) and the latter seems the revalued reformulation that escapes the trap of identity. I think that neither characterization is always accurate and that the supposed trajectory from the first to the second employs a potentially dangerous teleology of progress and liberation. . . . [Nonetheless] to the extent that we can contextualize our desires broadly rather than thinking of them strictly in line with or in opposition to other desires, we can potentially achieve a rewarding queer subject position outside of—but not out of sight of—sexual identities. (52, 54)

The first thing to note about this discussion is that Brim does affirm the teleology he questions, though in the modified form of a desirable rather than necessary progression; the positive value placed on nonidentity, "so privileged by queer poststructuralists" (53) remains as hoped-for achievement, though nonidentity will retain some awareness of identity. The second point to note, prior to questioning the positive valuation of nonidentity as such, is how poorly Baldwin's depictions of same-sex and opposite-sex desire fit this valuation. In the discussion above, specifically about John in *Go Tell It*, Brim concludes that "John is probably gay, but . . . also, and perhaps more importantly, queer" (53), apparently meaning that John's sense of his identity is not sexually specific.[1] More probably, John is in an interim moment before crystallizing a specific sense of who he is sexually, rather than moving toward nonidentity in Brim's terms.

The value queer theory accords nonidentity is further called into question by a host of Baldwin characterizations: by David's anguished but definitive acceptance of what he has always been (*Giovanni's Room*); by characters who come to realize homosexual or heterosexual desire, bisexual capabilities notwithstanding, and regardless of social strictures, as true to their deep being (Eric, Vivaldo, Hall, and others). Characters who seem bisexual in some true sense (Giovanni, possibly Crunch at first) have their own deep natures, but are a minority. Baldwin, then, presents sexual nature in a partly, but only partly, divided way. Abstractly and in principle, in essays and interviews, he presents desire as malleable and noncategorizable. (This in itself does not mean everyone's individual sexuality is or could be malleable, but that the range of human sexualities is.) But in fiction, and thus in his sense of experiential reality, he shows people with deep and unwilled natures that they come to terms with to their benefit, and ignore or change only as a self-mutilation (Crunch, Sidney). Despite queer appropriations, such as Robert J. Corber's statement that Baldwin acknowledged "the limitation of identity categories without discarding them altogether" (168–69),[2] in fiction Baldwin is closer than most queer readings admit to seeing sexual behavior as an evolving deep preference, even if Jimmy, in *Just Above My Head*, is the first Baldwin character—in a backhanded statement, "They want you to believe . . . that *we are psychological*"—to specifically affirm a homosexual identity (575).

The third, most fundamental question Brim's approach prompts is whether queer theory's critique of identity and preference for "nonidentity" are themselves limiting and restrictive. Here, one must qualify the term *identity*, and for this reason I refer below to sexual "identifications," perhaps a less totalizing, ontological term.

People bridle, of course, at being defined by a single quality, but from here to nonidentity as a desirable position is not a necessary or obviously positive step. That identities are multiple and overlapping—a root Baldwin idea that Corber stresses in the essay just quoted (167, 169)—does not mean personal sexualities should (or should not) be indeterminate or that a settled sexual identification amounts to a "normative oppression" (Brim 52). Most people live according to such identifications, whether from youth or in adulthood, and these acceptances are not always of loss or compromise but may be accessions of self-knowledge, as Baldwin stresses in varied ways for Eric, Hall, and Arthur. Experience suggests, further, that people want and need identities, work to establish them, use them to define themselves and to push back against imposed identities, and strive to reestablish shattered identities, in their original or modified forms, as African Americans did historically. While not defined only by memberships in groups such as homosexuals or African Americans, identities usually do not ignore these either, but rather incorporate them within a total sense of self. ("Queer," in fact, even with its assumptions of nonidentity, is an adopted identity, as potentially restrictive or expansive as any other.) So, an ontology that reads "queerness" or sexual lability as intrinsically more free than settled identification may not only be oversimple (it is not so easy to attain such a state) but overrestrictive, in comparison to an acceptance of difference and an idea of truth to an unwilled essence as liberating in the limited ways possible in our world.

Further, any sense of sexual liberation needs to specify the kind of society in which it might flourish. However valid, an idea of sexual indeterminacy or nonidentity as positive value rather than object of contempt is, in our present society, largely limited to nontraditional persons, mostly in the world metropole—and fraught with danger even there. An idea of workable sexual plurality and tolerance is in fact somewhat more attainable, but still precarious. Baldwin's conjoining of the ideas of apocalyptic body and apocalyptic city, involving both the possibility of attaining a kind of sexual holiness in a remade society, and the difficulty of maintaining it in our present world, provides an idea of when and how the apocalyptic body may become general. In both respects—his idea of a plurality of sexual essences and that of their flourishing in a society still unknown—Baldwin offers material for instruction, not simply critique.

Baldwin's approach to sexuality, of course, has its own limitations. One, certainly, is its failure to explore lesbianism in an extended way, even if my identification of Ernestine in *If Beale Street Could Talk* is accepted. And, even as applied to male sexuality, Baldwin's ideas of committed sex as potentially sacred and casual sex as usually degrading, noted in a previous chapter, form their own binary that seems oblivious to the messiness and, often, anarchy and absurdity of sex as actually lived: to the social life in and liaisons formed in places like Guillaume's bar; the way so many men follow their dicks down strange streets; the role games people play with casual or serious partners or their own fantasies; the basic fact that sometimes we want a man in our life, sometimes only in our bed.[3] Sex's anarchic qualities, indeed, are part of its resistance to and disruption of social regulation, past and possibly future. Baldwin's seeming assumption that sex must be serious seems unaware of these qualities and unintendedly puritan, an approach within his own intellectual framework to the policing of the body he hated in Holiness churches. However, if he approaches this sort of moralism, Baldwin does not fully go there: Eric's and Leo's tricking in parks and movie theaters, for example, is shown as self-degrading in these characters' own eyes, but not as morally stained. (Baldwin is, also, partly writing historically: this is what many gay men in the 1940s and 1950s would have felt.) Further, Leo's later night with "the boy" is, implicitly, a step in self-realization (*TMHL* 307–8); Arthur's propensity for chance pickups (*JAMH* 21, 472–73) is shown simply as a fact of his gay life. Baldwin is more ambivalent, to the end, on the related matter of the milieu of gay bars and the gay subculture, which he views retrospectively through his early experiences of that culture as involving sexual and racial role-playing ("FAI" 814–29), and it may be significant that he avoids placing protagonists like Leo or Arthur in this setting. Baldwin, in sum, comes to a more humane acceptance of casual sex in later work, though still devaluing it in part.

With its limitations admitted, Baldwin's view of sexuality retains great utopian and prophetic significance. And this is because of the way discussions about homosexuality have developed in the last decades, at least in the United States and Europe. By most, exclusive or preferential homosexuality is not seen as a restrictive ideal in comparison with gender fluidity, but as one of numerous possibilities, including these as well as trans identities and others, that all deserve acceptance. At least a portion of today's youth recognize homosexual behavior as normative—that is, one part of human life among many, not needing specific explanation or justification. And because homosexual love, whether exclusive, preferential, or occasional, is normative in this sense, it acts, for this segment of twenty-first century youth, as a synecdoche for human love in general. To these readers, Baldwin's presentation of a homosexual love moving toward openness and affirmation suggests the same for all forms of love.

Nevi'im and Ketuvim

Looking at Baldwin's idea of a transformed world requires a broader vantage point, both because there is no sustained critical discussion on this issue as on Baldwin and sexuality,[4] and because the subject itself necessitates a broad cultural-historical perspective. As noted in my introduction, Baldwin participates, in part, in an alternative, nonsecular "working narrative" of U.S. culture (Brooks 441) reaching from the seventeenth and eighteenth centuries through to the twentieth (and beyond). Baldwin absorbed this inheritance from family background, general African American church practices, his early Pentecostal affiliations, and, later, the part-secular, part-religious outlook of the civil rights movement. Though just one part of this mix, the Holiness-Pentecostal element is particularly important. These trends in black and white worship arose over the time span in which dominant U.S. and European cultures were growing more secular, commercial, and (in the U.S.) focused on the country's new international power. In opposition to these tendencies, these religious cultures emphasized a coming time of the "latter rain" when the harvest of ages would ripen. These beliefs were nonsecular in content and nonempiricist in method—based on varied combinations of faith, inspiration, biblical study, and ministerial authority. Importantly, this alternative outlook provided a way of standing against the dominant culture, as in C. H. Mason's World War I preaching urging his hearers to "trust in God" rather than in the warring states.

Baldwin, we know, attacks this church culture for what, by his time, he saw as a hardened amalgam of sexual repression and withdrawal from active challenge of the surrounding world. Nonetheless, he arguably gained from this early milieu an intellectual practice of viewing dominant culture from outside, as both contingent and transient. And, like the traditions just mentioned, this intellectual practice was in important ways nonsecular in content and nonempiricist in method, incorporating a fundamental but unprovable belief in realizable possibility: "[W]e can all become better than we are. I know we can" (*James Baldwin: The Price*). This inheritance became the basis for Baldwin's ability to propose, early on, an eschatological alternative within existing reality.

We also know, however, that Baldwin was thoroughly at home in other, secular and empiricist, cultures. These included, variously, the mainly-white, second-generation immigrant, partly Jewish intellectual and literary atmosphere of his high school; the street-level African American life he admired but kept at arm's length—essentially the culture of the blues; and, finally, the secular, skeptical, again partly Jewish, liberal-radical political and literary cultures of his Greenwich Village days and early publishing. (The magazines he began publishing in, *Partisan Review*, *Commentary*, *The New Leader*, and others, were a microcosm of this culture.)[5] From these sources, he took a sense of life's continuity across time that, previous chapters have shown, jostled in his thought with his emphasis on the sacral and salvational.

These varying outlooks, both present in Baldwin's imagination, I have referred to using the biblical categories of the Nevi'im and Ketuvim, or Prophets and Writings. These, we remember, are the divisions of the Old Testament and Jewish Tanak whose essential standpoints are manifested in Arthur and Hall Montana's outlooks. Baldwin's cultural inheritance, then, drew partly on the viewpoint of the Ketuvim, as well as on the secularized Jewish culture around him, with its emphasis on ethical conduct in the present world, and partly on that of the Nevi'im, seen through a Christian lens as anticipatory of the New Testament, as well as on the New Testament itself and still-resonant church teachings stressing the future reality of new life.

Baldwin's simultaneous fluency in these dual narratives provides unique strengths. In one quite specific way, an aspect of his secularist thinking noted earlier, his Feuerbachian idea of God as a human construct, offers—seemingly paradoxically—a clue to the reality he seems to assign to the sacred and apocalyptic, qualities that, we have seen repeatedly, for him resist reduction to the metaphoric. In place of reading reductively, we can view such references partly as Feuerbachian projections: if God is, as Baldwin asserts, a human "creation" ("PI" 596), then the sacral and apocalyptic are parts of human need, real components of what humans seek and perhaps (Baldwin hazards) can create. Yet what Baldwin does *not* take from this view of God is also important. He does not—as does his character Hall (*JAMH* 335)—draw the conclusion that we should dispense with the holy altogether and rely on ethics and good conduct alone. Baldwin's biblically-derived language and paradigms, working on what I called in chapter 3 an "in-between level, neither specifically theistic nor simply secular," imply, rather, that in intelligible ways the world he envisions does genuinely embody sacral promise.

More broadly, the presence in Baldwin of both secular-empiricist and nonsecular-nonempiricist inheritances, and the viewpoints of the Ketuvim and Nevi'im, allows him to express two impulses present in all of us, regardless of which tradition we grew in: longing for a better world, with its unavoidable belief in what does not yet exist, and attachment to this one, both from life preference and from the effort and risk required to seek change. Baldwin's footing in both "narratives" grants him, then, an ability to give artistic form to clashing voices that exist in each of us.

But, they do not exist in everyone in the same proportions, or without change—not now, for example, as compared to the 1960s; and this fact complicates assessment of Baldwin's prophetic significance. In today's life, under the weight of a social construction of present reality as the only one possible, and in the tacit acceptance of powerlessness that passes for democracy, the voice of the Ketuvim is paramount and that of the Nevi'im can seem unreal. "Women," students will write, "have been oppressed since time began," a remark I usually answer with a joke (time began fourteen to seventeen billion years ago, women are more recent) but that makes the serious point that human life always has been and will be a structure of oppression. Or: "Racism will always exist." *Why?* Because that is the voice of the Ketuvim. Only rarely do today's youth hear the voice of the Nevi'im—perhaps when reading Baldwin on, say, a meeting for civil rights in Richmond, held "in the ordinary black church, Mount Olive or Ebenezer or Shiloh, a proud stone edifice with a yard and steps," where Hall becomes "aware of the music, coming from the choir, but pounding from the walls. . . . People are standing in the aisles" (*JAMH* 400–1). Then, readers realize, could the sun rise on a day of hope and set, that night, after a day of hope.

Baldwin's great merit as a novelist is to bring the world of the Nevi'im—of prophecy, warning, hope, redemption, and the city he thought possible—before us. It is his great merit to ask one of the great questions: can our lives change? But this has meant, given the predominance of the Ketuvim in everyday life, that this part of his meaning is not always grasped, by scholars or ordinary readers. Based on their experiences and backgrounds, student readers may find it easier to grasp his idea of homosexuality as sacred, for which there has been some social spadework in recent years, than his belief in a possible remaking of society by its own despised. That idea, once common coin, now can seem counterintuitive, even puzzling. African American students, in particular, seem today to believe, rather, in a future that will not change in any basic way, in which they will seek to live with dignity and gain social traction, and remain prepared to fight discrimination, but will never be truly equal or free.

A similar point emerges from some recent literary treatments of race, notably Ta-Nehisi Coates's 2015 book-essay *Between the World and Me*, modeled partly on Baldwin. Coates's conception of African American identity, an ecumenicized version of the Black Nationalism he grew up with, is U.S.-centered, as was Baldwin's despite his cosmopolitanism, later emphasis on Third World revolution, and increasing, if critical, interest in Africa.[6] "They made us into a race," Coates says of white Americans and the U.S. social system. "We made ourselves into a people. . . . [We] have voyaged through death, to life upon these shores" (149). What Coates does not share with Baldwin, he makes plain repeatedly, is transformative hope. In his experience, Coates tells his son, the universe's moral arc—referring to King's paraphrase of Theodore Parker—"bent toward chaos then concluded in a box," and so, "You must resist the common urge toward the comforting narrative of divine law" (28; 70). Coates refuses, then, to articulate a hope for positive change, besides the precarious survival of the embattled black beauty he celebrates.

Inferably, Baldwin realized the difficulty of making redemptive belief seem real in the time he and his characters had lived into. He countered this difficulty in deciding, through Hall, to give the greatest weight in his last novel to the time of hope and to his protagonist's commissioning as apocalyptic prophet. But it was also right and true for Baldwin to recognize the two great patterns in thought and, in a period of restabilization, to balance Hall's voice against Arthur's—and, in Hall's final dream, the two voices of his implied reference text: "Since the fathers fell asleep, all things continue as they were from the beginning of the creation" and "But the heavens and the earth, which are now, by this same word are kept in store, reserved unto fire" (2 Pet. 3:4, 7). So it is not easy to decide if Baldwin's prophetic significance lies most basically in revealing ("unveiling") possible transformation, or simply in demanding that "Israel"—his readers—choose. We will have to look elsewhere than at this novel's structure to find his preference.

Nonsecular, Postsecular, and Prophetic

Baldwin now seems more and more relevant, I proposed in my preface, because he is able through religiously-inflected language to evoke the crisis of the nation. If true, this point identifies a dimension of his present prophetic significance that suggests reviewing his relationship with the postsecular. My introduction suggested two points of relevant difference with the literary and political postsecular. First, Baldwin remains apart from models of the postsecular in his focus on basic change. This aspect of his work can stand not only as a difference but as a historically prior critique and correction. Fundamental in how a theorist like John A. McClure presents postsecular literature—and in many of the works he discusses—is what he variously terms a decoupling of religion from "projects of power and grandeur," a refusal of "imagined spiritual transcendence," and a repudiation of "anything like full redemption," along with the tentativeness of postsecular projects of community-building (13, 15, ix, 19–21). For McClure, this literature's distinctness from the prophetic and apocalyptic is basic. It derives both from the "finitude" and "fallibility" (13) he associates with "weak religiosity" and, more basically, from the historical conjuncture in which postsecular literature arose in the 1970s and 1980s, which he sees as one of crisis and collapse in secular politics. McClure, that is, relates this literature to a widespread sense, in the period from about the mid-1970s onward, that the historical "horrors" that marked the twentieth century, and "the comprehensive improvements that did not," mean that "the conventional political options of modernity are exhausted" (11, 21).[7]

This same conjuncturally derived sense of exhaustion—also, we know, the subject of *Just Above My Head*—can, however, be seen as the basis for critique; what McClure and those he cites see as a lesson of history can appear from outside its historical period as a viewpoint characteristic of that period, much as nineteenth-century ideas of progress that then seemed widely evident now appear simply as leading nineteenth-century ideas. So, the rejection of large-scale change that characterized postsecular literature and social thought can be regarded as a common, but not universal, response to a specific conjuncture, from about 1970 to 2010, in which the belief and energy needed to seek such change—including prophetic belief—receded, whether temporarily or not. One feature of the conjuncture that opened around 2010, in contrast, is a widespread, and extremely mixed, questioning of existing social-political norms and structures; and this questioning is a point of relevance for systemic critiques such as Baldwin's.

A further limitation in postsecular thinking emerges when its modeling of social change is placed in juxtaposition with Baldwin's emphasis on the importance of the utopian and prophetic-apocalyptic in the lives of the disfranchised. My example here is William E. Connolly's widely-cited *Why I Am Not a Secularist* (1999), which, to its merit, considers social change at length. Connolly outlines a model of "militant, experimental, and persistent political movement[s]," starting outside the normal political process, through which identities previously "not acknowledged" or "*below* the register of justice" seek recognition, and of the consequent shifts in dominant identities once they extend recognition (47–70, at 51, 63). This model goes beyond the frequent postsecular idea of dialogue between recognized secular and nonsecular identities to theorize how once-unrecognized groups gain inclusion. But its focus is limited to the recognition of "identities," a form of conceptual inclusion, and stops short of considering attempts to change institutional power, social relations, and street-level force and violence. Significantly, Connolly takes examples from movements of women, homosexuals, Native Americans, and others, but does not discuss the historical labor movement or the U.S. civil rights movement, struggles that sought not only recognition of identities, but changes in actual power and life conditions. When the former goal is satisfied without the latter, one portion of an identity achieves recognition while another, with different conditions, sinks again "*below* the register of justice," and for many African Americans and Hispanics, as well as working-class whites—though in different ways—something like this process occurred over the decades under discussion. Connolly, at least, fails to theorize how this outcome might be avoided.[8]

These aspirations to real change in power and conduct—to greater access, more secure rights, less exploitation and victimization, less subjection to violence—as well as more far-ranging hopes for a "social order of justice" and for "Babylon's" fall—are what the utopian and the prophetic-apocalyptic are about, whether in art or general culture. But, these aspirations are also rivaled and contested by regressive outlooks, such as jihadist fundamentalism and European-U.S. xenophobia and bigotry. So, to answer the question implied at the start of this section, contextualizing Baldwin in relation to the academic postsecular suggests that this interpretive category has been too conjuncturally based and too narrow in social scope to account for what has emerged in the last decades as a wide and mass-based rejection of things as they are, but one in which regressive ideals, as yet, far outweigh utopian. We cannot yet know, of course, if, in our no longer stable political world, the latter will grow strong and deep enough to challenge the former. We do know that Baldwin's emphasis on the systemic, as on the prophetic and eschatological-apocalyptic, is basic; by instinct, Baldwin thinks in terms of the large-scale oppositions that mark our period—international or national community, plural-inclusive or communal-exclusive culture, and more—and of general reformation, and these preferences are part of his present relevance. But this point by itself does not resolve the polarity between prophecy and doubt.

Blues and Gospel

Blues and Gospel, with their affinities to the Ketuvim and Nevi'im, are the music genres most consistently important to Baldwin—Gospel from childhood, blues in adulthood (Miller, "Using" 90–92). Arguably, they are coequal in his imagination. Yet, as noted earlier, commentaries on Baldwin and music have usually elevated blues (or blues and jazz) over Gospel as his primary affinity. One of the most thorough general discussions, D. Quentin Miller's "Using the Blues: James Baldwin and Music," notes the importance of the four genres of jazz, blues, classical music, and Gospel in Baldwin's works (83), emphasizes "the deep influence of gospel on Baldwin's aesthetic and on his thinking" (93), and gives a strong, sustained account of Gospel's participatory character (94–95). Yet Miller presents blues as primary over Gospel, not only through his title, but by emphasizing Gospel's blues-like qualities. Miller calls it "a form of the blues in a religious idiom" (92)—rather than, partly, a use of blues forms and techniques for religious expression—and argues that, in a song like "Savior, Don't Pass Me By," *Just Above My Head* uses "black suffering as expressed in gospel and blues music [as] a unifying, connecting force" (106–7). Miller calls this novel Baldwin's "fullest expression of the intersection of the blues, the tragic musician, and the African American experience" (102). Missing in this account is Gospel as an expression of hope, not suffering alone: "Savior, Don't Pass Me By" is not *only* "a cry for salvation" (Miller 106), even in Arthur's and the Trumpets' performance, but also an expression of the gospel's unifying power and of prophetic hope:

> When Jesus was passing by
> He heard the woman cry
> If I could but his garment touch
> I would go and prophesy. (Tharpe, "Saviour" 16–19)

So, ultimately, Gospel is misread, or read partially, if taken only in light of the Ketuvim, as part of the universality of suffering, and not also in that of the Nevi'im, as an expression of what is also universal, hope.

Baldwin himself, it is true, is partly responsible for this emphasis on blues' primacy in his thinking. He stressed the blues' influence in essays and interviews, as Miller notes ("Using" 90–91), and it is attested in titles (*Jimmy's Blues*), part-titles and epigraphs (*AC* Book One), and text quotations (Bessie Smith's "Shipwreck Blues," "Long Old Road," and "In the House Blues," *AC* 232–38). Gospel and hymn references may be less obvious to the general reader. Those in *Go Tell It* can be discounted as given by the setting and subject. Others may seem only characterization, such as Ida's use of "Precious Lord" and her fondness for "Just Above My Head" (*AC*

258, 313); some may simply be less known than familiar blues titles, like "Any Day Now" in *Another Country* Book Two as compared to "Easy Rider" in Book One. But cumulatively such references are substantial, act as counterpoints to blues allusions and quotations, and express important thematic shifts, as, for example, *Beale Street*'s "Zion" allusion and the appearance of "I'm Going to Run to the City of Refuge" in *Tell Me How Long* Book Three suggest redemptive-apocalyptic themes in these works.

The remaining question is what the relationship is, in Baldwin, between blues and Gospel, and between the standpoints of the Ketuvim and Nevi'im that these artistic forms embody. Here we observe a double paradox. First, I have identified a shift away from blues as fundamental to Baldwin's presentation of prophetic art. This shift is first heard in "Sonny's Blues" as one in style and expression, not genre—toward a music calmer in feeling that yet evokes past and future and tells us how we may "cease lamenting" (140). A similar transition occurs as a genre shift in Ida's move from "Since I Fell for You" to "Precious Lord" (*AC* 254, 258)—significantly, the move Arthur executes in the other direction in *Just Above My Head.* In *Just Above My Head* itself, the blues-to-Gospel shift occurs in Arthur's scene with Sonny Carr, and in Arthur's musical development a comparable evolution takes place from general to apocalyptic hope. So, some movement from suffering to hope, from endurance to victory, would seem a basic Baldwin musicological and thematic fingerprint. Yet, in *Just Above My Head,* what was already presented in this way in narrative Baldwin re-presents in the final dream as a juxtaposition *between* genres, as part of this novel's questioning of its premises and of Baldwin's challenge to his readers to choose between prophecy and doubt. Presenting the relationship of blues and Gospel in two ways, as thematic-generic progression and as juxtaposition and alternative, is the first paradox.

The second is that Arthur's turn from Gospel is ruinous for his musical direction and self-conception as an artist, so that the questioning of the blues-to-Gospel progression just mentioned is itself questioned by the effects of the shift for Baldwin's protagonist. Arthur's loss is not one of artistry, at least until his final months. The "standards"—the jazz and pop-based repertory that he embraces—can be the vehicle for supreme artistry. It is notable that Marvin Gaye, whose "crossover" history may have been one model for Arthur's change in direction, began experimenting with the "standards" in his later career; Harry Weinger, Universal-Motown vice president and archivist, remarked on this move, "Can you imagine? Imagine Marvin at sixty [doing] 'Bewitched, Bothered and Bewildered' and 'At Last'!" (Dyson, *Mercy* 20). These songs, sung decade after decade as great artists' home repertory, sublimely embody the repeating experiences of life: new love, loss of love, aging, choice of life paths. They are, then, an artistic expression of the life stance of the Ketuvim, and in critiquing Arthur's change in repertory Baldwin would seem to be critiquing this stance as well as presenting it as possibly true and valid.

Baldwin, then, has presented blues and Gospel—like Ketuvim and Nevi'im, and parallel to them—as fundamental and coequal modes of expression, embodying fundamental life stances. Baldwin's idea of individual life as tragic because inevitably lost—and, before its loss, *as* loss—makes blues foundational in human experience. And yet his idea of society, that the struggle for dignity is *not* bound to go down in darkness as one's own life is, means Gospel is also fundamental. Yet it is insufficient to note this double reality and leave matters there; when we compare these genres, we see other differences besides those already mentioned. Both reflect root experiences—of pain and hope—lived by many millions. But while blues shares its pain, it also retains ownership over it, holds the pain to itself. One can listen to or sing a classic blues, of course, but one does not join others in singing the blues. Blues is personal to the core, expressed individually as it is lived individually, at four in the morning. Gospel in contrast gives up ownership to a community, asks others to join in the expression, feeling, and hope that the song imagines.[9] While Gospel can be performed solo or with a group or choir to an audience, its essence is participatory, and in a church setting it is almost always sung this way. Miller notes that in Gospel "the audience is encouraged to join in the performance through singing and clapping . . . and although the vocal soloist temporarily breaks away from the group, the emphasis is on the communal production of music rather than on individual performances" ("Using" 94–95). This quality can be heard in a performance of "The Comforter"—the hymn Arthur sings in the church near Atlanta just before Peanut is kidnapped—by the choir and congregation of the Church of God, Greenville, Ohio: the six-minute recording begins with vocalists and choir but, gradually, the whole congregation comes in, singing and raucously shouting ("The Comforter"). Something like this tumult, we realize, may have been heard in Baldwin's fictional church.

If sung by a community, so is Gospel also music *of* a community and an effort to build that community. This is, so the singers hope, the community of those who "moved on the bloody road forever, with no continuing city, but seeking one to come" (*GT* 207). And since this music is communal by intention, it also risks the distortions and betrayals that can occur when sharing one's personal vision—the haughtiness, self-righteousness, and exclusiveness that Baldwin's views of the

Gospel and Holiness communities show so clearly. (Consider, for example, the theological "correction" represented by Baldwin's change in "The Comforter's" lyrics—"let every mortal voice proclaim" in place of "every Christian voice" [*JAMH* 447].) But these risks must be taken because of the nature and purpose of this music.[10] This communal essence means, then, that Gospel moves beyond the artist's control, and additionally that its goal may never be reached, since the goal is not simply an attitude but a change in how people live—here, in our world, since, we know, the heavenly city lies on the remade earth. And so the risks of Gospel are greater than for the blues.

So Gospel would bear comparison with Baldwin's idea of love. The essence of that idea is the willingness to risk: David may achieve love with Giovanni, Jacques tells him, "if only you will *not* play it safe" (*GR* 57); Eric tells Vivaldo, "The life you think you *should* want . . . is always the life that looks safest" (*AC* 336); most of all, Hall imagines for Arthur, "He dreams about Jimmy, and comes, almost, to prefer the dream because dreams appear to be harmless: dreams don't hurt. Dreams don't love, either, which is how we drown" (*JAMH* 471–72). Love, too, for Baldwin, involves a recovery of innocence within experience, so that Vivaldo with Eric feels "clear, washed, and empty, waiting to be filled" (*AC* 386). Love, then, is about the risk that may achieve a state approximating innocence within adulthood and experience.

These points are true as well of Gospel, which, without being too fanciful, can be said to be, in Baldwin's presentation, an act of risk to achieve a community of hope: Arthur, we remember, "sang to [his hearers'] love and their worry; he sang to their hope" (*JAMH* 267). Baldwin's Gospel is an act of risk in that all human history tells us its community of love cannot be, tells us the dreamers will die too far down a country road, the new planet of love will vanish on approach. Against that assurance of experience as loss and compromise, Gospel offers only a "dream" (*JAMH* 419) that is not a substitute for risk but its embodiment—of a new and complex innocence, a breakthrough in consciousness as in social power. So while for Baldwin blues and Gospel are each supreme, coequal ways of finding "order" within the chaos of experience (*AC* 302), Gospel stands higher because it reaches out and risks all in a double move toward a possible community and a possible future.

If this is true, if Gospel is in Baldwin's terms an act of love, then we can understand which choice, of those that end his final novel, Baldwin would wish us to make. We can understand, too, his self-referential choice of songs for Hall to remember from Arthur, for at the close of *The Fire Next Time*, based on the same Bible text as Arthur's song, Baldwin asks us, in his own person, to "dare everything" to rebuild our country and our world (105). And we can understand, lastly, Arthur as not just protagonist but—alongside Hall as chronicler—Baldwin's prophetic artist-hero, who also dared everything, only to lose his way and die in the salt of despair: for the sake of his "loving brother," for us, Baldwin's readers, in our own time.

Could he speak to us now from where he has been for over thirty years, Baldwin would have much to say about our present time. He would have no difficulty recognizing the online news—the arrogance and contempt of police, now slightly disguised by current political vocabulary; the stomach-churning malevolence, cowardice, and hypocrisy of political leaderships; the beauty of those who go into the street to march, and sometimes to trash and burn, for justice. All this would be too familiar, as, too, would be the long absence of prophetic hope, now, perhaps, beginning to break earth, nourished by the latter rain (*JAMH* 534; James 5:7). Baldwin would, I think, understand how impoverished we have been by this lack, how dry our throats and how lost our stares, would wish, for our sakes, that we might receive the gifts of hope and anger, and would say, with his namesake Jimmy (*JAMH* 538), "Welcome to the slaughter, children."

Notes

PREFACE

1. I refer to Clarence E. Hardy III's *James Baldwin's God* (2003) and Matt Brim's *James Baldwin and the Queer Imagination* (2014).

INTRODUCTION

1. Sondra A. O'Neale's contention that in the 1980s Baldwin became a member of "one of the largest Baptist churches in Washington, D.C." (131 and 122 n. 21), repeated by several others, seems to be a legend; none of Baldwin's main biographers, James Campbell, David Leeming (the most reliable), or W. J. Weatherby, mentions the point, and Baldwin did not live in Washington in these years. In email communications (July 9 and 15, 2014), Eleanor Traylor, whom O'Neale mentions as a principal in the incident, remembers specifics differently and states that so far as she recalls, Baldwin did not join the church.
2. Early essays by Shirley S. Allen ("Religious Imagery"), Charles Scruggs, and Rolf Lundén exemplify the first approach; several essays by Michael F. Lynch as well as book studies by EL Kornegay and Josiah Young, represent the second. For the third, besides Hardy, see Macebuh and O'Neale.
3. Kornegay argues implicitly against Hardy in rejecting the thesis of Baldwin's "rage against

an angry God" (3), and explicitly in some later references (e.g., 16–17). Young accepts much of the "angry God" idea but believes Baldwin supersedes it in *Tell me How Long* and elsewhere (141). Vincent Lloyd, similarly, argues that Baldwin "transformed, rather than rejected, his father's Christianity" (172).

4. Those affirming a "white God" include, for example, the culture that has brought the world close to nuclear destruction (*FNT* 57) and white people who cannot accept "the dark gods, who live in them at least as surely as the white God" (*NN* 136).
5. Examples include the churchgoers and scoffers in *Go Tell It* and the Rivers and Montana families in *Beale Street* and *Just Above My Head.*
6. See, for example, Zevit chap. 8; Weems.
7. Besides Petersen's essay cited here, see his *The Prophetic Literature*, 90. On apocalyptic literatures, see, for example, Blount, *Can I Get a Witness?*, especially chap. 2; Collins, *The Apocalyptic Imagination*, chap. 2 (on Daniel); Rowland, "The Book of Revelation."
8. On God's assumed enmity toward oppression, see, for example, Absalom Jones and Richard Allen as discussed below. On early African American Christianity overall, see at least Frey and Wood, Sobel, and Raboteau, *Slave Religion.*
9. For discussion, see LaRue 19, 114–15.
10. With specialized exceptions, notably the critical literature on *Go Tell It*, this process has not been studied in detail. Exceptionally, in a major book chapter and a later anthology essay, George Shulman explores Baldwin's use of prophecy models to announce "the conditions we *must* acknowledge *if* we are to flourish" (*American Prophecy* chap. 4; "Baldwin, Prophecy, and Politics" 117). Shulman's focus, however, is solely on nonfiction, and, in fact, largely on pre-1968 works.
11. "Weak religiosity" (or "weak religion") is a key idea for McClure, discussed throughout his book. McClure's is just one theorization, but similar to others. Manav Ratti, for example, discussing postsecular literature in India and Sri Lanka, says it values "a non-secular secularism, a non-religious religion" (xx), an idea similar to McClure's "weak religiosity."
12. Viswanathan focuses on the persistence of the nonrational and imaginative rather than on ideas of prophecy and apocalypse, but her point seems applicable to the latter.
13. I draw the phrase "taking authority" from an undergraduate thesis on Frederick Douglass by Joshua Bolden, "Inside the Mind" (2013). Bolden uses the phrase to characterize Douglass's penchant for turning oppressors' ideas to his advantage.
14. Since Luther's time scholars have considered Hebrews "deutero-Pauline," that is, by an author writing under Paul's guidance or in his tradition (see Craddock 6–7). But in common parlance Hebrews is by Paul, and Baldwin so cites it (e.g., *Evidence of Things Not Seen* [v]).

15. On this view of Paul, see the introduction in Wills, with instances from Jefferson, Nietzsche, Shaw, and others.
16. Uses of Paul's formula include, for example, Reverdy C. Ransom, *The Negro: The Hope or the Despair of Christianity* (1935): "Is not the day at hand when the weak may arise and confound the mighty?" (x–xi); Anna Julia Cooper, *A Voice from the South* (1892): "Do you *believe* that the God of history often chooses the weak things of the earth to confound the mighty, and that the Negro race in America has a veritable destiny in His eternal purposes[?]" (299).
17. See, for example, *Go Tell It* 105 (Deborah's rape brings "dishonor" in the world's eyes); *Giovanni's Room* 55 (David and Jacques debate who is more "despicable"). For Rufus's penis as "despised" and Eric's life as "filth" and without "honor," see chap. 3, as also for Arthur fearing to be "despised" by Crunch.
18. On varied senses of *apokalypsis*, see Rowland, "Revelation" 517–18. Older theories of apocalypse often saw end-time and transformation as constitutive ideas. Recent studies stress the heterogeneity of canonical and extracanonical apocalypses, some having no sense of change or a new age, and often reserve "apocalyptic" for the meaning of revelation. A further component of much apocalyptic thinking, a division between our world and a higher world of spirits or angels, common to apocalyptic literature as a whole, will concern me less (see Collins 5; Rowland, *The Open Heaven* 94–113). In what follows I distinguish among these senses as needed, but also, drawing on the fusion of meanings influenced by Revelation, use "apocalypse" and "apocalyptic" for the ideas of fundamental change and alteration from old to new.
19. Baldwin's study curricula as Sunday school leader and youth minister from 1938 to 1941 are not known, but from a later period, the *Official Manual* of the Church of God in Christ (COGIC), revised 1973, cites Paul's teachings, including First Corinthians 6:9, in its discussion of "Sex in Christian Life" (128–29), indicating these texts' place in the type of scripture study a leading Pentecostal church thought important.
20. For discussion, see Martin 108–17, 134–36, 168–79. For other commentaries, see Sampley 986–90, Fee 788–803, Conzelmann 283–92.
21. Martin makes this argument concerning the second half of Paul's verse (95).
22. On the emergence of Holiness thinking from John Wesley's doctrine of perfectibility, see John L. Peters, *Christian Perfection and American Methodism*, first published 1956 and still the fullest study. Peters does not discuss African American roles in the movement; on this point and on the movement's history and the emergence of Pentecostalism, see Vinson Synan, *The Holiness-Pentecostal Tradition*; Anderson 28–34 and later; Sanders chap. 1; Alexander and Yong. On Baldwin's early Pentecostal affiliations, see Leeming 24–25,

Hardy 4–5. For currents in present-day Afro-Pentecostalism, and trends away from strict focus on sanctification and noninvolvement in "the world," see Alexander and Yong 3–4, 6–8. The term "sanctified" generally refers to churches and beliefs fusing ecstatic worship and emphasis on personal sanctity; Sanders, for example, employs it to cover churches with these emphases in several denominations. Baldwin uses it in this same general sense (e.g., *BS* 19; *JAMH* 107, 119). Hurston's use (103–7) refers only to ecstatic worship. Hardy adopts "Holiness," instead, as his umbrella term.

23. In this section I adapt and reorder my own presentation in *The Mount of Vision* x–xii, 36–44, 82–90, 117–48.
24. Patterson, Ross, and Atkins 23–24. This work includes an account of Mason's life and ministry to about 1920, interspersed with first-person recollections from which I quote, and a précis of later church history. COGIC's pacifism, very important in early years, continues in a muted way today. For Jasper, see Randolph 53–69 and 142–57, and *The Mount of Vision* 131–44.
25. See Miller, *A Criminal Power* for a book-length study.
26. See *The Mount of Vision* xi–xv, 108–16, 191–95.

CHAPTER 1. PROPHETIC COMMISSIONING

1. Perceptive early readers could catch *Go Tell It*'s homosexual subtext: in a 1953 letter to Richard Wright after reading the novel in galleys, Ralph Ellison comments that it "is the best work on Negro religious conversion that I have seen thus far," and adds, in a note lined in from the margin, "actually it is a book 'about' *homosexual* conversion" (letter to Richard Wright, 21 Jan. 1953, Richard Wright Papers, JWJ MSS 3, Box 97, Folder 1314, Beinecke Rare Book and Manuscript Library, Yale University). Early reviews and essays, however, largely missed this theme; possibly the first published reference to John as homosexual is Eckman 30–31 (1966), citing Baldwin's statement to the writer. This view was argued in some detail in Macebuh 52, 54, 61–62, 67 (1973); for other early references, see Fabre 127 (1970); Bell; Giles (both 1974). The interpretation is now fairly standard, with differences over whether John realizes or represses his homosexuality and whether Baldwin attempts to repress it textually; see among others Boggs 138–39 (1999), Brim 50–54 (2014), Clark 56, 61 (2004), Powers (2005), Washington (1996). W. J. Weatherby's 1989 biography is responsible for the often-repeated assertion that Baldwin was "made to tone down" an initially more explicitly homosexual denouement under editorial pressure (93, 117). Extant drafts in the Baldwin Papers (Schomburg Center) show homoerotic-homosexual episodes in chapters on John's adolescence belonging to an earlier plan of the novel, but no more explicit

version of the John-Elisha material or the novel's ending (James Baldwin Papers, Boxes 12–13). Weatherby's documentation and quotations from editorial comments at Alfred A. Knopf, the novel's publisher, do not support his assertion, based on a recollection in the late 1980s by Baldwin's friend Emile Capouya of a version he might have read around 1951 (96; see 95–97, 99–100 overall). Possibly Capouya read an earlier manuscript (such as the incomplete typescript, c. 1950, also in the Schomburg Center) or was recalling "The Outing" (1951). Laura Claridge's account of Blanche Knopf's involvement in the final revisions also does not refer to excised homosexual content (280–82).

2. Despite casual references to John as a would-be prophet (e.g., Leeming 88–89, Scott 105), there has been almost no critical recognition of *Go Tell It*'s use of biblical ideas about prophecy or its concern with accession to prophetic mission. For contrasting early responses to religion in the novel, see, for example, Albert Gérard, who calls the church practices Baldwin describes "truly elevated" and John's conversion a "crisis, in which a man's soul is born" (152, 155) and Stanley Macebuh, who notes Baldwin's portrayal of the "millennialism and the metaphorical protest in Black Christianity" but argues that as a whole the book embodies "Baldwin's Quarrel with God" (49, chapter title). In the line of descent from Macebuh are O'Neale and Hardy. Lynch's "A Glimpse," arguing that Baldwin, in general, presents a "corrective" to Christian theology rather than a "repudiation" (52), is a riposte to such views. Allen, "Religious Imagery" (1975), Scruggs, "Tale" (1980), and Lundén (1981), all pioneering studies of biblical references, present relatively conventional views of Christianity and reject any idea of John as homosexual. (Scruggs slightly modified this point in revising for book publication; see *Sweet Home* 164.) For views of John's likely future as one of secular humanism, see, for example, Dixon 124–25; Miller, *A Criminal Power* 34; Warren 26. For the competing view that he will undergo religious sacrifice of his sexuality and individuality, see Montgomery 63, 55, Hardy 28, and others. Coleman represents a less prevalent viewpoint that continues to see the novel in relatively conventional theological terms. Hardy and Powers illuminate the novel's portrayal of Holiness beliefs and practices, as does Gerod Williams in a notable undergraduate thesis concluding that John's mission is to reveal a "new Holy city which will embrace the natural" (23). Kornegay and Young treat the novel *inter alia* in efforts to define an overall Baldwin theology.

3. See Exod. 3:4–4:17; Josh. 1:1–2; Isa. 6:1–12; Jer. 1:1–19; Ezek. 2:1–5; Amos 7:10–17; Hos. 1:1; Joel 1:1; Mic. 1:1; Zeph. 1:1.

4. See my introduction for general discussion; see Cone 1 for use of Matt. 11:28 in a basic theological statement. Baldwin uses Matt. 25:40 several times in nonfiction; see, for example, "WR" 749 and 756, as well as "Open Letter to the Born Again," in *Collected Essays*

784.

5. For biblical uses of "saints" in this sense, see, for example, Dan. 7:18 and 27; Rom. 1:7, 1 Cor. 1:2. Most sources now stress the Holiness and/or Pentecostal roots of the novel's church. (Possibly its name is a tribute to Baldwin's first church mentor, "Mother" Rosa Horn, once a member of the South Carolina-based Fire Baptized Holiness Association [Brooks 444].) The novel's chronology places Gabriel's early preaching at the start of the 1900s, before the Pentecostal upsurge in 1906–1909, but when the Holiness movement, including the original Fire Baptized Movement, was at its height (Synan 51–59). However, as I will indicate, Gabriel's early affiliations remain unspecified.
6. For Wesley's ideas, besides his own *Brief Account* (a compilation edited to reflect his later views), see Rack, esp. 156, 185, and chaps. 5.1, 9.2, and 11.1, 11.3; 202 for Whitefield's comment. See J. Peters chaps. 1–2 for a different emphasis. On the nineteenth century, see J. Peters chaps. 4–5; Synan chaps. 1–3.
7. Peters quotes a Doctrinal Statement included in the Declaration of Principles of the First General Holiness Assembly (Chicago, 1885).
8. This epigraph and the title and epigraph for Part Three entered the novel late, between the complete copyedited manuscript and the first galley proofs (James Baldwin Papers, Box 12, Folder 3; Box 13, Folder 1). Present in the 1953 first and some later editions, it is omitted from several reprint editions, including the 2013 Vintage edition used as copytext, but included in *Early Novels and Stories* (5). For commentary see Childs, *Isaiah* 310–11.
9. Set as shown in the Vintage edition, as a single verse in the AV, and as prose in *Early Novels and Stories* (7).
10. In the Vintage edition, "seen the King" is repeated; most other editions read correctly.
11. Compare Jer. 1:9 (God touches Jeremiah's mouth) and Ezek. 3:1–3 (Ezekiel is made to eat a scroll, that is, take its words into his mouth). On the "commissioning report" or "prophetic vocation account," see Petersen, *The Prophetic Literature* 20–21; Sweeney, *The Prophetic Literature* 36. Baldwin's late introduction of this epigraph in place of a prior one, "I know that my Redeemer liveth" (Job 19:25) accentuates the prophetic.
12. The threshing floor allusion, identified in Leeming 86, is especially apt for a member of this church, since John says he who comes will baptize "with fire" (Luke 3:16).
13. E. Peters 351, a variant text (for the more familiar version, see 217). The relevance of these lines is noted in Scruggs, *Sweet Home* 149. For the prophet as "watchman," see, for example, Isa. 21:6, 11, 12.
14. Lines from two later stanzas appear during John's conversion experience (202). Baldwin's use of this and other Tharpe lyrics, sometimes in variants from standard versions, suggests familiarity with her recordings. For background on Tharpe, see Heilbut 189–96,

313–16; J. Jackson.

15. The remaining chapter epigraphs are also thematically meaningful. Gabriel's (87), affirming that after his conversion he is "No stranger now," is later applied to John (209), indirectly raising the question whether John's prophetic vocation will be false, like Gabriel's, or genuine. Florence's (59), about Jesus's birth, probably refers to Royal's birth, mentioned in her chapter, and may suggest that Royal could have been a prophet or savior but for Gabriel's rejection. Elizabeth's (151), from the song "I Can't Stay Away," applies longing-for-Egypt imagery to her nostalgia for life before Gabriel, and is surely ironic, implying that only a false theology could see her life then as one of bondage.
16. See Coleman 50–51 for a contrary reading. The implications that safety is a false lure and that Elizabeth should have risked telling Richard of her pregnancy (168–69) presage a continuing preoccupation; see, for example, *Giovanni's Room* 57, *Another Country* 336–39, and *Fire Next Time* 105–6, and discussion in my Conclusion..
17. See von Rad, *Genesis* 49–51.
18. See, variously, Deut. 34:1; Zech. 14:4; Matt. 24:3, Mark 13:3; Rev. 21:10.
19. For representative views of this scene, see Dixon 131–33; J. Hughes 137–40; Scruggs, *Sweet Home* 151–53.
20. For these scenes, see 29, 31, 32–35. Scruggs ("Tale" 6–7) may have first identified the movie John sees as *Of Human Bondage* (1934; Leslie Howard, Bette Davis), based on the 1915 Somerset Maugham novel that deals in part with religious doubt and artistic apprenticeship and uses the protagonist's clubfoot as a fictional disguise for Maugham's homosexuality.
21. Gabriel's river baptism at age twelve (68–69) comports with Baptist practice. Some but not all of the terms relating to his post-conversion experience imply Holiness influence (Baldwin is not precise on these points). "Saints," as already noted, was in common use in "sanctified" churches; "elect" and "chosen" were more common among Calvinists than among Methodists, but non-Calvinists could speak of election resulting from free will and grace (see N. Hatch 235 for an example). Sanctification was Baptist as well as Methodist-Holiness doctrine, but, for Baptists, was a gradual process not conferring sinlessness in this life. Revivals and "field" preaching could belong to any evangelical denomination.
22. For example, 1 Sam. 24:6, 2 Sam. 23:1, Ps. 18:50, Pss. 105:15, 1 Chron. 16:22.
23. See Colbert 59–61 for a contrary view.
24. See Crummell 181–96, quotation at 194; Holsey 172–80. Their attitudes were not exceptional.
25. For discussion see Blenkinsopp 22–23, 32–34; Petersen, *The Prophetic Literature* 12–13; Sweeney, *The Prophetic Literature* 28–32.

26. For references to Handy, Oliver, Rainey, and others, see, for example, "Nobody Knows My Name," "Negroes Are Anti-Semitic Because They're Anti-White," "Last of the Great Masters," and "The Price of the Ticket," in *Collected Essays* 205, 742, 770, 831. In 1979 Baldwin felt deeply honored to meet Dorsey, then eighty; a recording of Baldwin singing Dorsey's *Precious Lord* was played at the writer's funeral (Leeming 343, 382).
27. For example, in Caleb's entering into a rigidly conventional marriage in *Tell Me How Long*, a work Field does not discuss in this respect and Brim does not mention at all.
28. For the "living rod" tradition, see, for example, *Bible Story Told in Verse* (1870): "Christ is the living rod held up by faith" (96). The phrase is nonbiblical.
29. See Rosso 24–31; Harris and Platzner 50, 65, 108–9. The linkage, originally argued by Hermann Gunkel in 1895 (Rosso 24), rests partly on etymological similarity between Hebrew *tehom*, "the deep," and Babylonian *Tiamat* (the sea, personified as a dragon or monster) and partly on passages that, unlike Genesis 1, mention God's destruction of a sea dragon in connection with the victory over the sea (Pss. 74:13 and 89:9–10, Isa. 51:9).
30. The voice has been taken as Satan's (Lundén 124, Allen "Ironic Voice" 35–37); Elisha's (Brown 62, 63); and that of John's authentic self-consciousness (Warren 25).
31. The "ironic voice" also mocks the so-called curse of Ham, which has troubled John (199–200). The voice's questions, seemingly pertinent, remain unanswered as John's mind turns toward identification with the sufferers, which provides the real answer. See Davis 64–69 for a brief discussion of the idea.
32. The song John recalls (204, 207) is similar to several traditional songs (e.g., "John Done Saw Dat Number," E. Peters 282), but differs in specifics.
33. On Baldwin's complex views of suffering, see Lee; Lynch, "Beyond Guilt and Innocence." For social and historical dimensions, see esp. *Fire Next Time* 98–100. For contrasting views of suffering's role in black redemption generally, see, for example, Pinn, *Why, Lord?* and Blount, *Can I Get a Witness?* 69–89, partly a response to Pinn.
34. This scene is itself prophetic in form, as the three character groups' simultaneous conversations focus successively on the past (Elizabeth and the church women), the present (Florence and Gabriel), and the future (John and Elisha).

CHAPTER 2. PROPHETIC ART

1. For a nonfiction exposition, see Baldwin's "The Creative Process" in *Collected Essays* 669–72.
2. Scholars recognize three segments with partly distinct focuses in Isaiah, originating in pre-exilic, exilic, and post-exilic times, later unified editorially, and often called First,

Second, and Third Isaiah. They are usually specified as chaps. 1–39, 40–55, and 56–66. For discussion, see Childs, *Introduction* 316–38.

3. Among recent studies presenting Baldwin as primarily inspired by blues, see Miller "Using"; Lordi chap. 3; Pavlić, who treats Gospel as one among many forms that Baldwin was interested in but not as one whose artistic vision spoke powerfully to him (4–7, 36). For a more balanced, though brief, discussion, see Field 109–12.
4. A creative sequence seems clear—*Amen Corner* adds to *Go Tell It on the Mountain*'s portrayal of the church, "Sonny's Blues" to the play's treatment of music. The textual sequence is less clearcut, since *Amen Corner* (1952–1953, revised 1955 for the Howard University production directed by Owen Dodson) was published only in 1968, while "Sonny's Blues," written "mostly in Washington" (Leeming 135) at the time of Baldwin's visit for this production, was published in 1957. Hence, I prefer to say the story "varies" rather than "revises" the play's ideas. For details, see Leeming 106–12, 135; Campbell 91–92 and associated notes; J. Hatch 197–202 (including the 1971 oral reminiscence by Dodson, Baldwin's put-upon host); Weatherby 111–12.
5. Ellison's discussion, in his now-famed essay "Richard Wright's Blues," first published in 1945, is probably not a source for Baldwin, as it was little known until reprinted later than this Jan. 1964 essay. Ellison expressed comparable views in 1958 and 1962 essays (Ellison 277, 264–65), which Baldwin might have seen. LeRoi Jones/Amiri Baraka's *Blues People* (1963), while affirming some of these qualities (50, 136), largely historicizes rather than universalizing.
6. For additional identifications, see Tracey.
7. Leeming's excellent brief remarks on this scene consider Sonny a "prophet" (in the general sense used throughout Leeming's biography) who plays "for his very life and for ours" (135–36). In contrast, Jacqueline C. Jones's "Finding a Way to Listen" (1999), on the artist's growth in "Sonny's Blues," apparently all that has been published of an important dissertation cited below, separates personal from social, arguing that "it is not the collective history of African Americans that the artist must confront but his own" (479). John M. Reilly's pioneer cultural contextualization (1970) stresses blues' embodiment of "the glorious capacity of human beings to take the worst and give it a form of their own choosing" (59) and relates Sonny to the postwar bebop development.
8. Baldwin's reference, probably first identified by Donald C. Murray (1977; 357 n. 3), has also been discussed by Byerman (371), Clark (46), Lobb (147), Mosher (59), Sanderson (94), and Tackach (117), among others, who treat the cup as signifying individual relief from pain, family reconciliation, or communion in or the universality of suffering, but not as communally significant.

9. See Albert, Reilly, Savery, and Sherard for views of the music's genre affiliations.
10. This reading differs from Houston Baker's view of the essays as based on "a contradistinction between *individual* and *society*" and as typifying "bourgeois aesthetic theory" (142).
11. See *Another Country* 97, 112, 152, 327 for Dostoevsky; 195 for Proust and others; 215–16 for Beethoven; 162 for Vivaldo's novel; 4–5, 8–9 for contrasting approaches to jazz; 162–63, 262 for television. The classic discussion of the saxophonist is Eugenia W. Collier's "The Phrase Unbearably Repeated" (1964).
12. See *Another Country* 88–90, 103–5, 109, which establish the time for Rufus's death; 331, 393, 429, which do the same for the closing events. Yves's ages, five when the Germans occupied Paris (June 14, 1940) and twenty-one as Eric prepares to leave France (late May), set the probable years (also noted by Cohen 219 n. 8); 1956–1957 is just possible.
13. For example, in "Freaks and the American Ideal of Manhood" (1985), Baldwin observes that "all of the American categories of male and female, straight or not, black or white, were shattered, thank heaven, very early in my life" ("FAI" 819).
14. See Lordi for an extended though differently focused analysis (113–14, 121–29). Other discussions include Harris, chap. 3, and brief but astute comments in Jones ("His Tale" 90–91).
15. The first songs are "Since I Fell for You" (Buddy Johnson, 1945), a Baldwin favorite also used in *Just Above My Head*, and "Betty and Dupree." There is an extensive literature on Dorsey and "Precious Lord."
16. Note Zaborowska's argument, based on sketchy evidence, that Ellis is Jewish and that Vivaldo's dislike is anti-Semitic (116–17, 123–26).
17. Cendrars (1887–1961) was an early modernist poet and student of African culture and "négritude"; Yves might be reading Genet's *Journal du voleur* (1949) or (anachronistically for the novel's time-frame) *Le Balcon* (1957) or *Les Nègres* (1959), dealing directly with revolution and race. On Baldwin's intermittent friendship with Genet, see White 350, 439, 544, 563. Eric's play seems to echo such socially concerned works as Arthur Miller's *All My Sons* (1947) and Elia Kazan's film *On the Waterfront* (1954).
18. Book One's epigraph, from W. H. Auden's "In Memory of W. B. Yeats" (1939), hints at this concern: Auden's subject, like Baldwin's, is the artist's responsibility in world crisis. Book Two's title, from Walter de la Mere's "The Listeners," alludes to the idea of belatedness implied in the novel's title, and Book Three's epigraph, from the Gospel song "I'm Going to Run to the City of Refuge," announces the apocalyptic theme that emerges at the novel's end.
19. On Ezekiel's dates and evolution, see Darr 1087–88; Petersen, *The Prophetic Literature*

137–40.

20. The title is probably taken from "Tell Me How Long the Train's Been Gone," recorded in 1950 by both Valaida Snow and Kay Starr (perhaps as a cover). In both, it is a jaunty uptempo blues about the effects of inaction and indecision: "Tell me how long the train's been gone [three times] / The people keep a-comin' but the train's done gone" (Snow). Mable Hillery recorded a slow-blues version, with different body lyrics, in 1966, when Baldwin was working on the novel. Baldwin explains the title through his general epigraph, "Never seen the like since I been born, / The people keep a-coming, / And the train's done gone," which he cites as "traditional." Scott (50–52 and nn.) attributes the epigraph to a song found in a 1926 source (Johnson and Johnson 2:124–25; Scott cites E. Peters 28) and the title to a distinct, rare 1948 Gospel recording; neither includes both title and epigraph phrases, as the blues songs do. Darcy A. Zabel speculates that the epigraph originated as a folksong during northward migrations via "exodus trains" in 1917 (28, 102). Her source for the period, Bontemps and Conroy, does not mention such a song, but the lines' near-contemporary appearance in Johnson and Johnson make her idea plausible. Baldwin is somewhat more likely to have known any of the blues versions than the sources Scott and Zabel suggest.
21. Leo is nineteen later this summer and the following winter (*TMHL* 200, 405). The war ends in between (363–65), making 1926 Leo's probable birth year and 1965 or 1966 the present time. Most details are consistent with these dates but not all—for example, when Leo is fourteen, he and Caleb see a 1942 movie (218, 227).
22. In Ezekiel, God asks the question and Ezekiel answers, "O Lord GOD, thou knowest" (37:3).
23. Travis recorded the song for the four-disc album *Folk Songs of the Hills* (1947). Baldwin misstates the title as "Down in the Dungeon." The novel's chronology places this scene about 1952.
24. On the four "Servant Songs" (Isa. 42:1–4, 49:1–6, 50:4–11, 52:13–53:12), traditionally thought to anticipate or refer to Jesus, see Childs, *Isaiah*; Childs stresses the second Song's continuity with the following material, 49:8–12 (386).
25. *If Beale Street Could Talk* probably takes place in 1974—Tish's parents met during the Korean War and her sister is twenty-three. Part One occupies a few weeks in May or June (Tish, three months pregnant, conceived shortly before Fonny's March arrest); Part Two moves ahead to Tish's labor. This time-span postdates Baldwin's inscribed completion date in Oct. 1973 (166) and *Beale Street*'s spring 1974 publication; it is not clear if Baldwin was careless or intended a future-time setting. The final paragraph (166), describing Fonny sculpting, that is, freed from jail, leads some interpreters to assume another shift

in time. Since this paragraph says the baby's cries are approaching "from far away," it most probably occurs during Tish's labor but envisions a future liberation. (Scott 195 n. 58 and Miller, *A Criminal Power* 148–49 summarize critical views; both see the point as ambiguous.)

26. Nathaniel Mills links Tish as inventive artist with Handy's "blind man on the corner," whose "representations of Beale Street" necessarily are "artistic constructions" (64, 69).
27. Most accounts agree that Baldwin draws on his involvement in the case of Tony Maynard; see Leeming and Baldwin's *No Name* for details, and Miller's detailed discussion, *A Criminal Power* 141–49.
28. See Mills 65–67 for a gender analysis of this material.
29. Though Baldwin is usually careful about such matters, *Just Above My Head* contains irreconcilable inconsistencies in chronology. Varied references, including Hall's inferred age of twenty-two on what seems the first Christmas of the Korean War, imply a 1927 or 1928 birth year, roughly consistent with a reference to *The Wiz* (1975) as a "big hit" in present time, when he is nearly forty-eight (100, 135; 5; 514). Early Baldwin notes specify 1928, and 1935 for Arthur (James Baldwin Papers, Box 28, Folder 14). But in Book Four, what seems a variant chronology specifies that Hall turned thirty "in the sixties" (335), making 1930 his earliest birth year; most events in Book Four are consistent with this chronology. The inconsistencies may reflect carelessness; however, they underline a major emphasis, noted later, on the unreliability of Hall's memory.
30. Blues are used sparingly in the novel, primarily for generic transition in the Paris scene discussed below (505–8). "Standards" appear briefly in several contexts, but mainly as the music of Arthur's "crossover" period and artistic decline. Gospel, however, is the music both of Arthur's sexual awakening and of civil rights and international radicalism (Books Three and Four). Commentaries emphasizing blues over Gospel include, for example, W. Carson 223–24; Miller, "Using" 102–9; Traylor. Bruck and Field (109–12) are exceptions, though Bruck believes Baldwin disregards Gospel's "eschatological dimension" (137).
31. Baldwin's words differ slightly from Tharpe's ("Saviour"). Here and in other lyrics below, my ellipses indicate omissions of narrative passages between song segments in Baldwin's text.
32. Baldwin substitutes "every mortal tongue" for "every Christian tongue" in the standard lyrics.
33. See John 14:16–17, 14:26, 15:26, 16:7–11 and a related passage, 16:12–15. For discussions, see O'Day 774–78; D. A. Carson.
34. See Chappell, *A Stone of Hope* (2004), especially chap. 5.
35. As often, Hall's memory is inconsistent: he imagines two different itineraries for Arthur

(*JAMH* 452; 473, 514) and distinct chronologies for Arthur's appearance at the Paris club (456; 458 and following).

36. This epigraph, in the first and later editions, is omitted in *Just Above My Head*'s text in the Library of America's *Later Novels* (2015)—by error, according to the LOA (email correspondence, Oct. 22, 2015). Though the epigraph is to Book One, this is the present-time setting for the whole novel, creating a sense that the epigraphs apply to the whole story. The epigraph's lineation varies from the text version and its last stanza differs. Both stanzas are traditional; see E. Peters 209–10, citing a 1926 source I have not traced, and 115 for a distinct version. (The other Book One epigraph, "Work: for the night is coming," from the hymn of that title by Anna Louisa Walker Coghill, 1861, probably represents Hall/Baldwin's sense of approaching age and the obligation to transmit memory)
37. The tradition is based on this passage and on Daniel's dream-vision of the kingdoms as beasts from the sea (7:1–27). For discussions see Collins 101–7; Rowland, *The Open Heaven* 178–83.
38. Summary in Randolph 142–57; for discussion see my *Mount of Vision* 140–43 and notes.
39. See Tharpe, "The End of My Journey," for full lyrics; "Another Building Not Made with Hands" has varying lyrics in different sources; words similar to Baldwin's appear in Hughes, *Black Nativity* 374.
40. Commentaries have not recognized the songs' importance or discussed their content. In an excellent overall treatment, Robert Reid-Pharr notes that Arthur "picks up the hammer that Sonny lays down," but does not describe Arthur's song (*Once You Go Black* 112–13). Scott's coverage of the scene (157–59) mentions "a gospel song about the prophet Daniel" without specific discussion (158–59). Miller's survey of music in the novel ("Using" 102–9), Traylor's early appreciation also focusing partly on music, and Young's discussion of religious themes (173–74) do not mention this scene. None of these writers mentions Baldwin's use of "Daniel" as an epigraph.

CHAPTER 3. THE APOCALYPTIC BODY

1. See my introduction; Martin chaps. 1 and 5, esp. 115.
2. Among representative views on David's evolution, Armengol (114), Chancy (185), Field (107), Henderson (324), and Young (75–77) agree in different ways that David finds a painful self-acceptance. But perhaps most commentators think he reaches no real acceptance of his sexuality, whether defined as homosexual, bisexual, or fluid (Beemyn, Bieganowski, DeGout, Frontain; Reid-Pharr, "Tearing"; Shin and Judson). With regard to David and Giovanni's bisexuality, Armengol, Beemyn, and Chancy endorse what

they variously see as the novel's presentation of gender "fluidity," of "unfixed racial and gender lines," or of "homosexuality and heterosexuality [as] one in the unconscious realm" (Beemyn 58, Chancy 185, Armengol 112); Mitchell offers a sharp dissent; Brim applies a meta-analysis arguing that queer theory, gay studies, and transgender analysis yield competing views of the text (see especially 56). Black masculinity theory has built a subgenre of criticism on the novel, with several writers (Abdur-Rahman, Armengol, Chancy, Mitchell; Reid-Pharr "Tearing") viewing the Italian Giovanni as symbolically or narratively black, or construed as nonwhite in 1950s Europe (Armengol, Chancy); Abdur-Rahman, Armengol, and Chancy additionally argue that David in some sense is or becomes black or racially indeterminate, whether through homosexuality's association with darkness and dirt, through self-acceptance as "other," or because Baldwin assumedly sees blackness and homosexuality as "interchangeable identities" (Armengol 107).

3. On the Wesleyan-Arminian view of grace, still standard in Methodism and many Holiness and Pentecostal churches, see Harper 220–25, 232–46; Coppedge 111–17; Rack 199–202, 388–93. Calvinists saw grace as a determinate selection for salvation; Arminians believed it conferred freedom to choose belief, but that the subject could refuse belief and, indeed, turn from it in later life.
4. Most commentaries agree that the knowledge Paul speaks of is to be attained at the eschaton, which for him was imminent. See Conzelmann 225–31, Fee 641–52, Sampley 954–55 for general commentaries on verses 8–13.
5. In a deconstructive reading, Kevin Ohi argues that *Another Country*'s moments of seeming revelation offer only "opacity" and thus that revelation "appears only in the guise of its failure." Eric's seeming revelation with LeRoy, for example, is a "tautology" that reveals only that it is a revelation (264, 274). Ohi does not consider that fiction commonly communicates by periphrasis (most readers will understand Eric's revelation as the discovery of his sexual nature) and, since he does not deal with Baldwin's religious language, also does not note that communication through suggestion is characteristic of Baldwin's model, Revelation.
6. In this scene and elsewhere, Vivaldo has attracted some gay/queer critical animus. Charles Toombs, for instance, considers him (as well as Rufus) a homosexual "passing" as bisexual (106); Brim finds his request for Eric's love when their sexual relationship will not continue, and Eric's acceptance, "peculiar beyond all patience" (116; see 105–18 generally). I read the characters' psychology as more complex, and Eric and Vivaldo's friendship as more mutually empowering, than these critics do.
7. See Haymes for historical context, including the song's early recording history. In recent times it has been recorded by Elvis Presley, Lavern Baker (a secular version with the refrain

"You must come into my heart"), and others. Presley's lyrics are very similar to Baldwin's.

8. References include "Take Me to the Water to Be Baptized"; "Somebody Touched Me (Must Have Been the Hand of the Lord)"; "This Train"; "peace like a river" (from "It Is Well with My Soul," 1873, by Horatio Gates Spafford; the biblical source is Isa. 66:12); "Run and Tell That" ("I looked at my hands and they looked new"); "Now We Are the Sons of God" (*JAMH* 199–200, 201, 207, 212, 216, 222).
9. See also Marlon Rachquel Moore's reading of *JAMH* in terms of "the salvific principle of sacred sensuality" (50–61, at 52).
10. On anointing, see W. Smith 41 (sense 1.2, "official"). As the passages on Tish and Fonny's lovemaking have been criticized for male-centeredness and patriarchalism (e.g., Spillers 97–99), it should be noted that Tish's anointment is to the book's primary salvational role. The "anointing" is also called "a tribal rite" (*BS* 68), suggesting African affiliations as well as the tribe of Israelite strangers represented by Lot's family in Genesis 18–19.
11. In Rev. 17:5, "mystery" is part of (alternatively, a description of) the name of Babylon as harlot, signifying false worship in collaboration ("fornication") with "the kings of the earth" (17:2).
12. See the similar comments, noted earlier, in "Freaks and the American Ideal of Manhood" ("FAI" 819).
13. On *le milieu*, the gay demimonde, see, for example, *Giovanni's Room* 26–27, 39–40, 77–78, 105, 109, 140. These comments function to characterize both David and Giovanni as overinvested in stereotyped masculinity; David, indeed, retrospectively says of Jacques, though not of *le milieu*, "I understand now that the contempt I felt for him involved my self-contempt" (23). But the passages also capture Baldwin's own responses to the gay world, described in his 1954 essay on Gide, "The Male Prison," as an "underworld in which [one] never meets either men or women, where it is impossible to have either a lover or a friend" ("MP" 234) and in his 1984 interview with Richard Goldstein, in reference to Greenwich Village in the 1940s, as involving "all the role playing" (174). *Giovanni's Room*'s picture of Guillaume's bar as containing only sad older men and flamboyant queens, no ordinary men pairing off or enjoying a few drinks, is itself a stereotype, one Baldwin partially but incompletely compensates for in later work.
14. See comments on this issue by Nelson and DeGout.
15. For a view of Hall as a "closet homosexual" in love with Arthur, see Harris 199–203, at 202. Hall's continuing sexual love for his wife Ruth and the failure of his assumedly repressed homosexuality to manifest itself in other ways over time argue against this analysis.
16. Baldwin, who has provided sketchy psychogeneses for David and Eric (*GR* 10–13, *AC*

197–200), offers almost none for Crunch—his interest from the start is in how the world misunderstands and mistreats Crunch's sexual magnetism (*JAMH* 85–86). For Baldwin at this time, then, the social and psychic accommodation and repression of sexuality, not its genesis, are of interest.

17. Eldridge Cleaver famously believed Rufus "let a white bisexual homosexual fuck him in the ass" (*Soul on Ice* 132), but this formula expresses Cleaver's own image of black male abjection; it is not consistent with Rufus reviling Eric "as a woman" and "inferior" to a woman (*AC* 46).
18. Hall cannot have heard details about the sermon at the time (he was in Korea) and in present time he says that Julia never before told him "what you've just told me" (*JAMH* 41), so we know the sermon presented later is an imaginative reconstruction. On Holiness churches' rejection of adornment, see Powers; Synan (e.g., 47, 58, 64, 81).
19. The imagined plea draws on the hymn "Take Me As I Am": "My only plea—Christ died for me! / Oh, take me as I am" ("Hymn" 7–8). But the hymn states this idea in terms of atonement (vicarious discharge of sin). Neither Julia's nor Arthur's words express this idea; their claim is unconditional.
20. On Baldwin's interest in prison homosexuality, see Zaborowska, chap. 3, supplemented by Plastas and Raimon; Miller, *A Criminal Power* 126–27.
21. Possibly they masturbate simultaneously but separately; the description is ambiguous.
22. Various elements in Leo's memories and future life fictionalize Baldwin's own, including the racketeer ("FAI" 818–19; Leeming 30); later relationships with a black woman and a white gay man (*TMHL* 346–47, 374–75; "FAI" 823–24, Leeming 45); and his long love relationship and friendship with Barbara, which they agree will not lead to marriage (272–78; Leeming 77)—however, Baldwin avoided a sexual relationship with this woman, Mary S. Painter, to whom he dedicated *Another Country*.
23. Speeches by Martha and Sidney (*JAMH* 328–30, 333–34) show similarities to Nation of Islam beliefs and Malcolm X's life (Malcolm, in prison, was guided toward the Nation by letters from his brother; Sidney is guided by his imprisoned brother). Martha mentions her intended role as Sidney's "helpmeet" (329), an accurate reflection of Nation of Islam ideas on marriage and a tragic outcome for this vibrant woman.
24. Scott notes that this scene and other comments by Hall and Paul deny the "permanence and genuineness of Arthur's homosexuality" (104).
25. In the 1950s and early 1960s, when these scenes take place, homosexuality was barely mentionable among polite people; euphemism was used, and only when necessary. The topic would if possible not be mentioned directly to the person concerned. Thus, Hall's reticence is not a personal matter, but almost inevitable in the discourse of the time.

26. Tish, Ernestine herself, and Frank (Fonny's father) all put others down as "faggots" (*BS* 56, 62, 160). Tish's comparison of New York to Sodom, too, may reflect the tradition that the city was destroyed for sexual and homosexual violations, though the alternative tradition of punishment for "pride" and "haughty" treatment of strangers (Ezek. 16:49–50) is also relevant.
27. For the views of Baldwin and patriarchalism in this paragraph, see for example Clark 58; Harris 156–63 (on Ernestine, 142–46, 162); Spillers; Scott 79–83, 116–19. For Cleaver's attack on Baldwin, see *Soul on Ice* 122–37, especially 124–31. Some recent commentaries are more nuanced. Mills (2012) argues, in part, that the novel implies a "queering of black nationalist constructions of masculinity" (66); Taylor (2010) believes Cleaver attacked *Another Country* because it critiques white liberalism more, not less, trenchantly than Cleaver himself. In a near-contemporaneous work, *One Day When I Was Lost,* Baldwin shows Laura, Malcolm X's former girlfriend, in later life as a prostitute who is affectionally lesbian (190–92, 267).
28. See Miller, *A Criminal Power*, for a treatment of Baldwin and the law. Miller, however, says little about the nexus analyzed here.
29. The initial sex may not have gone beyond groping (*GR* 61). The same passage indicates that Giovanni expects more "trouble." Giovanni's final confrontation, in which he submits to sex with Guillaume to get his job back and is then told he will not be rehired (155–56), is David's imaginative reconstruction and may not have happened as described.

CHAPTER 4. THE APOCALYPTIC CITY

1. Mack is speaking of the pattern of development in Pope's poetry, comparing it to that of "the book [Pope] was accustomed to call Scripture" (3). See also Abrams 32–46.
2. See Poore, Hicks. The latter uses "hate" or "hatred" ten times in a short review.
3. Published as "Yellow Dog Rag" (1915); republished in 1919 under the more familiar title.
4. My transcription. It is not certain that Baldwin had this version of the song in mind, but *Tell Me How Long*'s including Cooke's recordings among those Leo has in the hospital (315) seems to indicate Cooke's importance for Baldwin. Anyone following Gospel music in the 1950s would be familiar with Cooke, whose voice, still in youth, is radiant on this recording. On Cooke's career and significance, see Heilbut 87–93; Wolff et al.
5. See Rev. chap. 13. Two beasts appear, and Yeats's sphinxlike figure does not match either, but these points are not relevant here.
6. Even Book Two's epigraph, from Conrad's *Victory* (1915), contributes to the pattern: Lena, the heroine, urges her lover, "Why don't you take me into your arms and carry me out of

this lonely place?" (part 4, chap. 3; *AC* 181, slightly misquoted), but she has been fatally shot: her "other country" will be heaven.

7. Ironic uses are found, for example, in "Fifth Avenue, Uptown" and *The Devil Finds Work* (*Collected Essays* 179, 514), both on white images of the antebellum South; other references are serious if metaphoric, as in the passage from "Preservation of Innocence" ("PI" 596) that I quote next in my text. David, in *Giovanni's Room*, satirizes Jacques's Eden as involving "football players" while Giovanni's involved "maidens," but Jacques's comment that provokes this dig poses the essential question: "Nobody can stay in the garden of Eden. . . . I wonder why" (25).
8. For discussions, see, for example, Collier 289–95, Feldman 90–94, and Toombs 110–18, all viewing Leona solely as victim. Dievler, exceptionally, faults Leona for unconscious race superiority and judges that Rufus and Leona as lovers "perceive only their racial selves—they are imprisoned in them" (113).
9. See, for example, "Alas, Poor Richard" and "Dark Days" (*Collected Essays* 265, 793), on Richard Wright and on Baldwin's elementary school teachers.
10. Lordi rightly sees this term as a sexist attack (126), but underplays (121–26) Ida's use of sexual barter to gain band dates.
11. The conclusion of *The Fire Next Time*, published less than a year after *Another Country*, echoes *Another Country* in several ways: the conscious few work together "like lovers" to change public consciousness and "end the racial nightmare"; if successful, they may "achieve our country" (105), paralleling the implication in the novel's title. On the Ezekiel tradition in prophecy, see my introduction.
12. See my *The Mount of Vision*, preface, chap. 3, and conclusion.
13. James M. Hughes sees the city on fire as "Babylon in flames" (232). On the context of 2 Pet. 3, see chap. 5; see Harrington 289 on textual problems in this verse.
14. For brief references, see Lordi 101, 128. Though Baldwin mentions only the album title, it is likely that Ida hears the title song, tracks A1 and A2 on the album.
15. Leo's morning with "the boy" (not named) occurs in indeterminate time (*TMHL* 307–9). Since the scene begins Book Three, "Black Christopher," one might assume "the boy" is Christopher, but when Leo and Christopher first speak seriously (they have briefly met before) there is no indication that they previously slept together (443–52). Leo's night with "the boy," then, is a random piece of his life showing that he is now largely living as a gay man. His sexual relationship with Barbara, which began in summer 1945 in New Jersey and continued over several years (306, 405–8), is not shown as active in present time, though the two remain life comrades. Leo's relationship with Christopher continues in immediate past time (456, 460–71, 475–76) and, apparently, present time;

Leo's active concern with black struggle, evidenced in the rally scene, develops with this relationship. Suggestions that the novel assumes bisexuality as a positive norm, though only as an idealized projection (Kilpeläinen 48–49) do not mesh with this timeline.

16. Though later than the book's mid-1960s present, Creedence Clearwater Revival's "Bad Moon Rising" (1969), with its apocalyptic imagery ("I feel the rivers overflowing / I hear the voice of rage and ruin"), can serve as an example.
17. Varying lyrics appear in Johnson and Johnson 1:136; E. Peters 299, 299–300; and a recording by the Carter Family; none includes the line about being with Jesus, possibly a variant from Baldwin's church background.
18. Leeming 282 and Scott 53–55 note the revision of *Go Tell It*; Scott notes the scene's "apocalyptic" tone (55).
19. For discussion, see Rowland, "Revelation" 630–33, 643; Schüssler Fiorenza 69–73, 75–76, 79.
20. I write here from memory and personal experience.
21. My transcription. No prior commentary has noted this source. The singer in Lomax's recording was Lillie Knox. For the prisoners see "Untitled News Summary."
22. The "Davidic-Zion" tradition influences Isaiah, Psalms, and a few shorter books, which together include over half the biblical uses of "Zion." The term is not used in the New Testament. For discussion, see Petersen, *The Prophetic Literature* 91–94; Sweeney, *The Prophetic Literature* 47–48.
23. "Firstborn of the dead" quotes Rev. 1:5 (New Revised Standard Version); see also Col. 1:18. "The beginning of the new creation," based on Rev. 3:14, is a phrase often used exegetically of Jesus.
24. Herb Boyd, though not thinking in apocalyptic terms, hears the baby's cries as "a wake-up call for a drowsy, apathetic Harlem" (140).
25. See, for example, Cleaver, *On the Ideology of the Black Panther Party*, referring to black people's "struggle against the system of racial oppression and exploitation in Babylon" (1); the usage was widespread in Black Panther literature.
26. Arthur and Jimmy become lovers soon after the Paris club scene (*JAMH* 514–40) and are together "almost fourteen years" (577); present time is two years after Arthur's death (5), leaving aside the time for writing the book.
27. On Daniel's dating and textual history, see Childs, *Introduction* 611–18 and Collins 87–90, both noting probable use of older material in chaps. 2–6.
28. See, for example, 136, 203, 381 (Korea); 535–36 (white moral blindness); in contrast, 413 on whites liberated in and by the civil rights movement.
29. Biblically, the "latter rain" is the spring rains that nourish the crop, following fall rains

before planting. Biblical metaphoric uses include, for example, Deut. 11:14, Prov. 16:15, Joel 2:23, Zech. 10:1, James 5:7, the last three with apocalyptic-eschatological meaning. The term has been associated with Pentecostalism since D. Wesley Myland's *The Latter Rain Covenant and Pentecostal Power* (1910); see also Synan 148, 212–13.

30. The conversation takes place the day Hall returns from army service, in "the fall of the year that Arthur turned eighteen" (287), 1953 according to *Just Above My Head*'s dominant chronology—too early for the text's discussion of desegregation in Washington, D.C. Book Four's chronology would imply a 1955 date. The desegregation case, *Bolling v. Sharpe*, was decided May 17, 1954, the same day as *Brown v. Board of Education*, but involved only school desegregation, while Baldwin focuses on social integration.
31. See at least Ida on grinding the United States to powder (*AC* 351, above); Leo's "I'd rather drop dead than fight for this miserable country" (*TMHL* 178).
32. Reid-Pharr views the meditation somewhat differently, highlighting voluntary choice of identity. His overall judgment that Baldwin's formulation contributes to viewing "black American identity as a process of choosing and re-choosing" (*Once You Go Black* 113) is similar to mine.
33. In Hughes's well-known formulation, "I was only an American Negro—who had loved the surface of Africa and the rhythms of Africa—but I was not African. I was Chicago and Kansas City and Broadway and Harlem" (*The Big Sea* 325).
34. Field traces Baldwin's ambivalence toward Africa, primarily in nonfiction, arguing that in his last decade he grew "increasingly open to a transcultural—or, to use his term, interdependent—relationship between the African and the African American" (42–44, at 44). The point meshes with recent emphases on the transnational in Baldwin. Equally, however, Baldwin's fiction depicts limits to transnational solidarity of race (here) and gender (*Beale Street*, on which see Norman).
35. For commentary, see my *The Mount of Vision*, 91–93; 90–103 on the emigration debate in general. For a contrary view, see Newman 258–61.
36. See, for example, "This Train": "This train has left the station [three times] / This train takes in every nation."

CHAPTER 5. PROPHECY AND DOUBT

1. The notes, jotted on a jazz club table-card, state in part (square brackets are Baldwin's; angle brackets show my interpolations): "The key to Arthur's disaster is involved < . . . > with the fantasies of the Old Testament<,> which connect with the slave, or sorrow

songs: <and> his subsequent, [fatally inevitable <?>] abandonment of the New [the failure of Good News]<,> which connect<s> with the history of the slave, and his descendants, in America" (James Baldwin Papers, Box 28, Folder 14). The question mark qualifying "inevitable" is Baldwin's, written above the word; the "which" clauses are written separately, marked to go where included. The undated notes must be early; they include characters' birth years (with marginal math to check consistency), showing that Baldwin was working out basics. They are important but not determinative clues to Baldwin's early intentions. The "Good News" comment is closest to *Just Above My Head*'s development; the phrase, a frequent evangelical rendering of "Gospel," probably signifies both the New Testament message and the music expressing it. What Baldwin means by the "fantasies" of the Old Testament is less clear—perhaps ideas of prophetic office, promised redress, or apocalyptic transformation as such, all questioned in the final text, but as part of the double-voiced treatment I analyze here. If Baldwin intended to elaborate a New-Old Testament opposition, this purpose did not jell.

2. The chronological inconsistency between most of Book Four and the rest of the novel was covered in chapter 2. Other contradictions include the manner of Arthur's death (hemorrhage on 3–4, heart symptoms on 579–82); no commentary I am aware of has noted the difference. Some inconsistencies may be slips, given the novel's much-interrupted composition, a change of editors, and Baldwin's resistance to revising (see Weatherby 307, 313, 325, 329, 333–38). But the text itself emphasizes the unreliability of memory.
3. Events Hall all but omits include, besides much of Arthur's later life, the reasons for his own breakup with Julia, promised early (*JAMH* 49) but never given. Events he massages in his own favor include the family's and his feelings about Arthur's homosexuality.
4. The three references concern Julia's sermon for Mother Bessie, Hall's use of conjecture in his narration, and the location of a dinner involving Hall, Julia, Arthur, and Jimmy.
5. This phrase becomes the part-title for Book Five, reflecting the "hells" of the South (537) and of Arthur's decline and death, and yet this use balances, rather than negating, the phrase's biblical meaning. See chap. 4 for the context of Grimké's statement.
6. See Sweeney, *The Prophetic Literature* 17–20, and, for fuller exposition, "Tanak versus Old Testament"; see Levenson chaps. 1–3 on the tension between faith and doubt in the Ketuvim. Technically, the Prophets (Nevi'im) include the historical books, in which prophets play major roles ("former prophets"). Common usage, which I adopt, refers to the books from Isaiah to Malachi; it is these that follow the Writings in Christian orderings. Daniel, part of the Jewish Ketuvim, is among these books in Christian placements.
7. Ellison, whose view of blues we have noted as similar to Baldwin's, feels that blues "fall

short of tragedy" in that they "provide no solution, offer no scapegoat but the self" (Ellison 143)—blues do not bring a communal restoration through sacrifice of the tragic figure. For Baldwin, tragedy is less formally specific.

8. Scott 169 cites E. Peters 179–80, with slightly differing lyrics; Lynch, "Just Above My Head" (epigraph and 293) and Lee (93) quote the lyrics as they appear in *Another Country*. Bruck (epigraph) quotes a variant.
9. A few echoes elsewhere seem pertinent: Arthur, as a boy, feels safe when "his father and his elder brother were beside him, conferring together above his head"; Julia, trapped in her sexual relationship with Joel, hears his footsteps "above her head" in their brownstone; and in an application of the apocalyptic body, Arthur is much taken with Jimmy's "two dimples just above his ass" (*JAMH* 71, 250, 574).
10. The song is delivered antiphonally, with second voice singing distinctly a moment after the first, except in the final unison repetition of "heaven somewhere." Tharpe's is the first voice in stanzas 1–2 and 4–5; Knight's in stanza 3. The difference between Tharpe's earthy voice quality and style and Knight's purer contralto makes distinguishing their lyrics easy.
11. They first kiss in Nashville, during the Trumpets' summer tour, and, after stints in Birmingham and Atlanta, tour for another ten days before the group engagement ends, when they stay on briefly in Washington. Back in New York, they continue together until Crunch is drafted and leaves within a week, still before summer ends (*JAMH* 191, 195–95, 210–12, 217, 219, 255, 263).
12. Arthur is sixteen when he becomes Crunch's lover (*JAMH* 222); Hall is thirty-two, and Arthur therefore twenty-five, in the year of Peanut's murder, Arthur's Paris visit, and the start of his relationship with Jimmy (392; 558).
13. For a contrary judgment, see Scott 161.
14. See Scott 148–49 and nn.; Clark 59–60; Wolff et al. 90.
15. We do not know when Arthur began renting the loft. It is first mentioned (*JAMH* 369) shortly after Hall's thirtieth birthday (i.e., about four years after Crunch and Arthur's breakup).
16. For an early, highly homophobic example, see Lash; for a recent analysis, see Brim 105–18, which critiques the idea, as applied to Vivaldo and Cass, as queer abjection toward heterosexuals. Brim does not focus on later novels, and so does not discuss Baldwin's reworking of the "savior" pattern in *Just Above My Head* or, more generally, his depictions of non-abject, lasting sexual relationships between black bisexual (*TMHL*) and homosexual (*JAMH*) males.
17. The first three events occur within a few months of Arthur's return from Paris (*JAMH* 514–40). According to the chronology in Book Four, the year would be c. 1963; the

chronology elsewhere would suggest an earlier date. The sketch of Arthur and Jimmy's early years together (540–69) seems to cover an indefinite time of several years.

18. We do not learn when Crunch lost his teeth or went mad; the lack of reference to either event in the past-time narration implies times after the book's main action. We also do not know if Crunch's teeth were kicked out during a protest of some kind or some other confrontation. If I am right in speculating that Crunch avoided repairing his teeth out of "hate and rage," he exemplifies Baldwin's dictum that hate "never failed to destroy the man who hated" ("NNS" 84), but this point does not alter the significance of the police officer's action.
19. Baldwin paraphrases "Keep Your Hands on That Plow," noted as a song of "the Holiness people" (Lomax and Lomax 44–45), or quotes a version from his church background.
20. Oatman (1856–1922), composer of over three thousand hymns, also wrote "Higher Ground," mentioned earlier.
21. See Heilbut 193–94, supplemented by J. Jackson 237–38, on Tharpe; Wolff et al. 178–79, 261–62, on Cooke. The reality of Gospel shunning may be more modest than the legend: Wolff et al. note that despite feelings of betrayal among some Gospel stars, Cooke kept a foot in Gospel and remained loved by audiences; they rebut (178–79) a well-travelled story of his being booed off a Gospel stage, accepted as fact by Heilbut (90). Miller, in "Using" 108–9, suggests Mahalia Jackson as Baldwin's model for Arthur, but the parallels seem weaker, especially as Jackson never traveled far from Gospel.
22. "Feelin' Alright" was recorded by Traffic, Dave Mason's group, in 1968 and became a major hit when covered by Joe Cocker in 1969. Standard versions lineate differently; here as elsewhere, Baldwin's line breaks indicate breath and delivery.
23. In an alternative view, Scott argues that Arthur experiences artistic alienation because he moves from audience-participatory music (particularly in the southern scenes) to performing before passive audiences. The Paris scene, Scott believes, shows that rather than "an integral member of a community," he is becoming "a kind of ambassador to foreign nations" (159). However, a similar quality has been noted in much Gospel-related performance, a desire to reach mass audiences that is analogous to the "call to preach" with its "mandate to reach a crowd for Christ" (Gallien 121). About Arthur's final performance, Warren Carson comments that he "pours a lament" into his song and that the line, "Boy, you sure took me for one big ride," may be "addressed to God" (224). This reading misses the issue of musicianship—performing the song as lament is itself a sign of musical, as well as personal, collapse.
24. On Smith, see Albertson 132–39. Reid-Pharr recalls childhood family acquaintances saying about Jackson, "You know. They say she was funny" (*Once You Go Black* 106).

25. Here I take issue with a secondary but important point in Reid-Pharr's discussion, that *Just Above My Head* places value on moving beyond "the old intimacies . . . of the racial community" (*Once You Go Black* 101). As with Reid-Pharr's discounting of the "unanswering and unanswerable thunder and truth of history" in the matter of U.S. identity, I think Baldwin sees a given and not chosen quality of cultural identity in black racial affiliation, similar perhaps to the inner truth he perceives in sexual affiliations.
26. This dream and Hall's of the descending ceiling (*JAMH* 15) are based on real ones Baldwin and his brother David told each other at Baldwin's home in St. Paul de Vence sometime during the 1970s, which may have provided the novel's impetus (Leeming 345). The earlier dream was Baldwin's, the closing one David's. Baldwin has added and rearranged details. Scott (142) notes that "the road, the driving rain, the country house, even the dream itself," derive from *The Wizard of Oz*, which Hall's family has recently seen in its Gospel version, *The Wiz*.
27. The lines Hall remembers, or very similar ones, have been used by many different artists; Jimmy Rushing's "Going to Chicago Blues," for example, has a version close to Baldwin's.
28. The song was copyrighted under the first title by Homer Rodeheaver in 1928 (Rodeheaver no. 67), but may be older. It is better known under the more descriptive title, used in a 1930 recording by The Carter Family. The lines Hall remembers (usually sung as part of the second or third stanza, not the first) are followed by the two refrain lines included in my epigraph, "Hide me over in the Rock of Ages, / Rock of Ages cleft for me," which accentuate the eschatological element: God will safeguard the faithful until the end-time passes.
29. I owe this point to my student at SUNY Old Westbury, Michael Catania.
30. Fire imagery, common in apocalyptic passages of the New Testament, usually signifies punishment of the wicked and/or purification (e.g., Matt. 3:12, 13:40; 1 Cor. 3:15, Rev. 3:18). In verse 10, modern translations say the earth and its works will be "brought to judgment," "laid bare," or "disclosed," but the elements still dissolve or are destroyed in "fire" or "flames."
31. The sermon was delivered June 23, 1974. Criswell (1909–2002), originally a segregationist, repudiated segregation in 1968 (Chappell 114–15). He was pastor of First Baptist, which he built into one of the first "megachurches," from 1944 to 1990, holding honorary posts until his death. The website devoted to his ministry contains a large library of transcribed sermons.
32. See Harrington 235–37; Watson 323–24, partly summarizing work by Richard Bauckham.
33. Rosso's quotation (30) first brought this passage to my attention.

CONCLUSION. BALDWIN'S PROPHETIC ART TODAY

1. For the view that African American family structure resists heteronormativity, on which Brim bases his argument, see chapter 1.
2. Corber qualifies his statement, made in a 2001 review of two Baldwin anthologies, by noting that Baldwin thought identity issues "needed to be complicated and reconceived" rather than "transcended or replaced" (172), but his emphasis is on Baldwin's critique of set identities. Brim's reference (12) led me to this essay.
3. For a similar point, see Cohen 209–10.
4. For partial exceptions, see Shulman, *American Prophecy* chap. 4 and "Baldwin, Prophecy, and Politics," as cited in my introduction; Scruggs, *Sweet Home* 137–66. Kevin Ohi's previously discussed deconstruction of revelation in *Another Country*, "'I'm Not the Boy You Want,'" though dealing only with bodily and emotional revelation, is a serious effort to assess the issues.
5. For an extended treatment, see Field chap. 1.
6. On these points see Field 130–44.
7. I am joining together parts of McClure's discussions of Gianni Vattimo, Alasdair MacIntyre, and others, but not, I think, in a way that violates his ideas.
8. Connolly's prescription of a "democratic ethos of generosity" (16 and later) works well for the first sort of issue, not well for the second, in which preservation of institutional power usually is paramount for power-holders. Connolly uses the idea of generosity (introduced on 15 and frequently reiterated) almost always in the sense of recognizing identity claims rather than of adjusting or ceding real power.
9. I am indebted to Nicholas Powers for the ideas introduced here.
10. Secular equivalents of this kind of communal effort involve equivalent risks—the arrogance, elitism, and intolerance of so much of the Left, for example. But to discuss these would take me too far from my topic.

Works Cited

Abdur-Rahman, Aliyyah I. "'Simply a Menaced Boy': Analogizing Color, Undoing Dominance in James Baldwin's *Giovanni's Room*." *African American Review* 41.3 (2007): 477–86.

Abrams, M. H. *Natural Supernaturalism: Tradition and Revolution in Romantic Literature*. New York: Norton, 1971.

Albert, Richard N. "The Jazz-Blues Motif in Baldwin's 'Sonny's Blues.'" *College Literature* 11.2 (1984): 178–85.

Albertson, Chris. *Bessie*, rev. ed. New Haven: Yale University Press, 2005.

Alexander, Estrelda Y., and Amos Yong. "Introduction: Black Tongues of Fire: Afro-Pentecostalism's Shifting Strategies and Changing Discourses." In *Afro-Pentecostalism: Black Pentecostal and Charismatic Christianity in History and Culture*, edited by Amos Yong and Estrelda Y. Alexander, 1–18. New York: NYU Press, 2011.

Allen, Richard. "Letter from Bishop Allen." *Freedom's Journal* (New York), 2 November 1827, 2.

Allen, Shirley S. "The Ironic Voice in Baldwin's *Go Tell It on the Mountain*." In *James Baldwin: A Critical Evaluation*, edited by Therman B. O'Daniel, 330–37. Washington, DC: Howard University Press, 1977.

———. "Religious Imagery and Psychic Reality in Baldwin's *Go Tell It on the Mountain*." *CLA Journal* 19 (1975): 173–99.

Anderson, Robert Mapes. *Vision of the Disinherited: The Making of American Pentecostalism*.

New York: Oxford University Press, 1979.

Armengol, Josep M. *Masculinities in Black and White: Manliness and Whiteness in (African) American Literature*. New York: Palgrave Macmillan, 2014.

Baker, Houston A., Jr. *Blues, Ideology, and Afro-American Literature: A Vernacular Theory*. Chicago: University of Chicago Press, 1984.

Baldwin, James. *The Amen Corner*. 1968. New York: Vintage International, 1998.

———. *Another Country*. 1962. New York: Vintage International, 1993.

———. *Blues for Mr. Charlie: A Play*. 1964. New York: Vintage International, 1995.

———. *Collected Essays:* Notes of a Native Son, Nobody Knows My Name, The Fire Next Time, No Name in the Street, The Devil Finds Work, *Other Essays*. New York: Library of America, 1998.

———. "Come Out the Wilderness." 1958. *Going to Meet the Man*, 197–225. 1965. New York: Vintage International, 1995.

———. *Early Novels and Stories:* Go Tell It on the Mountain, Giovanni's Room, Another Country, Going to Meet the Man. New York: Library of America, 1998.

———. *The Evidence of Things Not Seen*. 1985. New York: Owl–Henry Holt, 1995.

———. *The Fire Next Time*. 1963. New York: Vintage International, 1993.

———. "The Fire This Time: Letter to the Bishop." In *The Cross of Redemption: Uncollected Writings*, edited by Randall Kenan, 215–18. New York: Pantheon, 2010.

———. *Giovanni's Room*. 1956. New York: Vintage International, 2013.

———. *Go Tell It on the Mountain*. 1953. New York: Vintage International, 2013.

———. *If Beale Street Could Talk*. 1974. New York: Delta, 2000.

———. *Just Above My Head*. 1979. New York: Delta, 2000.

———. *No Name in the Street*. 1972. New York: Vintage International, 2007.

———. *One Day When I Was Lost: A Scenario Based on Alex Haley's* The Autobiography of Malcolm X. 1972. New York: Vintage International, 2007.

———. "The Outing." 1951. *Going to Meet the Man*, 29–57. 1965. New York: Vintage International, 1995.

———. "Sonny's Blues." 1957. *Going to Meet the Man*, 103–41. 1965. New York: Vintage International, 1995.

———. *Tell Me How Long the Train's Been Gone*. 1968. New York: Vintage International, 1998.

———. "The Uses of the Blues." Jan. 1964. In *The Cross of Redemption: Uncollected Writings*, edited by Randall Kenan, 57–66. New York: Pantheon, 2010.

Baldwin, James, and others. James Baldwin Papers. Manuscripts, Archives, and Rare Books Division, Schomburg Center for Research in Black Culture, New York Public Library. MG936.

Beemyn, Brett. "'To Say Yes to Life': Sexual and Gender Fluidity in James Baldwin's *Giovanni's Room* and *Another Country*." In *Bisexual Men in Culture and Society*, edited by Brett Beemyn and Erich Steinman, 55–72. New York: Harrington Park Press, 2002.

Bell, George E. "The Dilemma of Love in *Go Tell It on the Mountain* and *Giovanni's Room*." *CLA Journal* 17.3 (1974): 397–406.

Bible Story Told in Verse. Edinburgh: William P. Nimmo, 1870.

Bieganowski, Ronald. "James Baldwin's Vision of Otherness in 'Sonny's Blues' and *Giovanni's Room*." *CLA Journal* 32.1 (1988): 69–80.

Blake, William. *Jerusalem the Emanation of the Giant Albion*. In *The Complete Poetry and Prose of William Blake*, rev. ed., edited by David V. Erdman, 144–259. New York: Anchor–Doubleday, 1988.

Blenkinsopp, Joseph. *A History of Prophecy in Israel*, rev. ed. Louisville: Westminster John Knox, 1996.

Blount, Brian K. *Can I Get a Witness? Reading Revelation through African American Culture*. Louisville: Westminster John Knox, 2005.

Boggs, Nicholas. "Of Mimicry and (*Little Man Little*) Man: Toward a Queer-Sighted Theory of Black Childhood." In *James Baldwin Now*, edited by Dwight A. McBride, 122–60. New York: NYU Press, 1999.

Bolden, Joshua. "Inside the Mind of Frederick Douglass: Logically Speaking." BA thesis, SUNY Old Westbury, 2013.

Bontemps, Arna, and Jack Conroy. *Anyplace but Here*. [Rev. ed. of *They Seek a City*, 1945.] New York: Hill and Wang, 1968.

Bottome, Francis. "The Comforter." In *Songs from the Parsonage*, 85–86. New York: Anson D. F. Randolph and Co., 1894.

Boyd, Herb. *Baldwin's Harlem: A Biography of James Baldwin*. New York: Atria, 2009.

Brim, Matt. *James Baldwin and the Queer Imagination*. Ann Arbor: University of Michigan Press, 2014.

Brooks, Joanna. "From Edwards to Baldwin: Heterodoxy, Discontinuity, and New Narratives of American Religious-Literary History." *American Literary History* 22.2 (2010): 439–53.

Brown, Joseph A. "I, John, Saw the Holy Number: Apocalyptic Visions in *Go Tell It on the Mountain* and *Native Son*." *Religion and Literature* 27.1 (1995): 53–74.

Bruck, Peter. "Dungeon and Salvation: Biblical Rhetoric in James Baldwin's *Just Above My Head*." In *History and Tradition in Afro-American Culture*, edited by Gunter H. Lenz, 130–46. Frankfurt: Campus Verlag, 1984.

Byerman, Keith E. "Words and Music: Narrative Ambiguity in 'Sonny's Blues.'" *Studies in Short Fiction* 19.4 (1982): 367–72.

Campbell, James. *Talking at the Gates: A Life of James Baldwin*, rev. ed. Berkeley: University of California Press, 2002.

Carson, D. A. "The Function of the Paraclete in John 16:7–11." *Journal of Biblical Literature* 98.4 (1979): 547–66.

Carson, Warren J. "Manhood, Musicality, and Male Bonding in *Just Above My Head*." In *Re-Viewing James Baldwin*, edited by D. Quentin Miller, 215–32. Philadelphia: Temple University Press, 2000.

Chancy, Myriam J. A. "Brother/Outsider: In Search of a Black Gay Legacy in James Baldwin's *Giovanni's Room*." In *The Gay '90s: Disciplinary and Interdisciplinary Formations in Queer Studies*, edited by Thomas Foster, Carol Siegel, and Ellen E. Berry, 155–90. New York: NYU Press, 1997.

Chappell, David L. *A Stone of Hope: Prophetic Religion and the Death of Jim Crow*. Chapel Hill: University of North Carolina Press, 2004.

Childs, Brevard S. *Introduction to the Old Testament as Scripture*. Philadelphia: Fortress, 1979.

———. *Isaiah: A Commentary*. Knoxville: Westminster John Knox, 2001.

Church of God in Christ. *Official Manual with the Doctrine and Discipline of the Church of God in Christ*. Memphis: Church of God in Christ, 1992.

Claridge, Laura. *The Lady with the Borzoi: Blanche Knopf, Literary Tastemaker Extraordinaire*. New York: Farrar, Straus, and Giroux, 2016.

Clark, Keith. *Black Manhood in James Baldwin, Ernest J. Gaines, and August Wilson*. Urbana: University of Illinois Press, 2004.

Cleaver, Eldridge. *On the Ideology of the Black Panther Party. Part 1*. San Francisco: Black Panther Party, 1969.

———. *Soul on Ice*. New York: Delta, 1999.

Coates, Ta-Nehisi. *Between the World and Me*. New York: Spiegel and Graf, 2015.

Cohen, William A. "Liberalism, Libido, Liberation: Baldwin's *Another Country*." In *The Queer Sixties*, edited by Patricia Juliana Smith, 201–22. New York: Routledge, 1999.

Colbert, Soyica Diggs. "Go Tell It on the Mountain: Baldwin's Sermonic." In *The Cambridge Companion to James Baldwin*, edited by Michele Elam, 56–69. New York: Cambridge University Press, 2015.

Coleman, James W. *Faithful Vision: Treatments of the Sacred, Spiritual, and Supernatural in Twentieth-Century African American Fiction*. Baton Rouge: Louisiana State University Press, 2006.

Collier, Eugenia W. "The Phrase Unbearably Repeated." *Phylon* 25.3 (1964): 288–96.

Collins, John J. *The Apocalyptic Imagination: An Introduction to Jewish Apocalyptic Literature*. Grand Rapids, MI: Eerdmans, 1998.

"The Comforter." By Francis Bottome. Performed by Church choir and congregation, Church of God, Greenville, Ohio. YouTube. Https://www.youtube.com/watch?v=MU98khZAz2g.

Cone, James H. *A Black Theology of Liberation*. 1970. Maryknoll, NY: Orbis, 2010.

Connolly, William E. *Why I Am Not a Secularist*. Minneapolis: University of Minnesota Press, 1999.

Conzelmann, Hans. *1 Corinthians: A Commentary on the First Epistle to the Corinthians*. 1969. Translated by James W. Leitsch. Philadelphia: Fortress, 1981.

Cooke, Sam. "Any Day Now." Recorded 2 March 1954, Sam Cooke (vocal) and Faidest Wagoner (piano). *The Legends of Specialty Series. Sam Cooke with the Soul Stirrers*. Specialty Records, SPCD-7009-2, 1991, CD.

Cooper, Anna Julia. *A Voice from the South: By a Black Woman of the South*. Xenia, OH: Aldine, 1892.

Coppedge, Allan. *Shaping the Wesleyan Message: John Wesley in Theological Debate*. Nappanee, IN: Evangelical Publishing House, n.d. [c. 2003].

Corber, Robert J. "Everybody Knew His Name: Reassessing James Baldwin." Review of *James Baldwin Now*, edited by Dwight A. McBride, and *Re-Viewing James Baldwin: Things Not Seen*, edited by D. Quentin Miller. *Contemporary Literature* 42.1 (2001): 166–75.

Craddock, Fred B. "The Letter to the Hebrews: Introduction, Commentary, and Reflections." In *The New Interpreter's Bible*, vol. 12, 1–173. Nashville: Abingdon, 1998.

Criswell, W. A. "The World on Fire." 23 June 1974. *Criswell Sermon Library*. Https://www.wacriswell.com/sermons/1974/the-world-on-fire.

Crummell, Alexander. *The Greatness of Christ and Other Sermons*. New York: Thomas Whittaker, 1882.

Darr, Katheryn Pfisterer. "The Book of Ezekiel: Introduction, Commentary, and Reflections." In *The New Interpreter's Bible*, vol. 6., 1073–1607. Nashville: Abingdon, 1994.

Davis, David Brion. *Inhuman Bondage: The Rise and Fall of Slavery in the New World*. Oxford: Oxford University Press, 2008.

DeGout, Yasmin Y. "Dividing the Mind: Contradictory Portraits of Homoerotic Love in *Giovanni's Room*." *African American Review* 26.3 (1992): 425–35.

Dievler, James A. "Sexual Exiles: James Baldwin and *Another Country*." In *James Baldwin Now*, edited by Dwight A. McBride, 161–83. New York: NYU Press, 1999.

Dixon, Melvin. *Ride Out the Wilderness: Geography and Identity in Afro-American Literature*. Urbana: University of Illinois Press, 1987.

Dyson, Michael Eric. *Mercy, Mercy Me: The Art, Loves and Demons of Marvin Gaye*. New York: Basic Civitas, 2004.

———. "Soul Stirrer: The Gospel Sounds of Sam Cooke." Review of *You Send Me: The Life and Times of Sam Cooke*, by Daniel Wolff, with S. R. Crain, Clifton White, and G. David Tenenbaum. *Christian Century* 112.18 (1995): 572–73.

Eckman, Fern Marja. *The Furious Passage of James Baldwin*. New York: Evans, 1966.

Edelman, Lee. *Homographesis: Essays in Gay Literary and Cultural History*. New York: Routledge, 1994.

Ellison, Ralph. *The Collected Essays of Ralph Ellison*, edited by John F. Callahan. New York: Modern Library, 1995.

Fabre, Michel. "Fathers and Sons in James Baldwin's *Go Tell It on the Mountain*." 1970 (in French). Translated by Keneth Kinnamon. In *James Baldwin: A Collection of Critical Essays*, edited by Keneth Kinnamon, 120–38. Englewood Cliffs, NJ: Prentice Hall, 1974.

Fee, Gordon D. *The First Epistle to the Corinthians*. Grand Rapids, MI: Eerdmans, 1987.

Feldman, Susan. "Another Look at *Another Country*: Reconciling Baldwin's Racial and Sexual Politics." In *Re-Viewing James Baldwin*, edited by D. Quentin Miller, 89–104. Philadelphia: Temple University Press, 2000.

Field, Douglas. *All Those Strangers: The Art and Lives of James Baldwin*. New York: Oxford University Press, 2015.

Frey, Sylvia R., and Betty Wood. *Come Shouting to Zion: African American Protestantism in the American South and British Caribbean to 1830*. Chapel Hill: University of North Carolina Press, 1998.

Frontain, Raymond-Jean. "James Baldwin's *Giovanni's Room* and the Biblical Myth of David." *CEA Critic* 57.2 (1995): 41–58.

Furnish, Victor Paul. *The Moral Teaching of Paul: Selected Issues*. 3rd ed. Nashville: Abingdon, 2009.

Gallien, Louis B., Jr. "Crossing Over Jordan: Navigating the Music of Heavenly Bliss and Earthly Desire in the Lives and Careers of Three Twentieth-Century African American Holiness-Pentecostal 'Crossover' Artists." In *Afro-Pentecostalism: Black Pentecostal and Charismatic Christianity in History and Culture*, edited by Amos Yong and Estrelda Y. Alexander, 117–38. New York: NYU Press, 2011.

Garnet, Henry Highland. *The Past and the Present Condition, and the Destiny, of the Colored Race: A Discourse*. Troy, NY: J. C. Kneeland, 1848.

Gérard, Albert. "The Sons of Ham." Translated by Judith H. McDowell. *Studies in the Novel* 3.2 (Summer 1971): 148–64.

Giles, James R. "Religious Alienation and 'Homosexual Consciousness' in *City of Night* and *Go Tell It on the Mountain*." *College English* 36.3 (1974): 369–80.

Goldstein, Richard. "'Go the Way Your Blood Beats': An Interview with James Baldwin (1984)." In *James Baldwin: The Legacy*, edited by Quincy Troupe, 173–85. New York: Touchstone

Books, 1989.

Grimké, Francis J. *The Works of Francis J. Grimké*. Edited by Carter G. Woodson. 4 vols. Washington: Associated, 1942.

Habermas, Jürgen. "Notes on Post-Secular Society." *New Perspectives Quarterly* 25 (Fall 2008): 17–29.

Handy, W. C. "Beale Street." New York: Pace and Handy, 1917. Archive of Popular American Music, UCLA Digital Library. Http://digital.library.ucla.edu/apam/librarian?ITEMID=SY118689.

Hardy, Clarence E., III. *James Baldwin's God: Sex, Hope, and Crisis in Black Holiness Culture*. Knoxville: University of Tennessee Press, 2003.

Harper, J. Steven. "A Wesleyan Arminian View." In *Four Views on Eternal Security*, edited by Stanley N. Gundry and J. Matthew Pinson, 207–55. Grand Rapids, MI: Zondervan, 2002.

Harrington, Daniel J. "Jude and 2 Peter." In *1 Peter, Jude and 2 Peter*, by Donald P. Senior and Daniel J. Harrington, 161–299. Collegeville, MN: Michael Glazier–Liturgical Press, 2008.

Harris, Stephen L., and Robert L. Platzner, *The Old Testament: An Introduction to the Hebrew Bible*. Boston: McGraw-Hill, 2003.

Harris, Trudier. *Black Women in the Fiction of James Baldwin*. Knoxville: University of Tennessee Press, 1985.

Hatch, James V. *Sorrow Is the Only Faithful One: The Life of Owen Dodson*. Urbana: University of Illinois Press, 1995.

Hatch, Nathan O. *The Democratization of American Christianity*. New Haven: Yale University Press, 1989.

Haymes, Max. "Fatted Calf's Blues—The First Golden Age (African American Gospel & Sacred Songs, 1902–1942)." *EarlyGospel.com—Essays and Articles*. Www.earlygospel.com/eg-essays-fatted%20calf%20blues.htm.

Heilbut, Anthony. *The Gospel Sound: Good News and Bad Times*, 25th anniversary ed. New York: Limelight, 2002.

Henderson, Mae G. "James Baldwin: Expatriation, Homosexual Panic, and Man's Estate." *Callaloo* 23.1 (2000): 313–27.

Hicks, Granville. "Outcasts in a Caldron of Hate." Review of *Another Country*. In *Critical Essays on James Baldwin*, edited by Fred L. Standley and Nancy V. Burt, 149–52. Boston: Hall, 1988.

Hobson, Christopher Z. *The Mount of Vision: African American Prophetic Tradition, 1800–1950*. New York: Oxford University Press, 2012.

"Holiness Churches." *World Council of Churches*. Www.oikoumene.org/en/church-families/holiness-churches.

Holsey, Lucius H. *Autobiography, Sermons, Addresses and Essays of Bishop L. H. Holsey, D.D.* Atlanta: Franklin, 1898.

Hughes, James M. "Black City Lights: Baldwin's City of the Just." *Journal of Black Studies* 18.2 (1987): 230–41.

Hughes, Langston. *The Big Sea: An Autobiography*. 1940. New York: Hill and Wang, 1963.

———. *Black* Nativity*: A Gospel Song-Play for a Variable Cast. The Collected Works of Langston Hughes*, vol. 6, *Gospel Plays, Operas, and Later Dramatic Works*. Edited by Leslie Catherine Saunders, 356–78. Columbia: University of Missouri Press, 2004.

Hurston, Zora Neale. *The Sanctified Church*. New York: Marlowe, 1981.

"Hymn—Take Me as I Am." *AllGospelLyrics.com*. Www.allgospellyrics.com/?sec=listing&lyricid=10856.

"I'm on My Way to Canaan's Land." The Carter Family, performers. MP3 download.

Jackson, Jerma. "Sister Rosetta Tharpe and the Evolution of Gospel Music." In *Religion in the American South: Protestants and Others in History and Culture*, edited by Beth Barton Schweiger and Donald G. Mathews, 219–45. Chapel Hill: University of North Carolina Press, 2004.

Jackson, Mahalia. "In the Upper Room." *In the Upper Room with Mahalia Jackson*. Apollo Records, LP 474. Released May 1957.

James Baldwin: The Price of the Ticket. Directed by Karen Thorsen. New York: Mayles Films, 1989.

Johnson, James Weldon. "Lift Every Voice and Sing." In *Complete Poems*, edited by Sondra Kathryn Wilson, 109–10. New York: Penguin, 2000.

Johnson, James Weldon, and J. Rosamond Johnson. *The Books of American Negro Spirituals*. [Reprint of *The Book of American Negro Spirituals*, 1925, and *The Second Book of Negro Spirituals*, 1926.] N.p. [Boston]: Da Capo, n.d. [2002].

J[ones], A[bsalom], and R[ichard] A[llen]. *A Narrative of the Proceedings of the Black People, during the Late Awful Calamity in Philadelphia, in the Year 1793* [etc.]. Philadelphia: William W. Woodward, 1794.

Jones, Jacqueline C. "Finding a Way to Listen: The Emergence of the Hero as an Artist in James Baldwin's 'Sonny's Blues.'" *CLA Journal* 42.4 (1999): 462–82.

———. "His Tale to Tell: James Baldwin and the Artist as a Hero in Fiction." Ph.D. Diss., City University of New York, 1996.

Jones, LeRoi [Amiri Baraka]. *Blues People: Negro Music in White America*. New York: Morrow, 1970.

Kilpeläinen, Pekka. "Transcending the Boundaries of Race and Sexuality: James Baldwin's Vision of Postcategorical Utopia." In *Post-National Enquiries: Essays on Ethnic and*

Racial Border Crossings, edited by Jopi Nyman, 47–61. Newcastle upon Tyne: Cambridge Scholars, 2009.

King, Martin Luther, Jr. "I Have a Dream." In *King's Dream*, by Eric J. Sundquist, 229–34. New Haven: Yale University Press, 2009.

Kornegay, EL, Jr. *A Queering of Black Theology: James Baldwin's Blues Project and Gospel Prose*. New York: Palgrave Macmillan, 2013.

LaRue, Cleophus J. *The Heart of Black Preaching*. Louisville: Westminster John Knox, 2000.

Lash, John S. "Baldwin Beside Himself: A Study in Modern Phallicism." In *James Baldwin: A Critical Evaluation*, edited by Therman O'Daniel, 47–55. Washington, DC: Howard University Press, 1977.

Lee, Dorothy H. "The Bridge of Suffering." *Callaloo* 18 (Spring–Summer 1983): 92–99.

Leeming, David. *James Baldwin: A Biography*. New York: Knopf, 1994.

Levenson, Jon L. *Creation and the Persistence of Evil: The Jewish Drama of Divine Omnipotence*. Princeton: Princeton University Press, 1994.

Lloyd, Vincent W. "The Negative Political Theology of James Baldwin." In *A Political Companion to James Baldwin*, edited by Susan McWilliams, 171–94. Lexington: University Press of Kentucky, 2017.

Lobb, Edward. "James Baldwin's Blues and the Function of Art." *International Fiction Review* 6.2 (1979): 143–48.

Lomax, John A., and Alan Lomax. *Our Singing Country: Folk Songs and Ballads*. Mineola: Dover, 2000.

Lundén, Rolf. "The Progress of a Pilgrim: James Baldwin's *Go Tell It on the Mountain*." *Studia Neophilologica* 53.1 (1981): 113–26.

Lordi, Emily J. *Black Resonance: Iconic Women Singers and African American Literature*. New Brunswick, NJ: Rutgers University Press, 2013.

Lynch, Michael F. "Beyond Guilt and Innocence: Redemptive Suffering and Love in Baldwin's *Another Country*." *Obsidian II* 7.1–2 (1992): 1–18.

———. "A Glimpse of the Hidden God: Dialectical Vision in Baldwin's *Go Tell It on the Mountain*." In *New Essays on James Baldwin's* Go Tell It on the Mountain, edited by Trudier Harris, 29–57. Cambridge: Cambridge University Press, 1996.

———. "Just Above My Head: James Baldwin's Quest for Belief." *Literature and Theology* 11.3 (1997): 284–98.

Macebuh, Stanley. *James Baldwin: A Critical Study*. New York: Third Press, 1973.

Mack, Maynard. *The Garden and the City: Retirement and Politics in the Later Poetry of Pope, 1731–1743*. Toronto: University of Toronto Press, 1969.

Martin, Dale B. *The Corinthian Body*. New Haven: Yale University Press, 1995.

McClure, John A. *Partial Faiths: Postsecular Fiction in the Age of Pynchon and Morrison*. Athens: University of Georgia Press, 2007.

Miller, D. Quentin. *A Criminal Power: James Baldwin and the Law.* Columbus: Ohio State University Press, 2012.

———, ed. *Re-Viewing James Baldwin: Things Not Seen*. Philadelphia: Temple University Press, 2000.

———. "Using the Blues: James Baldwin and Music." In *A Historical Guide to James Baldwin*, edited by Douglas Field, 83–109. New York: Oxford University Press, 2009.

Mills, Nathaniel. "Cleaver/Baldwin Revisited: Naturalism and the Gendering of Black Revolution." *Studies in American Naturalism* 7.1 (2012): 50–79.

Mitchell, Keith. "Femininity, Abjection, and (Black) Masculinity in James Baldwin's *Giovanni's Room* and Toni Morrison's *Beloved*." In *James Baldwin and Toni Morrison: Comparative, Critical and Theoretical Essays*, edited by Lovalerie King and Lynn Orilla Scott, 261–86. New York: Palgrave Macmillan,. 2009.

Montgomery, Maxine Lavon. *The Apocalypse in African-American Fiction*. Gainesville: University Press of Florida, 1996.

Moore, Marlon Rachquel. *In the Life and in the Spirit: Homoerotic Spirituality in African American Literature*. Albany: SUNY Press, 2014.

Morrissey, Lee. "Literature and the Postsecular: *Paradise Lost?*" *Religion and Literature* 41.3 (2009): 98–106.

Mosher, Marlene. "Baldwin's 'Sonny's Blues.'" *Explicator* 40.4 (1982): 59.

Mossman, James. "Race, Hate, Sex, and Colour: A Conversation with James Baldwin and Colin MacInnes." In *Conversations with James Baldwin*, edited by Fred L. Standley and Louis H. Pratt, 46–58. Jackson: University Press of Mississippi, 1989.

Mowinckel, Sigmund. *The Spirit and the Word: Prophecy and Tradition in Ancient Israel.* Edited by K. C. Hanson. Minneapolis: Fortress, 2002.

Murray, Donald C. "James Baldwin's 'Sonny's Blues': Complicated and Simple." *Studies in Short Fiction* 14.4 (1977): 353–57.

Nelson, Emanuel S. "The Novels of James Baldwin: Struggles of Self-Acceptance." *Journal of American Culture* 8.4 (1986): 11–16.

Newman, Richard S. *Freedom's Prophet: Richard Allen, the AME Church, and the Black Founding Fathers*. New York: NYU Press, 2008.

Norman, Brian. "James Baldwin's Confrontation with US Imperialism in *If Beale Street Could Talk*." *MELUS* 32.1 (2007): 119–38.

Oatman, Johnson Jr. "Lift Him Up." 1903. *The Cyber Hymnal.* Www.hymntime.com/tch/htm/l/i/f/lifthimu.htm.

O'Day, Gail R. "John: Introduction, Commentary, and Reflections." In *The New Interpreter's*

Bible, vol. 9, 491–865. Nashville: Abingdon, 1995.

Oforlea, Aaron. "Remaking and Making Tradition: Black Male Subjectivity in Baldwin's *Tell Me How Long the Train's Been Gone*." *Obsidian* 9.2 (2008): 62–76.

Ohi, Kevin. "'I'm Not the Boy You Want': Sexuality, 'Race,' and Thwarted Revelation in Baldwin's *Another Country*." *African American Review* 33.2 (1999): 261–81.

O'Neale, Sondra A. "Fathers, Gods, and Religion: Perceptions of Christianity and Ethnic Faith in James Baldwin." In *Critical Essays on James Baldwin*, edited by Fred L. Standly and Nancy V. Burt, 125–43. Boston: G. K. Hall, 1988.

Patterson, J. O., German R. Ross, and Julia Mason Atkins. *History and Formative Years of the Church of God in Christ with Excerpts from the Life and Works of Its Founder—Bishop C. H. Mason*. Memphis: Church of God in Christ Publishing House, 1969.

Pavlić, Ed. *Who Can Afford to Improvise? James Baldwin and Black Music, the Lyric and the Listeners*. New York: Fordham University Press, 2016.

Peters, Erskine. *Lyrics of the Afro-American Spirituals: A Documentary Collection*. Westport, CT: Greenwood, 1993.

Peters, John L. *Christian Perfection and American Methodism*. 1956. Salem, OH: Schmul Publishing, 1995.

Petersen, David L. "Introduction to the Prophetic Literature." In *The New Interpreter's Bible*, vol. 6, 1–23. Nashville: Abingdon, 1994.

———. *The Prophetic Literature: An Introduction*. Louisville: Westminster John Knox Press, 2002.

Phillips, Caryl. "James Baldwin: The Price of the Ticket." In *Colour Me English: Reflections on Migration and Belonging*, 239–50. London: Harvill-Secker, 2011.

Pinn, Anthony. *Why, Lord? Suffering and Evil in Black Theology*. New York: Continuum, 1995.

Plastas, Melinda, and Eve Allegra Raimon. "Brutality and Brotherhood: James Baldwin and Prison Sexuality." *African American Review* 46.4 (2013): 687–99.

Poore, Charles. "Books of the Times." Review of Baldwin, *Another Country*. *New York Times*, 26 June 1962, 31.

Powers, Peter Kerry. "The Treacherous Body: Isolation, Communion, and Confession in James Baldwin." *American Literature* 77.4 (2005): 787–813.

Raboteau, Albert J. "'The Blood of the Martyrs Is the Seed of Faith': Suffering in the Christianity of American Slaves." In *The Courage to Hope: From Black Suffering to Human Redemption. Essays in Honor of James Melvin Washington*, edited by Quinton Hosford Dixie and Cornel West, 22–39. Boston: Beacon, 1999.

———. *Slave Religion: The "Invisible Institution" in the Antebellum South*. Oxford: Oxford University Press, 1978.

Rack, Henry D. *Reasonable Enthusiast: John Wesley and the Rise of Methodism*. 3rd ed. London:

Epworth, 2002.

Randolph, E[dwin] A[rcher]. *The Life of John Jasper, Pastor of Sixth Mt. Zion Baptist Church, Richmond, Va., From His Birth to the Present Time, with His Theory on the Rotation of the Sun*. Richmond: R. T. Hill, 1884.

Ransom, Reverdy C. *The Negro: The Hope or the Despair of Christianity*. Boston: Ruth Hill, 1935.

Rasberry, Vaughn. "'Now Describing You': James Baldwin and Cold War Liberalism." In *James Baldwin: America and Beyond*, edited by Cora Kaplan and Bill Schwarz, 84–105. Ann Arbor: University of Michigan Press, 2011.

Ratti, Manav. *The Posecular Imagination: Postcolonialism, Religion, and Literature*. New York: Routledge, 2014.

Reid-Pharr, Robert. *Once You Go Black: Choice, Desire, and the Black American Intellectual*. New York: NYU Press, 2007.

———. "Tearing the Goat's Flesh: Homosexuality, Abjection, and the Production of a Late Twentieth-Century Black Masculinity." *Studies in the Novel* 28.3 (1996): 372–94.

Reilly, John M. "'Sonny's Blues': James Baldwin's Image of Black Community." *Negro American Literature Forum* 4.2 (1970): 56–60.

Robinson, Smokey. "Marvin Gaye." *Rolling Stone*, 15 April 2004, 95.

Rodeheaver, Homer, ed. *Convention Songs*. Chicago: Rodeheaver Co., 1937.

Ross, Marlon B. "Baldwin's Sissy Heroics." *African American Review* 46.4 (2013): 633–51.

Rosso, G. A. *The Religion of Empire: Political Theology in Blake's Prophetic Symbolism*. Columbus: Ohio State University Press, 2016.

Roth, Philip. *The Human Stain*. 2000. New York: Vintage International, 2001.

Rowland, Christopher C. "The Book of Revelation: Introduction, Commentary, and Reflections." In *The New Interpreter's Bible*, vol. 12, 501–743. Nashville: Abingdon, 1998.

———. *The Open Heaven: A Study of Apocalyptic in Judaism and Early Christianity*. 1982. Eugene, OR: Wipf and Stock, 2002.

Sampley, J. Paul. "The First Letter to the Corinthians: Introduction, Commentary, and Reflections." In *The New Interpreter's Bible*, vol. 10, 771–1003. Nashville: Abingdon, 2002.

Sanders, Cheryl J. *Saints in Exile: The Holiness-Pentecostal Experience in African American Religion and Culture*. New York: Oxford University Press, 1996.

Sanderson, Jim. "Grace in 'Sonny's Blues.'" *Short Story* 6.2 (1998): 85–95.

Savery, Pancho. "Baldwin, Bebop, and 'Sonny's Blues.'" In *Understanding Others: Cultural and Cross-Cultural Studies and the Teaching of Literature*, edited by Joseph F. Trimmer and Tilly Warnock, 165–76. Urbana: National Council of Teachers of English, 1992.

Schüssler Fiorenza, Elisabeth. *Revelation: Vision of a Just World*. Minneapolis: Fortress, 1991. Proclamation Commentaries.

Scott, Lynn Orilla. *James Baldwin's Later Fiction: Witness to the Journey*. East Lansing: Michigan State University Press, 2002.

Scruggs, Charles. *Sweet Home: Invisible Cities in the Afro-American Novel*. Baltimore: Johns Hopkins University Press, 1995.

———. "The Tale of Two Cities in James Baldwin's *Go Tell It on the Mountain*." *American Literature* 52.1 (1980): 1–17.

Shelley, Percy Bysshe. "A Defence of Poetry." In *Shelley's Poetry and Prose*, edited by Donald H. Reiman and Sharon B. Powers, 480–508. New York: Norton, 1977.

Sherard, Tracey. "Sonny's Bebop: Baldwin's 'Blues Text' as Intracultural Critique." *African American Review* 32.4 (1998): 691–705.

Shin, Andrew, and Barbara Judson. "Beneath the Black Aesthetic: James Baldwin's Primer of Black American Masculinity." *African American Review* 32.2 (1998): 247–61.

Shulman, George. *American Prophecy: Race and Redemption in American Political Culture*. Minneapolis: University of Minnesota Press, 2008.

———. "Baldwin, Prophecy, and Politics." In *James Baldwin: America and Beyond*, edited by Cora Kaplan and Bill Schwarz, 106–25. Ann Arbor: University of Michigan Press, 2011.

Simawe, Saadi A. "What Is in a Sound? The Metaphysics and Politics of Music in *The Amen Corner*." In *Re-Viewing James Baldwin*, edited by D. Quentin Miller, 12–32. Philadelphia: Temple University Press, 2000.

Smith, Abraham. "Paul and African American Biblical Interpretation." In *True to Our Native Land: An African American New Testament Commentary*, edited by Brian K. Blount, Cain Hope Felder, Clarice J. Martin, and Emerson B. Powery, 31–42. Minneapolis: Fortress, 2007.

Smith, William. *A Dictionary of the Bible*. Revised and edited by F. N. and F. A. Peloubet. Nashville: Thomas Nelson, 1986.

Snow, Valaida, vocalist. "Tell Me How Long the Train's Been Gone." With Jimmy Mundy Orchestra. Derby Records 741, MX: D-16. Recorded 1950. YouTube. Https://www.youtube.com/watch?v=f9CqjXbymNE.

Sobel, Mechal. *Trabelin' On: The Slave Journey to an Afro-Baptist Faith*. 1979. Abridged ed., Princeton: Princeton University Press, 1988.

Spillers, Hortense. "The Politics of Intimacy: A Discussion." In *Sturdy Black Bridges: Visions of Black Women in Literature*, edited by Roseann P. Bell, Bettye J. Parker, Beverly Guy-Sheftall, 87–106. Garden City, NY: Anchor, 1979.

SNCC. "Student Nonviolent Coordinating Committee, Statement of Purpose." In *Nonviolence in America: A Documentary History*, rev. ed., edited by Staughton Lynd and Alice Lynd, 222. Maryknoll: Orbis, 1995.

Sweeney, Marvin A. *The Prophetic Literature*. Nashville: Abingdon, 2005.

———. "Tanak versus Old Testament: Concerning the Foundation for a Jewish Theology of the Bible." In *Problems in Biblical Theology: Essays in Honor of Rolf Knierim*, edited by Henry T. C. Sun and Keith L. Eades, 353–72. Grand Rapids, MI: Eerdman, 1997.

Synan, Vinson. *The Holiness-Pentecostal Tradition: Charismatic Movements in the Twentieth Century*. Grand Rapids, MI: Eerdmans, 1997.

Tackach, James. "The Biblical Foundation of James Baldwin's 'Sonny's Blues.'" *Renascence* 59.2 (2007): 109–18.

Taylor, Douglas. "Three Lean Cats in a Hall of Mirrors: James Baldwin, Norman Mailer, and Eldridge Cleaver on Race and Masculinity." *Texas Studies in Literature and Language* 52.1 (2010): 70–101.

Tharpe, Sister Rosetta, vocalist. "The End of My Journey." [Lucie Campbell.] Recorded 1941. *Sister Rosetta Tharpe* Disc 1.

———. "I Looked Down the Line (And I Wondered)." [Traditional.] Recorded 1939. *Sister Rosetta Tharpe* Disc 1.

———. "Saviour, Don't Pass Me By." [Tharpe.] Recorded 1939. *Sister Rosetta Tharpe* Disc 1.

Tharpe, Sister Rosetta, vocalist (with others). *Sister Rosetta Tharpe: The Original Soul Sister*. 4-CD set, Properbox 51. Proper Records P13041. 2005.

Tharpe, Sister Rosetta, and Marie Knight, vocalists. "Up Above My Head I Hear Music in the Air." [Traditional, arranged Tharpe.] Recorded 1947. *Sister Rosetta Tharpe* Disc 4.

Toombs, Charles P. "Black-Gay-Man Chaos in *Another Country*." In *Re-Viewing James Baldwin*, edited by D. Quentin Miller, 105–27. Philadelphia: Temple University Press, 2000.

Tracey, Steven C. "Sonny in the Dark: Jazzing the Blues Spirit and the Gospel Truth in James Baldwin's 'Sonny's Blues.'" *James Baldwin Review* 1 (2015): 164–77.

Traylor, Eleanor. "I Hear Music in the Air: James Baldwin's *Just Above My Head*." *First World* 2.3 (1979): 40–43.

"Troubled About My Soul." Lillie Knox, vocalist. Recorded by Alan Lomax, South Carolina, 12 July 1937. "Lillie Knox—Troubled About My Soul." YouTube. Https://www.youtube.com/watch?v=yC6D13Jzw_s.

[Untitled News Summary.] Ogden (Utah) *Standard Examiner*. 10 Feb. 1931: 10. *Newspapers.com*. Www.newspapers.com/newspage/21671364.

Visser, Joop. "Sister Rosetta Tharpe: The Original Soul Sister." Liner notes. *Sister Rosetta Tharpe: The Original Soul Sister*. 4-CD set, Properbox 51, Proper Records, P13041. 2005.

Viswanathan, Gauri. "Secularism in the Framework of Heterodoxy." *PMLA* 123.2 (2008): 466–76.

Von Rad, Gerhard. *Genesis: A Commentary*, rev. ed. Philadelphia: Westminster, 1972.

———. *Old Testament Theology*. Vol. 1, *The Theology of Israel's Historical Traditions*. Translated by D. M. G. Stalker. Louisville: Westminster John Knox, 2001.

———. *Old Testament Theology*. Vol. 2, *The Theology of Israel's Prophetic Traditions*. Translated by D. M. G. Stalker. Louisville: Westminster John Knox, n.d. [2001].

Warren, Nagueyalti. "The Substance of Things Hoped For: Faith in *Go Tell It on the Mountain* and *Just Above My Head*." *Obsidian II* 7.1–2 (1992): 19–31.

Washington, Bryan R. "Wrestling with 'The Love That Dare Not Speak Its Name': John, Elisha, and the 'Master.'" In *New Essays on* Go Tell It on the Mountain, edited by Trudier Harris, 77–95. Cambridge: Cambridge University Press, 1996.

Watson, Duane F. "The Second Letter of Peter: Introduction, Commentary, and Reflections." In *The New Interpreter's Bible*, vol. 12, 321–61. Nashville: Abingdon, 1994.

Weatherby, W. J. *James Baldwin, Artist on Fire: A Portrait*. New York: Donald I. Fine, 1989.

Weems, Renita J. *Battered Love: Marriage, Sex, and Violence in the Hebrew Prophets*. Minneapolis: Fortress, 1995.

Weir, Stan. "Meetings with James Baldwin." *Against the Current*, January–February 1989, 35–41.

Wesley, John. *A Plain Account of Christian Perfection*. 1766. In *The Works of John Wesley*, vol. 13, *Doctrinal and Controversial Treatises II*, edited by Paul Wesley Chilcote and Kenneth J. Collins, 132–91. Nashville: Abingdon, 2013.

"When the World's On Fire." The Carter Family, performers. Rec. May 1930. *When the Roses Bloom in Dixieland. Complete Victor Recordings, 1929–30.* Rounder CD 1066. Cambridge, MA: Rounder Records Corp., 1995.

White, Edmund. *Genet: A Biography*. New York: Knopf, 1993.

Williams, Emlyn. *The Corn Is Green: A Comedy in Three Acts*. 1938. New York: Dramatists Play Service, n.d. [c. 1972].

Williams, Gerod. "Holiness Religion in Baldwin's *Go Tell It on the Mountain*." BA thesis, SUNY Old Westbury, 2011.

Wills, Garry. *What Paul Meant*. New York: Viking, 2006.

Wolff, Daniel, with S. R. Crain, Clifton White, and G. David Tenenbaum. *You Send Me: The Life and Times of Sam Cooke*. New York: Quill–Morrow, 1995.

Young, Josiah Ulysses, Jr. *James Baldwin's Understanding of God: Overwhelming Desire and Joy*. New York: Palgrave Macmillan, 2014.

Zabel, Darcy A. *The (Underground) Railroad in African American Literature*. New York: Peter Lang, 2004.

Zaborowska, Magdalena J. *James Baldwin's Turkish Decade: The Erotics of Exile*. Durham, NC: Duke University Press, 2009.

Zevit, Ziony. *The Religions of Ancient Israel: A Synthesis of Parallactic Approaches*. London: Continuum, 2001.

Index

A